In the Year of the Bull

Zen, Air, and the Pursuit of Sacred and Profane Hoops

R I C K   T E L A N D E R

Simon & Schuster

 SIMON & SCHUSTER
Rockefeller Center
1230 Avenue of the Americas
New York, NY 10020

SIMON & SCHUSTER and colophon are registered trademarks
of Simon & Schuster Inc.

Designed by Elina Nudelman

Manufactured in the United States of America

10 9 8 7 6 5 4 3 2 1

Library of Congress Cataloging-in-Publication Data is available.

ISBN 0-684-80946-X

Acknowledgments

I would like to present a postseason trophy to Frank Scatoni for showing intelligence, insight, persistence, and humor when each was sorely needed. I present the game ball to Jeff Neuman, coach and cheerleader, for keeping me on the court when I wanted to hide in the training room.

As I walked down the hall, I met Mr. Stebbins, the superintendent of buildings. I asked him if he had two boxes about eighteen inches square. Stebbins thought a minute, and then said: "No, I haven't any boxes, but I'll tell you what I do have. I have two old peach baskets down in the store room, if they will do you any good."

—JAMES NAISMITH
Basketball: Its Origin and Development

1

Sweet Jesus, the noise.

I look around this part of the stage to see if there is a shred of paper anywhere, some tissue, newspaper, toilet paper, a rag I can rip into small pieces, anything I can wad up and jam into my ears to deaden the screaming throb of drums, harmonica, organ, vocals, bass, and dentist-drill guitar of the band rocking away. But there is nothing. Nothing even in my pockets. And there's no way I can just put my hands over my ears and be the least cool guy in the house, the only backstage dude who can't handle the din of blues–funk band Liquid Soul, harpist John Popper from Blues Traveler, and Pearl Jam's bassist Jeff Ament.

So I turn my head to the least painful angle, and let the vibrations do whatever damage they are going to do to my aural cilia; I remind myself that I once stood on the tops of chair backs in the second row of a Rolling Stones concert at the old International Amphitheater with my childhood buddy Bill Blair, in front of twin mountains of amps that produced force that Bill and I leaned into sort of the way you lean into a strong wind. I handled "Street Fighting Man" like that, though of course my hearing has never been the same.

But what the hell. This is another celebration—Dennis Rodman's 35th-birthday party at Crobar, a dark and sweaty industrial dance barn—so once more I dive in headfirst.

I have arrived after finishing my column on the Bulls' 94–81 victory tonight, May 14, 1996, over the New York Knicks. The win made the Bulls 4–1 against the hated Knicks in the 1995–96 NBA playoffs. The Miami Heat had already gone down 3–0 to the Bulls. So the Bulls are now 7–1 in the playoffs and ready to take on their next foe, last season's Eastern Conference champion and this year's second-place finisher to the Bulls, the Orlando Magic. The lone loss to the Knicks—a brutal, draining 102–99 overtime defeat at Madison Square Garden in which the Bulls' Michael Jordan played 51 minutes, Scottie Pippen 49, and current birthday boy Rodman 52 minutes—had scared Bulls fans half to death. Oh my God, went the subliminal refrain, the Bulls' omnipotent and entertaining victory machine is about to get derailed by subhuman thugs from Manhattan!

But it didn't happen, and the sense of relief among the swells at the United Center after tonight's win was overwhelming. "That was one of those playoff games we call a mudder," tired head coach Phil Jackson said afterward. Mud, gunk, fouls, violations, bodies colliding—a beautiful game turned into a primitive grappling match. As my occasionally indelicate and hyperbolic fellow sports columnist at the *Chicago Sun-Times,* Jay Mariotti, would put it for tomorrow's readers, the Bulls "ventured into the armpit of basketball and survived."

Rodman, the tattooed, body-pierced, brightly coifed power forward who goes after errant shots the way a piranha goes after errant hamburger, did his part to make the series a sludgepit. He collected 12 rebounds in Game 5, as well as 6 fouls, 2 technical fouls, and an automatic ejection. As he walked off after picking up his final technical tonight, his seventh in the eight playoff games, he played the crowd for all he could. The United Center rowdies were already firmly in his corner, chanting, "New York sucks! New York sucks!" Rodman acted as though the officials had somehow betrayed *him,* victimized *him,* the pure, uncomprehending martyr. He rolled his eyes in amazement, turned away in disgust, then ever so casually sauntered the long way to the Bulls locker room, past the Knicks bench, where he taunted the New Yorkers, including coach Jeff Van Gundy, before tossing his wadded-up jersey into the stands to be fought over by adoring ticketholders.

Then he split for Crobar.

Having written most of my column as the game progressed, I arrived at the Near North Side club at almost the same time as Worm. Crobar is in an area south of North Avenue frequented mostly by moving vans, freight trains, packing crates, and bums. That is, except for the high-tech strip club a couple buildings away. I looked over there: lots of glitz, but not much action tonight.

I parked my car in a muddy lot and fought my way up to Crobar, toward the searchlights that stirred the midnight sky like neon swizzle sticks. I trudged past strangely dressed teenagers, autograph seekers, people of indeterminate gender, and policemen on horseback. Sullen cops tried to herd me into a mob of waiting revelers penned to the left of the main entrance like cattle.

"I have an invitation," I protested, holding up my "Dennis Rodman's Birthday Party Hosted by Crobar" card, No. 2758, with the tiny silhouette of a man in a welding suit in the center and the words "VERY GOOD" stamped in red.

"You and everybody else," the cop snorted.

After a few minutes another cop, this one no doubt a *Sun-Times* sports page reader, spotted me and said I was okay to cross the barricade to the front door. There I had the privilege of paying $10 to get in, after presenting my invitation. Of course, "a good portion" of the fee would be going "to a charity Dennis will select," somebody said. Of course. No question about it. I wondered what I was supposed to do now that I was inside. I had run square into a wall of humanity. The heat, music, and smoke were overpowering. I felt like a chicken leg at a barbecue.

Abruptly, I was saved again. It was Dwight Manley, Rodman's personal manager, agent, and sometime housecleaner, appearing from nowhere. Tall, bespectacled, and proper as a banker. Manley said, "Follow me."

I did. Someone—it may have been one of Rodman's personal bodyguards, off-duty Chicago cops Kelly Davis or George Triantafillo— cleared a path to the back of the warehouse. Smoke machines shot random white jets into the dimly lit cavern. People danced to synth music that blasted out of the p.a. system the way rolling bombs fall from bomb bay doors. Men with women. Women with women. Men with men.

Manley led me to the entrance to the stage, where the band had set up and was getting in position to play. As we moved up the stairs to the side of the stage, past the security forces, a young man with spiked, bleached hair tried to stop me.

"He's with me," said Manley to the Green Day–lookalike dude. The punk eyed my straightness with contempt and then moved on.

I asked Manley who the guy was.

"A loser," he said. "Stay here. I have things to do."

And he was gone.

Now the band is playing, and my ears are caving in. I look into the crowd and see a tall, sunglassed black man approaching. He's wearing an open leather shirt, jeans, and a striped stocking hat about three feet long. Worm.

He walks up the stairs, a beer in his hand. He looks at me and nods. I am a speck in the storm. A Chicago fireman stops Rodman and hands him a T-shirt. Rodman peels off his leather top and slips the T-shirt over his many ink illustrations and metal body hoops. The shirt reads "Chicago Fire Department" on the front and has the firefighters' motto, "Taming the Beast," on the back

Worm looks to be in a great mood, drinking whatever anybody puts in his hand and smiling to all. He walks out onstage to riotous cheering. He takes the microphone and says to the crowd, "This is my fucking party, but it's a party for all of you, too!" Thunderous applause and screaming.

He introduces the rotund Popper, who had been at the game and is now ready to blow nasty harp. Then he talks about the Bulls machine and how it is going to continue to kick ass. The Bulls are going "all the fucking way!" He introduces Ament, a member of his favorite band on earth, Pearl Jam. Then Rodman grooves to the music as the band digs in.

After a spell, Rodman introduces a little bitty guy. This is the leader of Rodman's favorite band on earth, the lead singer for Pearl Jam—whose bellowing, deep-throated cries about pain and alienation have struck Worm to his core—former gas station attendant and now super-star Eddie Vedder.

Vedder leads the band and the entire house in singing "Happy Birthday" to Rodman, then he and Rodman drink beer and spray the crowd with suds. The crazed audience shoots beer and wine and mixed drinks right back on stage, and soon Worm is soaked. He takes the mike once more and proclaims, "I want to buy everybody in the house a fucking beer and a shot! On me!"

Wild screams of joy. Rodman leaves the stage and heads to another part of the hall to socialize. I find myself downing another drink and wondering, not for the first time: What am I doing here? Well, I'm writing a book, I remind myself. And this is a scene. This is part of the Bulls season, which I am documenting. But, but, please, I'm a sportswriter, not a war correspondent. Not a rock critic. What's this got to do with basketball?

I push my way from the stage, ready to take advantage of the offer of a gratis shot and beer. I elbow up to a beer tub, maintained by a young woman with tattoos and a nose ring (of course), and ask for my free stuff.

She is busy arguing with another worker, over spilled drinks or something, and when she turns to me she says or, rather, yells, "Management hasn't told us we can do that yet."

She says it so corporately I feel perhaps I've mistakenly entered the lounge on a cruise ship. But no problem: I see WMAQ-TV sports guy Tom Zenner approaching the tub, and either I buy him a beer or he buys me one, I don't remember. We nod, and shortly he is absorbed by the crowd.

I move closer to the stage and then stop several feet short. Along with the screeching tweeter-enhanced guitar assault on my ears, I can now feel the woofer-amplified bass notes thudding into my chest cavity like Mike Tyson roundhouses to the heart, and I am afraid for a moment that they are going to interfere with the natural functioning of that organ and kill me. So I retreat to another, more protected bar and order myself a shot of Jaegermeister, an evil tar-colored drink, to deaden the voltage. The natural undulating effect of the crowd slowly propels me away from the action toward the front of the building. I stop at another beer tub and am struck by the bar maiden's ethereal tattoos and the silver stud that pierces the flesh below her lower lip. I ask her the only question I have about the stud: "Doesn't that hurt?"

"Yes," she replies, pocketing my $2 sympathy tip.

There is noise coming from upstairs, and I look up at what I figure must be the inner sanctum. Wally, one of the United Center media room workers, stands on the stairs, motioning me upward. There are guards, but Wally tells them to let me through. The lounge on the second floor is almost as crowded as the main floor, but this is it, the hotspot.

Rodman is here, bouncing from well-wisher to well-wisher like a batted balloon. Most of his teammates are also here. Seven-foot-two center Luc Longley rises above everyone. Scottie Pippen is wearing a nicely tailored suit. Jud Buechler is dressed for the beach. Toni Kukoc stands at the edge of the throng, smiling. Not-on-the-playoff-roster power forward Dickey Simpkins is wearing even nicer clothes than Pippen. James "Buddha" Edwards, the ancient 7-foot former Detroit Piston Bad Boy, wears a grin as inscrutable as that of his namesake. Most of the Bulls are here, celebrating their teammate's birthday and their advancement to the Eastern Conference finals. Noticeably absent, though, is one fellow whose initials are M.J. Also unaccounted for are guard Randy Brown (though he is of such normal stature he might have been engulfed by the horde and invisible) and 3-point ace Steve Kerr, who had said post-game that late night insanity at a rehabbed warehouse with huge speakers was "not exactly my scene."

Absent, too, is the tribal chief, Jackson.

Passing him in the United Center corridor after tonight's win, I had asked him whether he was headed to Crobar for the event.

"Maybe." Jackson grinned. Maybe he went to a firewalk instead.

I get my photo taken with Eddie Vedder, who is no bigger than Spud Webb. The photographer is renowned sports picture-taker Bill Smith, who at 6'6" stands above the fray like one of the players. Bill is an old pal of mine from our *Sports Illustrated* days. He has been hired by Manley to be the exclusive photographer for this bash; no other cameras or note-taking hacks have been allowed. I've been drinking beer with a man who is a lawyer by trade, but who got his invitation to this gig by being the hundredth caller to phone a sports radio station this morning. "I made the last call on my cellular as I was walking into my office building," he told me cheerily. "And I got it—a game ticket and a pass to the party!" Now I leave my drinking buddy and ask Smith to snap me and Worm together. I want documentation. Will Dennis do it? I don't know. Are we pals? Maybe not, since he got mad at me after a trip we took to Crobar a couple months ago, when I wrote about Shyra, a dancer from an M. C. Hammer video who was in his entourage that night.

There was another female friend, I guess, whom I was supposed to be saving from embarrassment, though who that woman might have been I hadn't a clue. Maybe it was the naked babe who appeared with Rodman in the January 1996 issue of *Playboy,* the woman named Stacey something-or-other, described in the piece as Rodman's "model-dancer-bassist-helicopter-pilot girlfriend," her arms placed behind her and around him, and his right hand and wrist covering her bare breasts, his gigantic left palm shielding her uncovered mons pubis. I had been asked to write the accompanying piece for *Playboy,* had even received a contract to do it from articles editor Peter Moore in August, but I was too busy, my heart wasn't in it, and I let the project dissipate from inertia. Back then Rodman was just a bad-attitude guy, still a part of, but unwanted by, the San Antonio Spurs. I'd written about him once for *Sports Illustrated* when he first arrived with the Spurs, and I wasn't sure I wanted to go through any of that again. I did make a preliminary call to him in August, however, tracked him down at his new buddy Manley's house in California, and asked him what he thought about possibly doing the *Playboy* story together. He sounded so lethargic, so brain-dead, so uncertain about anything at all, that I quickly said goodbye and never called back.

Now I say hi to him, and he looks down at me with eyes that seem darn near partied-out. I try to talk to him, but either the music and crowd are too loud or else he is blabbering in a foreign tongue. A flash goes off, Worm worms into the crowd, and I'm left to boogie onward.

I find myself buying some people shots of Jaegermeister, partaking of too much myself, asking a woman with short hair and a feather boa who is dancing on a table whether indeed she is a woman. She doesn't take offense at the query. There is another androgynous little partyer I had spotted earlier in the bash, who is now dancing atop the bar next to two gorgeous women. One of the women, a very young and wholesome-looking blond, is a new friend of Worm's, I've heard. The other is a black-haired, coffee-and-cream-skinned dancer clad in a bejeweled bustier the likes of which Cleopatra might have worn on her royal barge. It's Shyra. I yell at her, pointing to her outfit, "Egyptian?"

She nods. "*I'm* Egyptian."

The little guy is the prize, though. He is dressed like a character from *A Midsummer Night's Dream,* in tights, leotard, silvered hair, makeup, and a pair of large gossamer butterfly wings. I'd asked him earlier if he could fly. He just smiled and flapped his wings. Then I asked him if he was from the Baton, the female impersonator bar on Clark Street.

"When?" he asked.

I began writing notes on napkin scraps and matchbook covers at that point, not trusting my long-term memory anymore. I look at them now.

One says, "Smoke everywhere. Wasted Worm." Another says, "Best team ever?" Another says, "Nostril, oh well" and "Camel" and then something indecipherable, and then "Salley with stogie." The last jot refers to Bulls backup center John Salley, another resurrected Detroit Bad Boy, and the great pleasure with which he leaned against a wall and puffed a massive cigar during the festivities. He could have been a model in an ad for the posh cigar shop he intends to open.

But my mind keeps returning to the fairy. He was the kicker, an adult Tinkerbell, and one of the last things I remember clearly was Rodman sizing the little fellow up, rising on his toes, and giving him a big wet kiss on the lips.

Then it all went dim.

2

FLASH BACK TO A YEAR BEFORE RODMAN'S CROBAR BIRTHDAY, late May 1995: The Bulls have just been shot down in the Eastern Conference finals, four games to two, by the young and snappy Orlando Magic.

For me it's the damnedest coincidence, or confluence, or nasty omen, because I have just started my new job at the *Sun-Times* after 14 years as a senior writer for *Sports Illustrated,* and in my first venture out onto the old newspaper prediction limb I've written that the Shaquille O'Neal/Penny Hardaway–led Magic had no chance against the Bulls.

I typed the words after the Bulls and the Magic were tied at one win each, with the series moving to Chicago from Orlando after the first two games. I had had a long chat with TNT playoff analyst and former Bulls coach Doug Collins in Orlando about the strengths and weaknesses of each team, and with his absolute assurance that I was right in my judgment (indeed, he steered me toward some of the juicier stats), I wrote the following:

If the Orlando Magic were a turkey, it would be browning up nicely now.

Honey, can you open the cranberry sauce? And call in the kids.

Yep, it's just about mealtime for the Bulls, because the Magic are about 10 minutes from being taken from the oven and carved into lunchmeat.

I don't say this to be mean. I have actually grown to like this collection of men-children who are getting a fine reputation as the NBA Champs of the Future. Just when that future might be, I couldn't tell you.

But I do know it's Not Now.

And there are reasons for this that go far beyond Shaq's apparent unfamiliarity with basketball moves that do not involve crushing or pulverizing.

To wit:

• The Magic have a losing road record. True, they have a marvelous home winning record, 39–2, best in the NBA this season. But NBA champs almost always have winning road records, indicating they can play tough in ugly places. The last NBA champ that lost more on the road than it won was the 1977–78 Washington Bullets.

• The Magic are the highest-scoring team in the league, with a 110.9 points-per-game average. This would seem like a plus, but something works against gunners once the stress of the playoffs begins. Teams see each other again and again, defense is jacked up a notch, and a lot of the midseason fireworks get snuffed in the process.

The last NBA champs who led the league in scoring were the 1974–75 Golden State Warriors. Rick Barry was the main gun for that team, and the Magic have no one close to him in sheer, unconscious, guilt-free shooting ability.

• *The Magic are the worst free-throw-shooting team in the NBA, making just 67 percent of their shots. I don't think I need to explain to you why that can be a problem. Just consider that Shaq is now being touted as a free-throw-shooting wizard because he only missed 7 of 20 free ones Wednesday. That's 65 percent, by my calculation.*

When asked after Game 1 against the Bulls how he had improved so much that night, Shaq grunted, "What playoffs you been watchin'?" Comfortable so quickly!

And yet the last team with the worst free-throw percentage to win an NBA title was the 1981–82 Los Angeles Lakers. And they had fellows named Kareem and Earvin doing everything but varnishing the floor.

• *Until this season, the Magic had not won a playoff game. Orlando beat that spell (sort of) by beating the hapless Boston Celtics 3–1 in Round 1 of this year's playoffs. That a team might take comfort in being considered superior to the current Celtics reminds me of an old line from Dick Schaap. "Being called an intellectual next to Joe Namath," said Schaap, "is like being called a weightlifter next to Truman Capote."*

These are just the facts, folks. The Magic have about as much chance of overcoming all these odds as Michael Jordan has of growing an Afro.

Down there in central Florida, people are not much taken with Magic coach Brian Hill's game plans, either. As one distressed fan said to me after Game 2, "He's the worst fourth-quarter coach in the league."

Well, I don't know about that. But I do know that for some reason Shaq almost disappears in the final 12 minutes of many games. The Bulls' 252-Inches-of-Flesh-Toned Monster, its pale center by committee, has done quite well against this man whose shoes are so large that I borrowed a left one before Game 2 and put my entire foot and size 11½ shoe inside it, easily. Truth.

And there are other failings on this team of youngsters. Not the

*least of which is the fact that one of its stars, Horace Grant, is not
exactly young anymore. And Shaq backup Tree Rollins? Lord, he's
a sliver of material from the Petrified Forest. Penny Hardaway
could use a lethal mid-range jumper. Dennis Scott could use consistency. Donald Royal could use an identity. Nick Anderson could
use a vacation from Mr. Jordan.*

*A team cannot always be Young and Learning. At some point it
must be Rough and Ready.*

But the Magic are not ready yet. But let's check that oven.

Perfect.

Fork, please.

Smartass.

After the Bulls were knocked out in Game 6, despite having had an
8-point lead with 3:42 to play, I didn't know what to think. Horace
Grant, the former Bull who had left Chicago the year before after an
ugly contract fight with chairman Jerry Reinsdorf, simply killed the
Bulls with his rebounding and his critical and impeccable jump-shooting.
The Bulls would collapse on Shaq, Toni Kukoc would double down on
the huge man with Luc Longley or Bill Wennington or Will Perdue, the
ball would circle around to the open man—Grant—and he would bury
the j. His blue goggles never fogged up, they just zeroed in.

During a loose-ball scramble with Longley in the first quarter, Grant
actually had his goggles knocked off his head onto the court. Old pal
Pippen snatched them and stuck them down the front of his own shorts.
That was funny. It seemed to point out that, sure, this was an important
game, but it was still really just a stage set for the amazing march of the
Bulls.

Why, Michael Jordan himself was back after a year and a half off!
The great cosmic adventurer had quit the Bulls in the fall of 1993, said
he had reached a crossroads in his life, was "going to watch the grass
grow," and then had tried to become a major league baseball player. His
jersey number, 23, had been retired; he had been honored at a tacky and
overblown retirement event at the United Center, and a scary bronze
statue of him dunking over what appeared to be souls burning in hell
had been erected by Gate 4. The statue's legend proclaimed, "The best

there ever was. The best there ever will be." At times during Jordan's retirement, people could be seen kneeling and praying before the sculpture.

But Jordan had come back to his true calling two months ago, on March 18, and had played 17 regular-season games since then. The Bulls had gone 13–4 during that stretch, a 76 percent win rate, compared to 34–31, a 52 percent rate, before his return. Critics said Jordan was rusty, couldn't fly like before. Oops. In his fifth game back, he torched the Knicks for 55 points at Madison Square Garden. It was the second-highest point total in the league that season.

But still there were doubts that Jordan, now 32, was the same man who had left the game at the pinnacle, after leading the Bulls to three consecutive NBA titles. He even wore a different number—45—because good old 23 was hanging from the rafters. In Game 1 against Orlando, the Bulls had the ball and a 1-point lead with 18 seconds remaining. As Jordan dribbled upcourt, certain the Magic would foul him to stop the clock, he had the ball stolen from behind by Nick Anderson. Hardaway picked it up and passed to Grant, who dunked for the Magic lead. The Bulls got the ball back with 6 seconds left, but Jordan threw it away on a bad pass to Pippen. The Magic had won a game it didn't deserve. Jordan had 8 turnovers and looked oddly mortal.

"I'm shocked," said Bulls guard Steve Kerr of the loss, speaking for all the Bulls. "I thought we had it gift-wrapped."

Number 45 wasn't number 23, went the buzz. Anderson's steal was played endlessly on television sports shows around the country. *Would the real Michael Jordan have done this?* Even when Jordan came out in his old 23 jersey for the next game, it didn't quell the rumors.

When Hardaway saw Pippen messing around with Grant's goggles in Game 6, he walked over to Pippen, shook his head in disgust, and yanked the goggles out of Pippen's trunks. No, Hardaway was saying to Pippen, Jordan, and the Bulls, this is not your moment. Your time has passed.

And as I watch the rest of the 1995 NBA finals, watch as upstart Orlando gets steamrolled by the Houston Rockets, I feel that maybe the Bulls are a ship whose sails no longer catch the full breeze. If frisky, up-and-coming Orlando gets whacked 4–0 in the 1995 finals by a Houston team with Hakeem Olajuwon and not much else, what does that say about the Bulls' chances for renewed greatness?

Why would I want to write about this team? I asked myself. Their golden moment was history. Rock-solid center Bill Cartwright from the Three-Peat days was gone. So was sharp-shooting guard John Paxson. And playmaker/long-range ace B. J. Armstrong. And, most noticeable of all, power forward Grant.

Slender 6'11" finger-rolling expert Toni Kukoc was no power forward. He'd filled the spot for the Bulls in Grant's absence, but it was like using a flower vase as a sledgehammer. Kukoc had sixth man written all over him.

So who could do the rough work at that spot? Dickey Simpkins and Corie Blount were inexperienced and unexceptional. The Bulls would soon draft 6'8", 255-pound Jason Caffey out of Alabama, but he, too, was inexperienced, and baffled by the offense to boot. Without a fierce, rebounding power forward, the Bulls were headed nowhere. But who was out there? Almost nobody.

Before the Magic series I had mentioned to Bulls Vice President, Basketball Operations Jerry Krause, a.k.a. the Sleuth, that the Bulls probably could use a serious power forward. He agreed, or at least grunted seeming acceptance of that obvious point. "Funny thing is," I said, "you had one. But now he plays for the other team."

Krause then explained how Grant had reneged on the handshake contract that Reinsdorf had made with him; otherwise he'd still be a Bull. I knew this part was coming, so I sort of listened but mostly watched the officials and cops and Lovabulls and United Center workers coming and going here in the restricted area underneath the stands. With the Sleuth you always pretty much expected revisionist history, and secrecy.

When he was done, I asked whether he was going to pursue a power forward.

"Do you have someone in mind?"

Just being goofy, I said, "How about Dennis Rodman?"

He looked at me as though I had nominated Jeffrey Dahmer for head chef.

"No, no. Never," he stated. "Not our kind of person."

I figured that. I had spent enough time with Rodman to know that he would be a tough nut for anybody to crack. And the Bulls prided themselves on having "good people" aboard. So the Sleuth and I talked about other things, and that was it.

What pleasure could there be in writing this book, I asked myself. What, really, was there left to write about Michael Jordan? As he said after the Game 6 debacle, "I have to take the blame, just as I would take the credit." Everything revolved around him, and, my God, it had all been documented. There were so many books out about Jordan that I stopped trying to collect them. *Rare Air* by Mark Vancil and Jordan and my old *Sports Illustrated* photo buddy, Walter Iooss. Then *Rare Air II.* Then *Airborne: The Triumph and Struggle of Michael Jordan,* by Jesse Kornbluth. And of course, *The Jordan Rules,* Sam Smith's best-selling book that showed Jordan had character flaws. (Still to come was Sam's not-so-best-selling Bulls/Jordan tome, *Second Coming.*) And Bob Greene's *Hang Time: Days and Dreams with Michael Jordan.* Which, of course was not enough for the prolific Greene, who had latched onto, as he often put it, the Elvis of our era. In *Hang Time* Greene wrote about Jordan having changed his—Greene's—life. Disillusioned by the nastiness he saw in the world and weary with middle-age ennui, Greene wrote of his spiritually uplifting Jordan encounter, "My life is better for having lived this time."

As you might expect, such epiphany would lead inexorably to book two in the Greene–Jordan metaphysical tango, *Rebound: The Odyssey of Michael Jordan.* In that one Greene described the minor league baseball–playing Jordan as "Elvis in the outfield," and let him ramble on about everything from Larry Bird to the Olympics. This Greene effort would eventually beget another edition of *Rebound,* one that boasted "With an Exclusive Update—A New Chapter Covering Jordan's and the Bulls' Extraordinary 1996 Season," even though the book came out before the 1996 playoffs started.

And there was *Transition Game: An Inside Look at Life with the Chicago Bulls* by Melissa Isaacson. In it Jordan says such things as, "Johnny (Bach) would say, 'Fuck the triangle, just take the ball and score.' " And there was the book my three daughters had read, *Michael Jordan,* by children's author Richard J. Brenner. It contained passages such as,

"The boy who had had trouble making his high school team had become a professional basketball player. And what a player he'd become!"

And there was, depending on how you looked at it, the sleaziest or strangest or most damning book of them all, *Michael and Me: Our Gambling Addiction, My Cry for Help,* by a golfing, celebrity-chasing, macho-posturing California oddball named Richard Esquinas. Jordan was either an out-of-control golf and poker gambler who hung around with unsavory characters and was well on the road to perdition, or he was not. Make your choice.

There were potential pluses to following the Bulls for a season, I had to admit. Phil Jackson was an interesting coach, a former hippie–NBA player who always had engaging tales to tell. And the players were varied and unique: a giant Australian, a skittish Croatian, a Canadian by way of Long Island, a surfer, a guy from a little town in Arkansas, a stutterer with a bad knee and a tattoo of Batman on his calf, a blond-haired shooter who was born in Lebanon and looked just like Beavis from the idiotic MTV cartoon show. And then there was Jordan. Even if he was in decline, he was more charismatic than any player in the league.

And then, too, what if the Bulls were reborn and went all the way to the top once more?

That could happen, too.

3

May 21, 1995, column (post–playoff elimination; pre–NBA draft)

I'm afraid to say it, but I think Orlando beat the Bulls for one simple reason—they're a better team.

These Magic fellows are so callow they make you wonder if championship teams aren't best built around near-adolescents.

Shaquille O'Neal is 23 and Anfernee Hardaway is 22, and they are going to be around a while.

So whatever time might heal for the Bulls, it better heal it with youth. Or with genuine substance.

The one thing that is certain about pro franchises is that when you have your moment to make your charge for the championship, you'd better charge full-tilt, and get there. To narrowly miss—a la the Phoenix Suns or Portland Trail Blazers—is to doom yourself to dropping back into the pack, unfulfilled, perhaps for a long time.

Bulls chairman Jerry Reinsdorf was aware of this phenomenon when he took over the club in 1985, with 1st-year man Michael Jordan already aboard. Reinsdorf knew that Jordan was a lightning bolt, a once-in-a-lifetime acquisition. But he also knew Jordan was surrounded by mediocre players, good enough to help the Bulls finish above .500, but not good enough to help them win anything important.

And not bad enough to override Jordan's brilliance and sink the Bulls to last place.

Which, crazily, is where great teams are built.

It's that draft thing, you know. Ineptitude rewarded as it never is in real life.

"I knew that with Jordan we'd never be bad enough to get a great center in the draft," said Reinsdorf, thinking back on those early days. "And we were trying to build a championship team around a two-guard, which had never been done before. So this was going to be tough."

It was tough. But it was done.

The most critical parts were getting power forward Charles Oakley in a 1985 draft-day swap with Cleveland, trading up to get Scottie Pippen in the 1987 draft, sneaking Horace Grant in that same draft, and then trading Oakley for coveted center Bill Cartwright in 1988.

Operations chief Jerry Krause deserves great credit for the tricks and stunts he pulled to get the Bulls to the back-to-back-to-

back championship stage. But that was then, and this is somewhere else.

Because Jordan ages daily, and when he's gone the Bulls' moment—long as it has been—is also gone.

The Bulls draft 20th this year, which is basically worthless, unless Krause knows something about somebody nobody else knows. B. J. Armstrong was the 18th player taken in the 1989 draft, remember. And Toni Kukoc was the 29th player taken in the 1990 draft.

But the scary thing is, look at the Bulls' most recent drafts and acquisitions. First-round picks Mark Randall, Byron Houston, Corie Blount, and Dickey Simpkins—power forwards all—haven't lit the world on fire. Haven't even lit a dark closet.

And free agent pickups Larry Krystkowiak and Ron Harper have been major disappointments.

I think Luc Longley, with an injection of adrenaline and some jumping lessons, can be a good center. I think Kukoc can fit in somewhere, maybe as the classic sixth man. Armstrong and Steve Kerr are all right, too. Paxson clones. There is no power forward anywhere that I can see, so the Bulls must trade or do something to get one. (Gee, Horace, could Michael talk you into a return trip north?)

As Jordan says, "I'm not worried about getting my net worth . . . Money comes and goes, but history books don't forget."

Like the rest of us, he can hear time whizzing past.

I look back on that and I think of two things right off: First, wasn't Jerry West a two-guard, more or less? Didn't he win a title with the 1971–72 Los Angeles Lakers? And what about Rick Barry of the 1974–75 NBA champion Golden State Warriors? What was Barry? A small forward, you say? Still, he finished second in the NBA in scoring, first in steals, and tied for fifth in assists. Excuse me, Mr. Reinsdorf, but maybe building around a smaller, non–point guard isn't that unheard of. Then, too, calling Jordan something as mundane as a two-guard is like calling Mozart a piano player.

Secondly, I couldn't see an available great power forward because, well, the one I had in mind had been removed from my sight.

■■■

Somewhere the Worm was turning. But where?

It was the late summer of 1993, and I had been searching for Dennis Rodman for days.

The Detroit Pistons were of no help; they had not seen their All-Star forward in months. To say the relationship between the Pistons and Rodman was strained would be to say the relationship between DDT and a mosquito is strained. Pistons player-personnel director Billy McKinney was at his wit's end with the fugitive forward. "My next move is to take a picture of him and put it on a milk carton," he said.

The roulette ball whirred through its arc. Worm stared at the spinning wheel, transfixed by the vectors, the possibilities, the forces involved. His money was on red. The ball clattered, clattered, clattered, then came to rest. Black! The croupier raked in Worm's chips. Good, thought Rodman. That's good. Take my money.

Worm's agent at the time, Bill Pollak, did not return my calls. "Mr. Pollak is in a meeting," said his secretary. "He'll get back to you this afternoon." That afternoon the secretary said, "Mr. Pollak is on a two-week vacation." Where? "Italy."

Worm's off-court business enterprise, Rodman Excavation Inc. in Frisco, Texas, had lost touch with its elusive owner. "We don't know where he is," the receptionist said. "No one knows." Another voice came on the phone, the voice of a higher-up. "We haven't seen him in four weeks," the woman said.

Worm put his money on the green felt of the craps table. A hundred dollars' worth of chips, two hundred, five hundred. He didn't know how much. Somebody rolled the dice, and the cubes bounced off the padded green wall. A number was established. The dice were thrown again. Wrong number. Worm has crapped out. The pitman raked in Rodman's chips. Take it, he thought. Take it all.

"I'm on the Rodman hunt too," said Pistons PR man Matt Dobek. "Rumor is he's in Sacramento. But there's also a theory he's in Denver. Somebody told me he had come back to Detroit, but he's not here. There's a 'For Sale' sign in front of his house in Bloomfield Hills, a

Corvette without license plates parked in the drive. His phone is disconnected. We've also heard he's in Las Vegas. Somebody saw him there. Staying at the Mirage. Supposedly he's got—what do you call those things?—dreadlocks."

The receptionist at the Mirage hotel says, "Mr. Rodman is not listed here, and if he is not registered, he is not here. Have a nice weekend."

But Rodman was in Vegas. His money was on the table. The dice were ricocheting off the wall. Rodman had wagered on the losing line, crapped out again. The croupier harvested everything Worm had left. The 32-year-old basketball star, who once worked the night shift as a janitor at the Dallas–Fort Worth Airport, had performed a symbolic act of penance, a cleansing of spirit that he felt would allow him to recapture, however fleetingly, the innocence and freedom of a former self that haunted him like a ghost. In a matter of days he had lost all he came with, close to $35,000, which is what he wanted to do.

"I hate money," he said later. "I went to Las Vegas to lose. So I could feel normal."

■ ■ ■

Normal.

The word bounces off Dennis Rodman like a clanger off the rim. Nothing about Rodman—nicknamed Worm years ago by his hometown friends in Dallas because of the way he squirmed while playing video games—is normal. His background is so bizarre that it could never work as fiction. And his oncourt accomplishments defy logic.

He joined the Pistons in 1986 and helped them win back-to-back NBA championships in 1988–89 and 1989–90, even though he had been little more than a benchwarmer during his half a season of high school basketball. He had been named to the NBA All-Defensive first team five straight years, and he routinely guarded centers, power forwards, small forwards, and shooting guards even though his college career game was limited to stints at a junior college and an NAIA school. He had led the league in rebounding the last two seasons (1991–92 and 1992–93), averaging an incredible 18.5 per game during that stretch, 4 boards a game better than his closest challenger. He had led the league in offensive rebounding the last three seasons, averaging a persistent 5.5 per game over that period, and yet he almost had to be pistol-whipped

into shooting the rock. "There were times when he'd get an offensive rebound right under the basket," said former Pistons teammate Isiah
Thomas, marveling at the image, "and he'd come all the way out to the
three-point line and hand me the ball."

In a league where scoring is everything and flash is worshipped, Rodman was a star who did not score or flash. Who did not *want* to score or
flash. "I have become a superstar from doing stupid, crazy shit," he said.
"I have the job nobody wants." Once, at the Silverdome, he flew into the
stands after a loose ball with such recklessness that he injured a female
spectator, who sued him. The court awarded her a reported $60,000 for
her injuries, which included the loss of several teeth.

"He brought back the concept of 'garbage player,'" said former
teammate Scott Hastings. "But he's made it an art form."

Worm did garbage so well that when things blew up with the Pistons
in 1992–93—when he was trying in vain to explain why he kept missing practices, when he was telling anyone who would listen that he
wanted to play somewhere else (it was never clear where), when he was
seeing a psychiatrist, when he was found by the police sleeping in his
truck in the parking lot at the Palace of Auburn Hills at 5 A.M. with a
loaded rifle under his front seat, when he kept adding more and more
tattoos to his body, when he took his shoes off in the middle of games,
when he shaved slogans into his scalp—even then there were half a
dozen teams clamoring for his services.

"There's never been an NBA player like him," said former Piston
coach Chuck Daly. "I love him. I'll endorse him anywhere."

Being on the gym floor seemed sacred to Rodman. There was the
night in 1990 when he cried on the court while playing the Houston
Rockets. Hakeem Olajuwon was going to dunk on him, had him beat to
the basket in the last moments of a tied game, and Worm knew he was
whipped by the much taller and stronger man, but he spun to the hoop
anyway, as hard as he could, never giving up, and leaped, and *blocked
the dunk*. It was transcendent. His eyes filled with tears.

Crying at such moments was nothing for this most unrefined and delicate of men. There was the night in 1992 when Rodman grabbed 34
rebounds against the Indiana Pacers, breaking Bob Lanier's 20-year-old

Pistons single-game record, and he cried like a baby. Broke a record held by a 6'11", 265-pound center. "This is not my greatest achievement," Worm said later. "The greatest achievement was turning my life around."

Which was true. But where was that life headed now?

"I think he's been overwhelmed with success," said TV analyst Dick Versace, who was a Pistons assistant coach when Rodman broke into the league as a 25-year-old rookie out of Southeastern Oklahoma State. "But nothing has ever affected his desire to win. He's never violated the sanctity of the game."

And yet when a team acquired Worm and his rebounds, defense, hustle, and fire, it had to ask itself: What else have we gotten? The San Antonio Spurs, who obtained Rodman from the Pistons in a trade on October 1, 1993, were asking themselves that, and more.

■ ■ ■

"I love pain," Rodman told me back then, as he steered his big Chevy truck onto a San Antonio freeway. "It makes me feel like I'm accomplishing something. I can't stand being in a game and not getting knocked down."

Once, guard Darrell Walker, then of the Washington Bullets, grew so disgusted with Rodman's tenacious play that he tried to kick him and then spat at him. The spit missed, but Rodman said he wished it had hit him so he could have rubbed it on his jersey and got "pumped up."

Pain, Rodman was telling me, made him feel whole, assured him that he was working as hard as he could. It made him feel that for the moment, at least, he was not, as *USA Today* columnist Bryan Burwell once put it, "tumbling back into that frightening old world."

But the pain he felt on this particular day was different.

"Man, my head's on fire!" he told Fred Baldarrama, the hair designer at Olga's Salon in a San Antonio mall. Baldarrama smiled gently as he dabbed soothing cream on the front of Rodman's scalp, where the gooey bleach was eating away at hair color and flesh. This was Rodman's maiden voyage into the world of hair-coloring, a practice he would eventually raise to pop art.

He sat as still as he could amid the old ladies and manicurists. Why was he going blond? All the way here he talked about wanting to blend in, to be normal, to get, as he put it, "solid." He pondered the question. "Why?" he said. "Because I don't give a damn."

He was so hurt in the 1992–93 preseason over Chuck Daly's departure from the Pistons, over the breakup of his two-year marriage to Annie, and over his inability to spend more time with their five-year-old daughter, Alexis, that he locked himself in his Bloomfield Hills home and refused to answer the door or the phone or attend practices or games, emerging only long past midnight to buy food or to work out at Gold's Gym. At one point he got a new phone number, but he didn't listen as the operator told him what it was. If he didn't know his own number, he reasoned, how could anyone find him?

He wanted to be traded, he told the Pistons. He felt betrayed. By whom? By everyone. All his friends from the old days were gone. Daly, "the miracle worker," as Rodman described him, the man who told him about life, was gone. GM Jack McCloskey, the man who had drafted Rodman, was gone. Trainer Mike Abdenour and assistant coach Versace were gone. His wife and child were gone.

He said that all he wanted to do was spend time with his daughter, but he wouldn't visit Sacramento, where she lived with her mother. He made little sense. He was late for practices. He was fined and suspended at various times. He missed games due to a lingering, questionable calf injury. He would not talk to new coach Ron Rothstein. But when Worm played, the Pistons were a different team. At one point in 1993 they were 17–12 with him, 0–10 without him. McKinney even stopped fining Rodman for breaking rules. "Why cut off your nose to spite your face?" he said. But this was all so wrong. Where was the joy Rodman had once brought to the arena?

"When he came into the league, he was this wide-eyed, frenetic, incredibly naive guy who just cherished it all," said Dick Versace. "Dennis would get the ball two feet from the basket and give it up. He was so thrilled—it was like, Wow, I'm playing with Isiah Thomas!"

"Those first few years he was the model Piston," said Thomas. "On time. Never complained. Followed instructions. If any of us had known how to make him happy at the end, believe me, we would have done it."

In mid-February 1993, police got a late-night phone call from a friend of Rodman's, warning that the player had left home in his truck depressed and possibly suicidal. That's when police found Rodman in the Palace parking lot at 5 A.M., unharmed, the rifle under his seat. He had broken no laws, but he scared the Pistons brass plenty. As Dobek, the PR man, was driving Rodman to a psychiatrist an hour after the incident, he got a call on his cell phone from his own mother. She had heard the news on the radio. "Are you okay?" she screamed to her son. "Did Rodman shoot you?"

Rodman said later: "Why was the rifle there? It's always there. I was depressed, but I wasn't going to kill myself. I was just hurting, ripped to shreds. You butt heads with reality and it's like having a stroke. I didn't lose touch with reality, but I put it on pause."

Rodman had used other terms to describe how he felt during dark times. He talked of sinking into "black holes," of feeling like a "mummy." His alienation never left completely, never left him in peace, except when he was immersed in the game on the hardwood, where, he said, "everything makes sense."

At some point, of course, this no longer generated sympathy from coaches or GMs or anybody else in the league. The NBA is not a charity; everybody plays hurt, and if you can't play, get the hell out of the way. In Rodman's case the Pistons had finally had enough. He was set to be traded to the Phoenix Suns in 1992 for forward Richard Dumas, but that deal fell through when Dumas was suspended for drug use. The Spurs wanted Rodman because they had finished last in the league in offensive rebounding the year before. General manager Bob Bass, who sent All-Star forward Sean Elliott and forward David Wood to Detroit for Rodman and Isaiah Morris (quickly waived), figured Rodman could take some of the rebounding pressure off center David Robinson and also help the Spurs lose the "soft" label they'd been tagged with for so long. Bass said, "We need somebody gambling on steals and diving on the floor."

And Rodman's personal baggage? "We'll just have to wait and see how that goes," Bass said hopefully.

■■■

Rodman's skull was still burning, as the toxic goop turned his hair from black to a sickly orange. He pulled up his shirttail and used it to fan his scalp, thereby revealing the gold ring that pierced his navel like a tiny door knocker. He had gotten the ring recently because his ex-wife had one and because he said he still loved her, even though their split had been bitter. He spoke wistfully about remarrying Annie, though he had not asked her how she felt about the matter.

And how *did* she feel about it? I called her and asked. "I will never marry Dennis," Annie said. "I will not go through that suffering again."

Rodman's body art—tattoos and more tattoos and more pierced body parts and soon hair-as-a-palette—could be interpreted as a form of self-mutilation, a quasispiritual mortification of the flesh, a way to show the world that he is doing penance for his sins, like a pilgrim, publicly. But mostly it's a manifestation of his flamboyant streak, a part of him that revels in being noticed and in showing that he is different from the crowd. And yet another part of him detests it. "He likes attention, and he doesn't like it," said Chuck Daly. "His whole life is a dichotomy."

Annie, a former model who fell for Rodman because of his "sensitivity, his innocence, and his vulnerability," grew angry at the spectacle Rodman had made of their private world. "He has a tattoo of his child on his forearm," she said, her voice cracking, "but he sent her nothing for Christmas. He didn't call on her birthday. He missed her first day of kindergarten. When she had chicken pox this summer, it took us three days just to *find* him. Sure, he lost thirty-five thousand dollars in Las Vegas on purpose, but why didn't he just set up a trust fund for Alexis instead? Have you seen the tattoo he has that says 'Linda,' one of his girlfriends? Talk about a knife in my heart." (When *Sports Illustrated* ran its 1995 cover story on Rodman, posing him in leather and chains, Annie wrote to *SI*, "I am embarrassed and ashamed of myself for ever being married to him.")

Raised in a tough part of Dallas in a family with an absent father and a mother who doted on Rodman's two younger sisters, both of whom were far better basketball players than he was, Rodman never felt particularly good about himself. As a bored, reticent, and bullied kid, he had a vague dream of someday playing for the Dallas Cowboys, but he did nothing toward making that dream come true. In high school he drifted, and he succumbed to the lure of the streets. Only 5'11" after graduation, with no marketable skills, he saw his life slipping away from him. Then, two years later, he abruptly grew 9 inches. While working that janitorial job at the airport, he stole a bunch of watches and gave them to friends. He was arrested, and though the charges were eventually dropped because he returned all the watches, he realized that if he didn't get his act together he was doomed to a life in what he refers to as "the netherworld." When he went off to Southeastern Oklahoma State in 1983, at age 22, following a year at Cooke County College in Gainesville, Texas, he vowed "I will never come back to Dallas until I have made something of myself."

He was a three-time NAIA All-America, averaging 24.4 points and 17.8 rebounds per game as a senior, and the Pistons drafted him in the second round—as a project. He was a primitive basketball marvel, people said, something like an idiot savant, the Rainman of the NBA. "Who are you?" a reporter asked early in Rodman's career. "I'm nobody straight out of nowhere," Rodman answered.

Small wonder, then, that he would one day be overwhelmed by his bounty. Certainly he had worked and prayed for this good fortune to occur. But did he *deserve* it? As we spent time together in San Antonio, Rodman's oddly silent new girlfriend, Kim, from L.A. or Vegas or somewhere always tagging along, it struck me that Dennis was never really mentally *here*. Distracted, nervous, self-absorbed, he seemed always to be looking for something that was nowhere to be found.

So it was that after his last Detroit season he vanished from the NBA world and reappeared at that holiest of American shrines, Las Vegas, to purge himself and to make amends. "I was getting rid of everything that had meaning in my life and starting over," he said of his ritualistic gaming losses. He had behaved that way before on a lesser scale, just given things away. He would do it because he never wanted to forget where he came from and because the unfairness of the world genuinely troubled him. In Detroit he would sometimes drive through the streets of the toughest parts of town, giving out money to homeless people—once, he struck up a conversation with a homeless man, then simply emptied his pockets to the poor soul, giving him close to a thousand dollars. "So many people need so much," Rodman explained. Sometimes he'd take a vagrant home with him, cleaning the man up, feeding him, and sending him off in good spirits.

When Worm's 'do was finally done, after three and a half hours of anguish, his coif resembled a yellow scrub brush. I was antsy the whole time he was in the chair, reminding him often that the Spurs' shootaround, the team's 1993–94 season debut in front of team owners and the public at the sparkling new Alamodome, was getting closer and closer. As he stood and stretched, I told him, horror-stricken, that the shootaround had started 30 minutes ago.

"Just some investors," he said, shrugging.

As we left the salon, people stopped dead in their tracks to gawk. At the Alamodome, Rodman was now 40 minutes late. There was tension in the air as 5,000 fans watched the team run through drills without the one player everyone had come to see. Behind the stands Rodman slowly walked toward the dressing room. I found myself trying to pick up the pace, saying "Come on, come on" to move him along; then I drifted behind, not wanting anybody in the Spurs organization to blame this debacle on me. Team officials tried to hurry him without offending him in any way.

Finally, shoes untied, jersey out, a RODMAN EXCAVATION baseball cap worn backward over his new golden swatch, Rodman jogged onto the floor to wild cheering and a smattering of boos. His teammates looked on silently, uncertain what to feel.

"Last, but not least," said master of ceremonies David Robinson into the stadium microphone. "He can rebound and play defense almost as well as I can . . . the Demolition Man . . . Dennis Rodman!"

The cap came off for an electrifying moment, then it went back on. Screeches filled the arena air. Rodman took the microphone. He looked into the recesses of the cavernous building, his face blank.

"You can like me or you can hate me," he said. "But all I can say is, when I get on the damn floor, all I'm going to do is get solid." He dropped the mike onto the polished wood. That was it for the day.

After changing back to his customary sweatpants, T-shirt, construction boots, cap, and shades, Rodman joined Kim and me and looked over where head coach John Lucas, the former NBA star/drug addict/

turned inspirational speaker, was talking engagingly to the two dozen or so team investors who were seated in front of him in the stands.

"Look at him," said Rodman with contempt. "Kissing ass."

The player yelled toward his coach, "Hey, Luke!" Lucas did not hear him and continued to talk to his audience.

"Hey, Luke!" Rodman called again. This time Lucas heard him, and he and the investors turned to see what was up.

"Hey, Luke!" Rodman shouted, with a nasty grin. "Need some Chapstick?"

■■■

When Rodman came into the league, the Pistons coaching staff named him Worldclass because, according to Dick Versace, "if he ran the four-forty, he'd be world class. The guy can run on his toes, all day, like a sprinter."

Rodman always could run all day, and in basketball he studied players' shooting tendencies, noting where the caroms of their shots were likely to go. He took early lessons in that from Detroit teammate Bill Laimbeer, learning "tenaciousness and how to tap the ball like a volleyball." But most of Rodman's rebounding success came from simple want-to. "I work my ass off, that's all," he said. "People ask how you dig a fifty-foot hole? You dig."

The sad thing was that now people were talking less about Rodman's skill and ferocity than his weird tonsorial statements. On the day of the Spurs' first preseason game, the *San Antonio Express-News* carried a report on the cover of its Lifestyle section about his "futuristic platinum blond flattop, which could be on the cutting edge of hair fashion."

On the sports page was an ominous "open letter" to Rodman from veteran columnist Dan Cook, who ripped him for his tardiness and posturing, reminding him that when he left the Pistons, the *Detroit Free Press* carried a huge headline reading simply DE-WORMED. "Dennis, you didn't come here with a chip on your shoulder," Cook wrote. "You're carrying a telephone pole, daring anyone to give it a tap."

"This summer when he came to see me, he seemed suicidal," said Annie. "He came here looking like a transient. He was in old clothes, he'd lost about fifteen pounds, he couldn't sleep. He had a designer design a twenty-five-thousand-dollar wedding dress for me, but he'd just been in Las Vegas with his girlfriend. Whatever Dennis Rodman can't have, he wants."

It struck me a day later, after bidding farewell to Worm and then boarding my plane to fly home from San Antonio, that perhaps Dennis Rodman would never feel at ease until he had lost everything that set him apart from what he once was. That what he would have to do was lose it all, and start over.

4

SUCH A HOT SUMMER IN CHICAGO. THE PAVEMENT SEEMS TO hold in the vibrating molecules the way a mattress holds in feathers. It's late July 1995, and in a few more days it will get so hot that hundreds of city residents will die from heat-related causes. Dogs seldom venture out of the shade. Air conditioners roar incessantly.

But here in the blazing sun, down a cracked sidewalk along Hoyne Street, west of the United Center, come the dignitaries.

Michael Jordan is followed by Chicago mayor Richard Daley, who is followed by Illinois governor Jim Edgar. As I wipe the sweat from my eyes I figure that if Bill Clinton were in town, he'd come next.

The occasion is the ground-breaking ceremony for the James H. Jordan Boys & Girls Club and Family Life Center. Funded largely by a $4 million donation from the Bulls, the club named in memory of Michael's father is being built on a weed-and-glass-covered vacant lot. As every NBA fan in the world now knows, James Jordan was murdered by robbers two years ago as he slept in his car on the shoulder of a highway outside Lumberton, North Carolina. The crime was so inexplicable, so improbable, so cold-blooded and grotesque—the victim was missing for weeks before his body was found in a South Carolina swamp and identified through dental charts—that many people felt there had to be some deeper meaning to the crime. Extortion perhaps. A message to Michael for God knows what. Punishment over bad debts. Something to do with Michael's or James's gambling habits.

The two hapless local teenagers who had been charged with the crime looked like the fall guys for some large conspiracy. Why hadn't the Jordan family reported its senior member missing sooner? Why had the body been cremated so quickly? The attorneys for one of the defendants even filed motions suggesting that James Jordan was still alive and on the lam. An article in *GQ* magazine in March 1994 all but proclaimed the case an elaborate fraud, quoting an unidentified source as stating "These kids were shut up."

Such speculation was rife until two months ago, May 1995, when the truth reared its insipid little head. While the Bulls were flying to nearby Charlotte to play the Hornets in the playoffs, Larry Demery, one of the defendants, pleaded guilty to robbing and murdering James Jordan. Nothing tricky; according to Demery, he and his pal, Daniel Andre Green, the other defendant, just up and killed a man and took his things. And the man happened to be Michael Jordan's father. Demery made the plea in hopes of avoiding the death penalty. Nothing noble. No remorse. Just trying to save himself.

I took time off from covering the Bulls–Hornets series and drove one sunny day the three hours to Lumberton. What a godforsaken, depressing town it was: so sleepy and rural-sounding, but it was a hellhole. Angry faces everywhere. I asked Hubert Rogers, one of Demery's attorneys, why the plea came in just as Michael Jordan arrived in the state. "Absolute coincidence," Rogers said. "We had been working toward this a long time." Statements Demery had made when he was first arrested were too damaging to overcome, Rogers explained.

"Those statements did it; they really took away our ability to blow some smoke," the attorney added with a down-home chuckle. "Otherwise, we would have just gone ahead and rolled the dice." Unless Green suddenly plea-bargained, he would come to trial for murder some time in the ensuing months, and Demery would testify against him. "Had this unfolded, we would have portrayed Larry as a follower," said Rogers of his no-longer-needed trial strategy for Demery.

I asked Rogers whether all the conspiracy theories were thus kaput, whether there was still any mystery to this crime. "I can't think how there would be," he replied.

I then drove to the Robeson County Detention Center to see if I could talk to Larry Demery. The grounds around the building sparkled in the sun; concertina wire sent light rays in all directions.

"Can't do nothing on the weekend," said the man in charge. "Try Monday."

It was then Saturday, and I'd be damned if I'd spend the night in this infernal place or drive back to Lumberton again. I put the hammer down and was in Charlotte before the sun set.

The effect on Michael of the speculation and innuendo was so unpleasant that it was one of the reasons he quit basketball a few months after his father's murder. Now he is here on this blistering Chicago street to pay homage to the man who used to accompany him to many Bulls games, often with a drink in hand and a wink for the pretty ladies. With each day, Michael—bald, getting older—looks more and more like his father. He says now to the small crowd that this soon-to-be-built club will give some poor kids the chance to hurdle bad luck and "evolve as people."

But there are more issues at work here today than just charity. Because of an ugly dispute between NBA players and management over the expired collective bargaining agreement between the two groups, the owners announced a lockout three weeks ago, suspending operations and halting player transactions. Jordan has come out fervently on the rebel side that has asked to decertify the union and start all over, paving the way for a strike that could be as nasty and debilitating as the one that crippled major league baseball. For a man who seldom speaks out on public issues, who does a fair amount of charitable work but very little in the social or political sphere, Jordan's leadership role in this salary dispute seems coldly mercenary to many critics.

It is ironic and sort of sad that Jordan praises Jerry Reinsdorf in his speech but then adds that Reinsdorf "could not be here because of my being here, I guess." He has guessed right, for under the terms of the lockout, management and labor may not mingle. Nor is Jordan ready to let the blame for the work stoppage be laid at the feet of greedy agents, who some owners have said are merely leading their clients like pigs with nose rings. No, Jordan wants us to know that the greediness, which may or may not be justified by the NBA's fabulous and growing popularity, is a concept fully endorsed by, among others, himself. "To blame David Falk [his agent] is almost an insult to me," Jordan said after the festivities.

Also absent is Jordan's indignant backcourt foe in this battle, Bulls player representative Steve Kerr. I called Kerr to get his take on Jordan and Company's militant stand to tear up the proffered contract and force the owners to open the kitty wide for players.

"I'm a baseball fan," Kerr said. "I've learned a lot from what's happened in baseball. That's why the contract is the best alternative for us. The league will go on for six more years, the players will make a lot of money, the owners will prosper. And we won't lose the respect of the fans." The NBA deal was not a wonderful one for players, but only if weighed in the rarefied ozone of the TV sports entertainment business. "Look," Kerr said, "some players want the owners to go broke, which is crazy. They're our employers. Why shouldn't we want them to do well? Jordan and those guys basically don't want any salary restrictions. But the owners have proved that without caps, they'll spend each other out of business. Owners in baseball tried to stop themselves, and they got hit for collusion. So they're in a bind."

And yet, Jordan and Co. have argued, it's a bind of the owners' own making. Kerr agreed. But then he asked the salient question, the one all players had to ask themselves: "How much is enough?" Jordan, probably the richest athlete in the history of team sports, says only the free market should limit a man's income. He says this at a time when he is starring in a movie for Warner Bros. (he is on hiatus from filming just now), an animated feature that might set new standards for merchandising tie-ins when it is released in the fall of 1996. Jordan has a point. But so do Kerr and the NBA majority.

"If we're slaves, we're pretty expensive slaves, I guess," Kerr said. "Every year I've been underpaid. I've never made a million dollars. But I feel rich beyond my wildest dreams. And then we have guys making three and four million, and they can't find happiness? I don't understand it."

Neither do a lot of folks. And as this ceremony concludes and everyone involved scurries off to air-conditioned automobiles, limousines, and offices, I find myself wondering whether there will be an NBA season this fall. The longer the lockout goes, the higher the stakes rise in this messy affair.

No power forward. No harmony. Maybe no games. And here I am, sweating like a donkey. Boy, it's great to be following the Bulls.

5

WELL, ISN'T THIS FORTUITOUS. I RUN INTO THIS GUY I KNOW named Wes in late September 1995 at O'Hare on my way home from a trip to New York, and Wes says he knows that Michael and some guys are running today at the Solheim Center at the Moody Bible Institute down on LaSalle Street. Wes is a black guy, skinny, with glasses, missing a front tooth. I know his full name, but he insists on being simply Wes ("No last name, man—just Wes, cool?"), and that's okay with me, because Wes always knows what's happening, what's cooking, what's shaking. He's a friend of Jordan's, and he's always got a cell phone to his ear, cruising in and out of places, checking the scene, nodding to people, smiling a lot with that gap-toothed grin, shaking hands with agents, players, coaches, writers, league officials, just being a guy in the know, hanging around, then splitting and showing up somewhere else— another party, another city, another hotel, another big game or news conference. I have no idea what Wes does for a living, nor does anybody else I've talked to. But he's cool, and I like him, and he says that Mike and them are probably gonna start running any minute now, and that's all I need to know.

So I thank him, get my bags, and drive straight downtown to Moody. My pal Sheldon Basett, the director of the Solheim Center, lets me into the place. There's no media here at all. No cameras. No autograph hounds. No spectators, except for a few Bible students and some gym workers. But man, oh man, this is the kind of thing you'd pay to see, my friends.

A full-court pickup game is in progress and the teams are filled with NBA players and street players and CBA hopefuls and college players. No coaches anywhere. No scouts. No nothing. And there is Jordan. Who knows what the score of the game is, but the guy with the chiseled ebony body and the sweet shoes is quietly lighting up the arena. His buddy and former Bulls teammate Pete Myers refuses to fall for any of Jordan's fakes, and so Jordan simply rises elegantly one, two, perhaps three feet in the air, and buries an 18-foot jump shot. Myers comes out too close to Jordan. Oops, there goes Air. Jam City. I haven't seen him in uniform since the last playoff loss in May, and gracious, does he now look pumped and ready to kick tail. This group of players is simply working out the kinks before training camp starts in early October, but Jordan seems not to have any kinks. Other players include NBA veteran Ken Norman and Juwan Howard, the young Washington Bullets forward who was raised in Chicago. Howard plays hard and looks very graceful for a big man, and it seems clear Jordan approves of his work ethic and skills. If Jordan didn't like the highly paid young Howard—and there are a number of highly paid youngsters Jordan doesn't like—he would bury him. No mercy. But even when he goes at Howard, there is an element of respect in his approach. It is Jordan's way of saying, You're okay, son.

When the games finally end, Jordan comes over to the cinderblock wall and sits on the floor next to his gym bag. Wes is wandering around, and the other players gradually disappear.

"Wanna talk a little?" I ask.

"Why not?"

He's back from L.A., he says, where he's been working most of the summer on *Space Jam,* the Warner Bros. movie starring him and a truckload of cartoon characters. He seems so good-humored and carefree that I barge right in and challenge him over this notion that because you can dunk you can act.

"I'm very nervous about it," he admits. "I think the movie's going to be good. Bill Murray's in it, and he's real funny. Nice guy, good golfer.

But me, well, I didn't sing. But I do a little dancing," and here he looks at me for a negative reaction, but getting none, continues, "and golf, and basketball, and baseball. It was a good experience, but it's hard. Start at eight, shoot till seven, six days a week." Most of his lines, he adds, were recited against a green screen, so that the smart-aleck rabbit, testy Martian, hungry Tasmanian Devil, and stuttering pig can be inked in later.

"Everybody tells me I'm good," Jordan says with a dubious look. "But I don't believe them."

He readjusts the ice bag on his left knee. He's not injured; this is just something you do when you're 32 years old. He seems to genuinely enjoy this sort of postgame ritual familiar to any gym rat: hanging, gabbing, icing, chilling. And Jordan, despite all his fame and money, is a gym rat at heart. His "love of the game" clause in his first Bulls contract—allowing him to play in hoops games anywhere, anytime he feels like it, insurance and league rules be damned—proved as much.

The movie people built Jordan his own bubble in the back lot at the Burbank studio, shipped a wooden floor from Long Beach State, put in some weights, exercise machines, golf nets, and a card table, just so their star wouldn't wander. All he had to provide were the players. And they came from everywhere, like subjects heeding the castle clarion.

"We played hard," says Jordan. Games started at 7:30 almost every night, witnessed only by a handful of Warner Bros. employees. The movie set and all access to Jordan were closed to the public and, especially, the media.

I ask Jordan whether the studio was going to keep the inflatable gym once the film was wrapped. "I doubt it," he says. "It costs ten thousand dollars a day just to air-condition it."

Well, there's that old money thing again. Funny, but most of Jordan's summer has been spent pursuing it, or at least trying to explain to his fellow NBA players why they should follow his lead, and not their union's, in pursuit of it. Of course, that is all—blessedly—water under the bridge, the new contract having been tentatively approved by both owners and players just days ago and the lockout lifted only yesterday. But Jordan has been burned a little in the process. I suppose he can be forgiven, then, if he doesn't believe the people who say his acting is swell. He thought he had made his case about the NBA union persuasively this summer, only to see the players do 180s once they left his presence.

There is, I point out, a perceived breach between the young superstar Shaquille O'Neal, who voted to accept the contract, and veteran demigod Jordan, Mr. Militant. Some people are saying Shaq won the economic and public relations battle, and his army will soon replace Jordan's as the main force in the league.

"Oh, man, that's all Shaq," Jordan says with a huff. "When I saw him, he was on my side. Then all of a sudden, I think his agent, Leonard Armato, got to him. Shaq switched. Because it was in his best interest." Contracts and ancillary deals made the difference for Shaq and a lot of others, Jordan says. He mentions one superstar who would have lost a huge balloon payment had there been a work stoppage. "You think he was going to lose that paycheck?" Jordan scoffs. He himself stood to gain much from a contract with a less restrictive salary cap and more player freedom than the accepted one, but he becomes quietly rock-firm when he ponders the issue of selfishness.

"Believe me, it was not for me," he says, looking sincere. "We're just trying to maximize our windows of opportunity. How long does even a good player get? Eight years? Maybe? Then he has to live like a normal person. Dick Versace said, 'Do you think Jordan's doing it for the other guys?' I was. Hey, my wealth has never been made on the basketball floor. I missed *my* window. But take Scottie as a prime example. He signed a three-year contract extension, and under the new deal he can't sign another extension until this one is up. What happens if he gets hurt in his third year? He deserves some security."

True, I reply, but then I toss out the philosophical question Steve Kerr had asked: "How much money is enough money?"

"Come on," says Jordan, punching me in the leg for emphasis. "You understand the industry. Three million isn't anything to the NBA. Okay, it's something. But Scottie, he's one of the five or six best players in the world. Is he paid like that? I mean, Patrick Ewing is getting eighteen million this year. So what should Scottie make?"

I play devil's advocate. So the free enterprise system should be unimpaired by any controlled spending, even in a league that set itself up to be autonomous?

"*We* didn't design the market," Jordan says, grimacing with exasperation. I am enjoying this, making him work, being less than a rubber stamp for everything he says—which, out of necessity, I always am when I'm part of the media pack in a typical time-is-precious "gang-bang" with him in the locker room or hallway. "[NBA commissioner David] Stern ought to talk to the owners and tell them to control themselves. That's not *our* responsibility. I mean, we should take a shitty deal because the fans don't want any problems, because the owners say they won't start the season? The owners use that against us. But it's not fair."

He shifts the ice bag on his knee. He's wearing a white Nike cap and white sleeveless T-shirt, designed by the fledgling Get Paid company of Chicago, that says "Lay Up" on the front and shows a player making a simple lay-in. Jordan has no deal with the company but wears the shirt because he thinks the design "is kinda cute." On him it looks cutting-edge. (Just this simple act, the megastar wearing a piece of clothing, could be enough to put the unknown company that manufactures it in the black. When I walked into the gym I saw the guy who claimed to be "representing" Get Paid—he was probably the owner, designer, and head salesman for the business—and he was positively quivering with optimism.) Jordan also has on black Air Jordan trunks, new generation white-patent-leather Air Jordan shoes with Carolina-blue soles ("out in about a month"), a genuine University of North Carolina sweatband on his left arm, and small-lensed Oakley sunglasses perched atop his cap.

Why the Oakleys? I ask.

"They're good." Jordan grins.

And? I know a little more about this than he reckons, having heard from a friend in the advertising biz that Jordan has just signed a serious Oakley gig.

"Well, we haven't officially announced it yet . . . " he says sheepishly.

So add Oakley to the Nike, Coca-Cola, Gatorade, Hanes, Chevy, McDonald's, Ball Park, etc., endorsement list.

"Anything else?" I ask, probing.

Jordan looks like a kid confessing to cookie theft.

"Ray-O-Vac batteries."

The game of basketball itself can almost get lost in the aura of otherness that swirls around Jordan like a long, twisting cape. He pulls a bottle of Gatorade from under the black Air Jordan sweatshirt at his side and opens it. He guzzles. I can't help wondering what it must be like going through life using products designed for, or associated primarily with, yourself. He senses the oddity.

"I mean, look at me," he says. He knows he's a human billboard. "Do you think the contract stance was for me? Two years down the road the players will be saying, 'Man, we shouldn't have made the deal.'"

"Well, then you can enjoy saying 'I told you so.'"

"I get no pleasure out of seeing people suffer," he says. "If we were all together, we could really do something."

I am reminded that Jordan, the greatest player ever, is currently the 31st-highest-paid player in the league, that he has never been No. 1, that he is paid less right now than slugs such as Benoit Benjamin, Danny Ferry, and even Stanley Roberts. His contract—which brings him about $3.9 million this year—is up at the end of the season. But even then, due to salary cap restrictions and a lack of a free market, he will never receive what he is worth. I ask him why he has stuck with his deal anyway. Everybody else renegotiates, holds out, threatens, malingers.

"Because I signed it," he says. "I'm in the last year of a six-year, and I was happy when I took it."

I remember the passage in *Rare Air,* his 1993 autobiography, where Jordan says he's a mixture of his mom and his dad, and their attitudes about life. "My father is a people person," he said. "My mother has always been more of the business side of the family. She has a kind of 'Get up and go get it' attitude. My father was more like, 'I don't need all those fancy clothes. I can wear these dungarees.'" Then Jordan added, "I'm happy with my contract with the Bulls. I signed the contract and I'll always be loyal to that deal. I'm not going to go in and complain about it or whine to the media about how I should make more money. I gave my word and my word is my bond."

It shouldn't strike me as odd that a star professional athlete should actually say what Jordan says. But it does.

I mention that he looks pretty fit.

"I've been working out for a month and a half," he replies. "I came in for the end of last season at 215, and I couldn't lose it. Now I'm 210, what I want to weigh." He looks lighter than that, lithe and fibrous. His trainer, Tim Grover, has been working with him constantly, he points out, getting him in basketball, not baseball, shape. Jordan's head, of course, is shaved and aerodynamic. A gold hoop earring glistens in his left ear. So was the Michael Jordan we saw for the final 20 or so games last season the best we can expect? Not that he was so bad or anything.

"Last season my mind and my body were not in sync," he answers. "I knew my shot was off. I'd think about doing stuff, and my body wouldn't do it. I'd try to go around guys I knew I could kill, but I couldn't do it. Yeah, people said it was age. But I hadn't practiced enough."

He chuckles. It's not a chuckle an opponent would want to hear.

"This year's gonna be fun for me."

So how, I wonder, will his teammates and fans respond to him?

"I'm not worried. I made the players aware of this whole business thing, raised their consciousness. And that's good. I'm a very happy person. I don't have hard feelings toward anyone. I talk to Stern. He did a job on the players' union by saying there wouldn't be a season, but we appreciate each other as businessmen. I'll never criticize Shaq or anyone for making a decision that benefits them. And the fans—why should they be upset with me? The games will be held on time. Why have any hard feelings?"

Jordan's so mellow that he even laughs when I bring up his baseball diversion and some of the, uh, lesser moments he had during that diversion. Yep, he admits, it was pretty dumb when he was running for home plate and he put his basketball moves on that minor-league catcher, and the guy just stood there with the ball, thinking, What an idiot—the plate's not going anywhere.

"But the best one was when I stole second and I wanted a timeout, and I did this." He taps both his palms to his shoulders. "I called a twenty-second timeout."

Now he's laughing good and hard. Pearly teeth, the whole bit. And it dawns on me: If he feels this good, boy, I feel good, too.

6

OMIGOD. WORM IS COMING.

Hell, he's not coming, *he's here.*

I am stunned. I'm at the Berto Center in the Chicago suburb of Deerfield on October 4, 1995, watching Jerry Krause and Phil Jackson present the one man I *knew* would never be a Bull. I have only myself to blame for this misconception. I listened to—nay, I believed—Krause when he said "never."

Dennis Rodman sits between Krause and Jackson like gunpowder between two blasting caps.

He's all done up. His fingernails are black and white, the old ebony-and-ivory motif, with the black in a V-shape starting at the cuticle and projecting up into the white so each nail looks like a tiny black patent leather shoe in spats.

Two hoop rings in the left earlobe.

One in the right.

Nose ring, left nostril.

Black stocking cap with what appears to be the Miami Heat logo on the turned-up edge.

Sweater.

Little red shades.

Crucifix on a neck chain.

Small leather pouch on a leather neck strap.

Sweatpants.

Black Nikes.

It's pretty much a normal outfit for Rodman. Certainly it is nothing as fine and haute couture as the silvery tank top and harem pants he wore to the MTV Awards last month. *Rolling Stone* asked Rodman whether he had been dressing for the TV cameras on that occasion.

"I just felt like looking a little gayish tonight," he replied, "so I looked in my closet and found this."

Vive le fashion! But no matter—whatever—here he is. The power forward of the Bulls' dreams. The demon of their nightmares. In a quick trade with the Spurs, Krause has sent much-maligned backup center Will Perdue down to San Antonio for Rodman. The talent-for-talent aspect of the deal is so out of balance that one realizes Rodman is obviously perceived by everybody in the NBA as an explosion waiting to happen. Certainly he had stirred things up with the Spurs: he helped lead them to the playoffs, then detonated and helped them get snuffed by the Houston Rockets. Technical fouls, odd displays of anti-management behavior, nearly palpable contempt for his own teammates—most notably for devout Christian family man and all-around fine citizen David Robinson—they were all there for the world to see. But Rodman has averaged almost 18 rebounds a game for the last four years, and what was it Jordan had said in the locker room after the final playoff loss last season? "I'd like to think we're a rebounder away, a power forward away." Check him out. The Bulls had gone to the edge, looked over, and then jumped.

The Bulls have picked up Rodman's gentle $2.5 million contract for one year, giving up virtually nothing (Perdue was merely "a journeyman center who just hasn't journeyed yet," I wrote in a column), and went for it all—a fourth title ring—in what could only be called a very delicate, dangerous experiment. They have acquired a 6'8" manchild who could mess with the chemistry of the team the way vinegar can mess with baking soda. Nor does it appear that Rodman has found the Lord, or changed his ways, or settled down, or done any of the other clichéd things that might indicate he has metamorphosed from the old Worm. He did say that he only recently had "found myself as a human being." But looking at him now, I wonder if what he had found wasn't a very tall androgynous grunge-rocker instead.

Could the Bulls have signed a bigger surprise? Scottie Pippen is asked.

"Yeah," Pip says. "Bill Laimbeer."

Pippen, who bears the chin scar from the seven stitches he received when Worm, then a Piston, cheap-shotted him into the stands back in 1991, is asked whether he has spoken to his new teammate yet.

No, he hasn't.

Well, had he ever had a normal conversation with the illustrated man at any time in either's NBA career?

"No," Pippen says without much levity. "Probably never will."

Jordan, fresh from wrapping his role in *Space Jam*, is a little more wait-and-see in his appraisal of Rodman. In fact, Rodman had joined Jordan in some of those high-level pickup games at the Warner backlot basketball arena. But had they conversed? Not really, Jordan admits.

"This kid, he wants to win," Jordan states of a man who, according to the passage of real time, is two years older than he. "I believe in giving a guy the opportunity to prove himself." But does Jordan have enough power to discipline Rodman should he go ballistic? "I don't know him well enough to do that," Jordan answers.

Of course, nobody in Chicago, or perhaps the entire planet, knows Rodman that well. And Pippen, at the very least, is quite wary.

"If he's going to be a negative to us," says Pippen, implying that Worm will be, "I don't think we need him."

Jordan responds, "Phil's probably got the toughest job of all."

And that is true. It was one thing for Krause to go after Rodman, another for Reinsdorf to give the go-ahead. But it's a whole different thing for Jackson to have to channel this lifelong rebel into the narrow confines of a team game. At some point Rodman's stocking cap comes off, revealing what might be a slight acknowledgment that perhaps he is willing to at least try to get with the program: bright red hair with a black bull's head in the back.

Three days before, when whisperings of a possible trade for Rodman had hit the media rumor mill, I wrote a column saying I was at best ambivalent about such a deal. You know, just being the conscience of the people, the fans:

> The deal is actually out there, dangling like forbidden fruit.
>
> Bulls optimists say the change of scenery would do the Worm good. The man can change. He just needs to be understood.
>
> People said the same thing about Darryl Strawberry, Chuck Muncie, Vernon Maxwell.
>
> When the Spurs tried to "change" Rodman during last year's disastrous playoff run, when he was acting like the tallest adolescent in the world, Worm stated, "I'm 34 years old. I'm a grown man. I know exactly what I'm doing."

More troubling words have seldom been spoken by someone so relentlessly juvenile.

Not that Rodman is all bad. I was with him one night in Texas when he stopped his car to hand a bum a $100 bill. I have seen him pass up layups to give the ball to teammates who needed to score. I have seen him disregard his own safety in fearless pursuit of rebounds, bad passes, and loose balls.

But I've also seen him miss practice, belittle management, disdain even the simplest and most harmless of team rules—such as catching a flight to the city where the next game will be played.

Folks think Phil Jackson's philosophical mysticism may reach the Worm and turn him around.

I think dropping Zen on Rodman will be like dropping a hug on Mike Tyson.

I've seen all the coaching techniques used on Rodman, seen them fail. Chuck Daly's rugged paternalism may have worked the best, until the father figure himself left town.

John Lucas' I-understand-you-because-I-was-once-a-junkie approach was a dismal failure, and nearly unhinged Lucas in the process.

Spurs coach Bob Hill's and GM Gregg Popovich's rules-are-rules approach was laughably ineffective. Telling Worm he can't do something is like telling a cat it can't go inside a cardboard box.

So the onus for Worm Control likely will fall to Michael Jordan himself. Jordan is more and more of a singular figure these days, and he has already suggested to friends he's not nuts about serving as a caretaker for a man who could help him immensely on the hardwood, but drain him immensely off it.

None of this is to say that I, personally, would mind seeing Rodman in a Bulls uniform this season. The wackiness alone appeals to my evil side.

But let me paint a quick scenario for you Bulls fans.

Rodman plays great. Bulls cruise to playoffs. Rodman skips a meeting, smarts off to Jerry Reinsdorf, gets into a slapfight at a female impersonator bar on North Clark.

*What do you do? How do you maintain order? How do you win
another ring?*
   Please send all suggestions to Bulls management.
   Or the American Psychiatric Association.

I didn't know then, but in time I would learn how the entire Rodman
deal had come to pass. It had started with everybody in the Bulls organization reaching the conclusion that the club had to get a real power
forward if it was going to have a chance at the NBA title. As Jackson
says, "Nobody would ever give us a center. And we knew our centers
couldn't do it, so power forward was it."

Then Krause and Jackson and the scouts, Jim Stack, Ivica Dukan,
and Clarence Gaines, Jr., put together a list of ten possible prospects
based on talent, availability, and cost. And liability. Rodman came in
around eighth place. For the obvious reason.

There had been some hope that either Dickey Simpkins or Jason Caffey would be the solution to the power forward dilemma, but that was
ruled out when Jackson got clear looks at each. When did he know the
oddly sluggish Simpkins wasn't the answer? "The first time I saw him
play," says the coach, without sugarcoating. And Caffey's problem?
"We need to give him an IQ test," Jackson says. "I'm not sure he should
have been in college." Of course, neither player was a high pick, so the
odds of either being the next Horace Grant or Charles Barkley were always long.

Then, in a meeting, Jerry Reinsdorf actually brought up the name of
Rodman as a serious candidate.

"People don't change," said Krause logically. "I can't do that to Phil."

Reinsdorf acknowledged the difficulty of taming, or even coexisting
with, this most nettlesome of players. But like everyone else, he knew
that if one could get full production and a semblance of cooperation
from Dennis Rodman, there was nobody else in the world who could do
the good things he could do. But who could control him?

"If anyone can do it, Phil can," said Reinsdorf.

After that it was Stack, the 6'6" scout who had played at Northwestern, who kept the Rodman idea alive. He kept bringing it up to Krause,

who drooled at the thought of Rodman acourt with Jordan and Pippen
and the 7'2", 285-pound Longley, but shivered at the thought of bringing in Rodman only to have the entire team blow up. It probably didn't
hurt that Stack's sister, Karen, a 6'1" former star basketball player at
Northwestern, was also Krause's special assistant. In time Krause decided it was a good idea, one that merited rolling the dice, primarily because Jackson was ready to give the crazy gamble a shot.

■ ■ ■

Lost in all the hoopla that accompanied Rodman's signing was the important fact that the Bulls had signed another player at the same time,
6'2" fifth-year free agent guard Randy Brown, a Chicago native. Late of
the hapless Sacramento Kings, Brown had not set the league on fire, averaging just 5.2 points and 2 assists as a substitute during his career. But
he was quick and hardworking, leading the league in steals per minutes
played in 1994–95. He would be the only quick small man on the Bulls
roster, the only player who physically could match up with smaller
point guards. "You watch this kid," Krause told me at the Rodman-fest,
as Brown stood quietly off to the side. "He's something. Oh brother, defense? This kid can play."

Though Krause was almost trembling with excitement, I disregarded
the insight, having no way of telling whether it was true or not. It was
Sleuth-speak. But then I heard Jackson refer calmly to the addition of
Brown. "The real key is that Randy knows how to play team basketball," he said. "He'll do whatever it takes to fit in."

So it was a counterattack. Two round holes to fill; Brown was the
round piece to buffer slightly the impossible trapezoid that was Worm.

Oh, and there was one other signing around the same time. The
strangest of all, really. A career stiff named Jack Haley, a former Bull,
was inked to the league minimum contract of $225,000 and promptly
placed on the injured list. Haley had been on the Spurs with Rodman for
two seasons, and had become known as Worm's cheerleader, comforter,
and offcourt pal. He clearly came along as packing material in the deal,
a cheap security blanket for the fragile genius. Nobody could envision
Haley actually playing for the Bulls. But he would be available to hold
Rodman's hand when necessary.

7

NOVEMBER 3. OPENING NIGHT. HOME, AGAINST THE CHAR-lotte Hornets.

People had observed the way the Bulls played in the preseason, had seen them make mistakes and correct them, had seen them fumble and adjust, and most of all had seen them look, at times, ungodly good.

And here in this game, everyone can see what's unique about the Bulls. It is, as it always was, a fellow named Michael Jordan. He scores 15 points in less than 11 minutes of the first quarter and leads the Bulls to a 105–91 rout. The Hornets, who had lost money-hungry All-Star center Alonzo Mourning—like Jordan, a David Falk client—to the Miami Heat earlier in the day, actually were ahead at halftime, 48–40. But the Bulls came out in the third quarter in a kind of controlled frenzy, built around a ferocious defensive attack, and outscored the Hornets, 40–18. In that critical period Jordan scored 19 points, 13 in the final 4:49. There was nobody like him on the floor, just like old times. He finished with 42 points, 7 assists, 6 rebounds, and only 1 turnover. High scorer for the Hornets was Larry Johnson with 19 points. The next highest on the Bulls was Toni Kukoc with 15.

Kukoc played quite a bit because Pippen went down with a groin injury after just 10 minutes, getting no points, no rebounds, no steals, no assists. Moreover, backup center Bill Wennington started for Luc Longley, the gentle Australian, who had been suspended for the opening game for, of all things, taking a swing at a player in a preseason game. The player was Chris Webber of the Washington Bullets, and the funny part was that Longley never loses his temper over anything. People were already pointing at Rodman, who came to Chicago saying he was going to transform the Big Wonder from Down Under into a scrappier mate. "I don't give a damn if Luc Longley turns around and punches me in the face," Worm said of getting the center jacked up. "If that's what it takes for him to get going, go right ahead and hit me."

The fight—a brief tussle under the basket that somehow left Webber with a hurt shoulder, one he would separate against the Indiana Pacers later in the preseason—delighted the Bulls faithful. Longley himself seemed somewhat amazed at the set-to. "I threw a couple of punches," he admitted. "I was lucky to get away with what I did."

Actually, he didn't get away with much, collecting a $7,500 fine in the process and losing $21,000 in salary because of the suspension.

So the Bulls, minus two starters, were almost as shorthanded as the Hornets in this opener. Rodman had 12 rebounds and 2 points in his 31 minutes. But more notable was the fact it took him exactly 4 minutes and 3 seconds to pick up his first technical foul of the season. He earned it by blatantly elbowing Charlotte forward George Zidek in the back. Basically, Worm was using Zidek as a sounding board to protest the shaky calls being made by the two replacement referees. The real refs (and there normally are three per game) were locked out by the NBA due to—what else?—a contract dispute. But what Rodman was showing was not something that would help the squabble. It was something that simply helped him vent displeasure.

It was a scary way to start the year. Jordan was back, obviously fed up with all the doubters from last season. But the vaunted triangle offense came apart like a cheap toy, perhaps because so many new faces were performing within it. "We were in disarray a little in the first half," Jordan summed up. He then added pointedly, "Some players got frustrated, got a technical." That would be Worm, the only Bull to get a T. "We just never really got into it," Jordan continued. "[The triangle] is sophisticated. Can't expect some of these guys to learn it in three weeks. It's just not gonna happen."

Which led directly to his third-quarter offensive outburst. "The triangle is like a college education," Jordan said. "It always gives you something to fall back on; you always have that system." Then why didn't he use it in the third period? "I felt like the triangle wasn't working."

So clear out, because here he comes. Jordan made 3-pointers and midrange jump shots and at least one flying dunk. No offensive scheme required. Indeed, the design of the NBA game—the 24-second clock, no zone defenses, relaxed traveling and palming rules—is perfect for an aggressive, elite athlete like MJ. Just give him the ball and take a seat. Then, too, what everyone was watching was a superstar who was clearly back.

"I feel totally different," he admitted postgame. "I've got rhythm in my jump shot, rhythm in my moves. This year I'm playing more off of instinct."

The ease he felt was certainly a relief to him. But it did not come by accident. Driven by the demands of his immense pride, Jordan had worked amazingly hard since last season's early exit from the playoffs. His movie gig was really just a day job sandwiched between his training and hoops at his fully equipped bubble stadium. When Nick Anderson had joked during the Orlando series that number 45 didn't have the rockets that number 23 did, it plainly had scorched Jordan to the bone.

One of his teammates, former union contract defender Steve Kerr, can attest to the fuel in Jordan's furnace this season. Indeed, though few people know it, Kerr still carries the faint markings of Jordan's fervor.

If you look closely, you can detect some discoloration around Kerr's right eye. It is the lingering result of a punch thrown by Jordan in the privacy of a Bulls preseason scrimmage. Phil Jackson had gone off to take a conference call in his office at the Berto Center, telling the players and assistant coaches to continue the run until he returned. With referees and authoritative supervision missing, the practice got more and more intense. Kerr and Jordan were on opposing teams and started jawing at each other. Kerr thought Jordan had fouled him, and the two debated the issue. Play resumed and this time they got truly tangled up and, raging, started swinging at each other.

There were many things being swung at, few of them personal, most of them symbolic. The 6'3", 180-pound Kerr and the 6'6", 210-pound Jordan were at opposite ends of the talent scale. They were also far apart on the pay scale: Kerr makes little more than his $750,000 salary; Jordan pulls in an estimated $40 million from offcourt ventures. There was the respect factor: Did a journeyman like Kerr even have the right to question a superhero like Jordan? Moreover, here were the two team leaders of the opposite sides in the recent players' union fight. Conservative, radical. Status quo, new era. Bicycle, space shuttle. Add to this the grind of camp itself.

But most of all there was the undying question that Jordan carried like a hated cross: Was he the same player he once had been?

"There was so much pressure on Michael," said Kerr one day when I grilled him about the fight. "There were all these articles in the papers reminding Michael that he didn't play well in the playoffs last season, wondering if he could return to what he was. There was pressure from the outside, pressure he put on himself."

Jordan's teammates could feel that pressure the way animals can sense an approaching tornado. "He came into camp like a man possessed," Kerr continued. "Every practice, every shooting drill, everything was just a huge competition. He was so competitive that it just set up the tone for our season. We all had to be that competitive every day."

So when the two players began brawling, it was clear what the result would be. "We threw some blows, and his landed and mine never came close," Kerr said with a smile. "Our teammates pulled us apart, and because of the frenzy, I didn't even know I'd been hit."

But he had, and his swelling eye was immediate evidence. Many emotions had coalesced for Jordan, and he was so overwhelmed by them that he left the floor and packed his things. Jackson had heard the commotion, and when he came out of his office, he saw Jordan preparing to leave. "I'm too upset," Jordan told his coach. "I'm just gonna get out of here."

That afternoon Jordan called Kerr at home and apologized. "He told me he felt horrible," said Kerr. "But still, the next day everything was a little uncomfortable, you know, because I had that shiner as a constant reminder." When the reporters began asking questions, the Bulls pretty much shrugged and said Kerr just got in the way of an elbow. "I made sure I never lied about it," noted Kerr, himself a former sports editor of his high school paper in Pacific Palisades, California. But he wasn't all that forthright, either. Why? "Hey, on an average NBA team that kind of thing happens three or four times a year. And to me it wasn't really that big a deal. The point is, I think, that training camp showed how it was going to be. There definitely was a purpose to Michael's competitiveness. He was trying to show us what we had to do to be champions."

Jordan's passion had a trickle-down effect on his lesser mates. In the Charlotte opener, with Pippen out, reserve forward Jud Buechler, a 6'6" beach volleyball and surfing enthusiast from San Diego with limited hoops skills, came off the bench and scored a remarkable 13 points in the second half to help the Bulls win. With a one-year contract for the league minimum, second-year man Buechler, a former teammate of Kerr's at the University of Arizona, had made this year's team on the last cut of the last day of training camp when much taller frontliners Jack Haley and Buddha Edwards were put on the injured list. But you could see the intensity with which Buechler played, a direct result of Jordan's fire. As Buechler admitted, perhaps his only game better than the season opener "was last season when I made that three-pointer that enabled all the fans to win a free pizza." United Center patrons still cheer him for that.

■■■

Game 2 is another home court victory, this one a 107–85 rout of the Boston Celtics. Pippen is miraculously back from the groin injury that 24 hours before seemed severe, and he is frisky with pent-up energy. He runs down Celtics guard Dana Barros from far behind to block his breakaway layup, and throws down a couple of monstrous jams of his own. He finishes with 21 points, 4 rebounds, 5 assists, 5 steals, and 4 blocked shots in just 29 minutes. "I almost took him out of the game earlier, he was doing so much," Jackson marveled afterward. "I was afraid he was going to jump out of the gym."

Game 3 is more of the same: a home 117–108 win over the expansion Toronto Raptors. The Bulls, however, start sloppy and, as will become something of a signature for them, trail their foe at the half before piling it on in the third and fourth quarters. Jordan finishes with 38 points, and between him and Pippen they have 64 points, 13 assists, and 7 steals. The Bulls look powerful, but they still aren't firing on all cylinders. They seem to have trouble stopping smaller point guards, such as Raptors rookie Damon Stoudamire, who has 22 points, 10 assists, and 6 rebounds. But yet another trademark of this squad is being revealed: intense, turnover-forcing team defense, even when the offense has come to a screeching halt. The Bulls have 13 steals to Toronto's 6, with 11 of them coming from the long-armed trio of Jordan, Pippen, and the quietly effective Ron Harper, who has 4.

Rodman works the boards and at times seems on the verge of snapping. When a late foul is called on him, he takes the ball and in a rage slams it hard off his forehead, just below the red swoosh he has had emblazoned in his now yellow hair. But nothing else happens. Jackson shrugs at such displays, and sometimes even laughs. He can afford to, since the Bulls are usually en route to winning when they occur. But the entire Bulls organization has the benefit of having been able to observe what *didn't* work with Worm on his other teams. Jackson, whose credo is firm guidance mixed with tolerance for eccentricities, seems just the man to stand behind Rodman.

"He's cool," Rodman recently told columnist Buck Harvey of the *San Antonio Express-News.* "Everyone was on pins and needles in San Antonio, watching to see when I did something wrong so they could overreact. Here, you just play."

Well, that's Worm's version, anyway. Pal Jack Haley told Harvey that the night before at dinner, he and Rodman had had the same argument they used to have in San Antonio. "He tried to tell me how the Spurs did him wrong," said Haley, "and I said, 'Hey, I was there.' Dennis caused 90 percent of the problems. That's why I don't blame Gregg Popovich, and I certainly don't blame Bob Hill. In fact, Bob did a tremendous job. I would have voted for him for coach of the year on the way he handled Dennis alone. He tried everything."

Phil Jackson continues to make good use of his cosmic-smile attitude. He sits back in his office at the Berto Center, which is appointed with Indian artifacts, and reads book after book about, well, everything under the sun. He is blessed, and he knows it. Though he is in the last year of his contract, for about $850,000 this year—far less than, say, Miami Heat coach Pat Riley's $3 million–per—with no guarantees from Reinsdorf about next year, he is not worried about the future. He wants to enjoy the hand he has been dealt. He has no desire to be falsely modest, either, about this team that some scribes are already saying has an outside chance to win a league-record 70 games. What does Jackson think about that?

"We're still on eighty-two–and–oh as our short-term goal," he replies.

8

RODMAN IS OUT. A CALF INJURY HE SUSTAINED IN THE THIRD game has worsened, and he says after missing the next game, against the Cleveland Cavaliers, "I'll probably miss the next month or two. I just jumped and felt something pop."

For some reason, I have spent a good deal of time staring at Worm's calves. They are well-defined and veiny, and bulbous only high up above his slender and sinewy ankles, and I have found myself wondering whether they are the reason he can jump so well—not all that high, though he can get *up* when he has to—but so quickly, relentlessly, and appropriately. I have decided that they are to Rodman as good eyes were to Ted Williams, as reaction time was to Muhammad Ali: part of the package, but not the genius of it. He uses his calves constantly, I know. I remember several years ago when I was watching a Detroit Pistons shootaround before the Pistons played the Bullets at the Capital Center in Landover, Maryland. While the Detroit starters were on the floor listening to coach Chuck Daly, Rodman was on the sidelines taking a break. But he never stopped softly running in place. Tap, tap, tap. Like water dripping. Finally, center Bill Laimbeer turned to him and hissed, "Stop it, Worm. You're driving me crazy!" So Rodman backed a few feet off the wooden floor onto the concrete, waited a moment, and then resumed his nonstop motion. Tap, tap, tap. At any rate, I can see why his calves in their overdevelopment might cause him problems at times. And I can see why his being injured should be a double concern to the Bulls management.

It was while he was sidelined with a calf injury back in the 1992–93 season that a depressed Worm took that fateful drive to the parking lot of the Palace of Auburn Hills with the rifle and ammo. Though he has been on a pretty even keel since arriving in Chicago, he could spring a leak at any time. And of course the Bulls will have problems replacing his board work while he is out.

The starting lineup, even with Longley back, now becomes a flawed one, just as it was last season when the lack of a true or aggressive

power forward became a major weakness. Though second-year, 6'9",
250-pound Dickey Simpkins starts in Rodman's absence, it has now become plain, after a year of training and watching and learning, that
Simpkins is not really a project in the making, but a dud in the offing.
And so Toni Kukoc comes off the bench to join starters Jordan, Longley, Pippen, and Harper for serious minutes. Thus the Bulls are much
the same as they were last year, when they just didn't quite have
enough. Except that now they are energized by Jordan's superb conditioning and want-to.

There is some concern that maybe Rodman is out with a "brain" injury, but nobody will say it publicly. The players themselves still do not
talk much with Rodman, nor do they inquire about such obvious things
as the meaning of his latest hairdo. "We never ask for an explanation,"
Jordan says with a shrug. "Even if he told us, we probably wouldn't understand it anyway."

Through it all, however, the Bulls keep rolling. They lose a close one
to their nemesis, the Magic, in Orlando, but it's not a true test of team
strengths. Rodman is out for the Bulls, and Shaquille O'Neal is out for
the Magic, for six weeks with a thumb injury. Moreover, the loss comes
at a place, the O-rena, where the Magic are nearly infallible. This fact is
one of the major reasons the Bulls want to have a better record than the
Magic come May, so they will have home court advantage against Orlando when the two teams meet in the playoffs.

On the night following the Orlando loss, the Bulls come back to the
United Center and beat the Cavaliers so badly that for the first time
some of the United Center regulars begin to suspect that a lot of the
games to which they have season tickets might not be very competitive
affairs. With the two new Canadian clubs—the Vancouver Grizzlies and
the Toronto Raptors—expanding NBA membership to 29 teams, a dom-
inant team like the Bulls will enjoy even more guaranteed W's. In the
Cavs game there is an almost festive mood to the Bulls' play. Pippen
throws in a 3-pointer from way outside and then grins and goes over and
gives Harper a big gangster chest bump. This is definitely not Phil the
Benevolent Warrior's style, and the next day Jackson promptly fines
Pippen for the display. "Leave that to the Knicks," he says firmly.

Off the floor, random rumors and gossip and speculation float around. Word is that the trial for one of James Jordan's alleged killers is set to begin sometime soon in North Carolina. Rodman was seen arriving at the game with a blond woman whom one observer described as looking "like she needed a shower." Jordan supposedly has spent close to a million dollars just on landscaping at his new mansion in the high-rent development Architecture Point in Highland Park, just a few miles northeast of the Berto Center.

Already leading the NBA in scoring with a 27.6-point-per-game average, Jordan has re-established his status as the icon of the league. On an off day he entertains 12 seriously ill boys at his Michael Jordan's Restaurant on North LaSalle. Most players in the league do charity work, but in a lot of cases the work is superficial, self-promoting, or tax-efficient. Sometimes it is all three at once. When Jordan does stuff like this, his million-watt smile and uncanny ability to make people feel blessed to be in his presence supersede any benefit to himself that might be involved. The looks on the faces of these Make-A-Wish Foundation kids pretty much tell the whole story. The executive director of the foundation stated that seeing Mickey Mouse is the No. 1 wish for most sick children, followed by a tie between Jordan and the cartoonish pro wrestler Hulk Hogan.

"If I had my druthers, I would see Mickey Mouse first, too," Jordan said.

But not everybody is convinced that Jordan is where he needs to be, charity work or no charity work. In a November column titled "The New Jordan Should Quit Trying to Be the Old Jordan," the *Chicago Tribune*'s Sam Smith wagged his finger at Jordan, stating, "He no longer has the high-flying, spectacular, take-it-to-the-basket-and-scare-the-heck-out-of-defenders ability he had—and was starting to lose—when he first left basketball." Smith then warned, "Jordan is about three months away from turning 33, the age at which all the great guards of the game, from Jerry West to Oscar Robertson, slowed down."

It seemed to me an odd criticism, the tone almost wishful that Jordan would get with the program and act his age, whatever that meant. *Of course* Jordan was older, and *of course* he had slowed down. But I didn't see him trying to be what he was not. He didn't drive to the hole as often as in the early days, but then nobody in the league did: You got killed when you did that. Ground to a pulp. In the last decade, the average weight of an NBA player had increased from 215 pounds to 223, and the old Pistons Bad Boys had shown that to stop a high-flying scorer, you just needed to put whatever weight you had on him and knock him into the seats. Take the fouls and the hell with it. But Jordan had mastered the fallaway jumper and was taking more 3-point attempts than ever. Those were smart responses to the changes in the game, which included moving in the 3-point stripe from 23'9" to 22', prior to the 1994–95 NBA season.

Smith was doubtless not alone in believing Jordan was in over his head. "Jordan doesn't need to average 30 points anymore because he's not the same player he was," Smith wrote. He then gave Jordan faint praise, calling him "one of the few elite players in the game after more than a decade of playing 40 minutes a game and a wonderful attraction because of the style and flair of his game." He concluded by saying, "And if he conserves himself a little and accepts all of that, the Bulls will be better when it counts next spring."

Myself, I didn't expect to see Jordan conserving himself at all. His scoring average was on its way up to 30, and beyond. I didn't see him giving a damn about what critics said he shouldn't do, only about what they said he *couldn't* do. By the end of the season he would have played 3,090 minutes in 82 games as opposed to 3,144 minutes in 82 games when he was a 21-year-old rookie. It would come out to 37.7 minutes a game in 1995–96 versus 38.3 minutes in 1984–85—a difference of 36 seconds per contest after 11 years. But that's getting ahead of our story.

Something more important than conjecture was about to occur, anyway. The Bulls were ready to take their 7–1 record on their annual Circus Tour—the extended road trip they are always forced to take in late November because of the arrival of the circus at the United Center, and before that at the Chicago Stadium (until that structure was torn down in 1994).

Jackson is being cool about the whole trip, saying that simply coming back with a winning record, 4–3, would be quite acceptable. "A team of our ilk likes to play over .500 on the road," Jackson says in his typically philosophical way. "If you asked a team, they'd probably say they don't want to lose any. But there is an acceptable level on the road."

If you asked Scottie Pippen, he would say the acceptable level is perfection. "I would love to go seven for seven," he states, "and really establish some dominance."

Before the season, but after the addition of Rodman, the Bulls were listed by *USA Today* oddsmaker Danny Sheridan as having a 1 in 5 chance of winning the NBA title. Those were pretty good odds, bested only by Sheridan's pick of the Orlando Magic at 1 in 4. But there were others who liked the Bulls even more. NBC analyst Bill Walton said that with the addition of Rodman, the Bulls were in a position to become "one of the greatest teams in NBA history." They were suddenly, said TNT analyst and former NBA coach Hubie Brown, "the best defensive team in the history of the game."

But they were embarking on this two-week road trip without a healthy Rodman, and all those glowing projections had been based on his having a productive and sane season. Moreover, no one knew how Jordan would do on his first big road venture after returning to the game. Jordan himself was confident.

"Last year, those seventeen games were not me," he had said. "It was a transitional Michael Jordan from baseball to basketball." He added that the problem was "baseball muscles" as opposed to basketball muscles. "I don't think people truly understand the difference in muscles. From fingertips to forearms, baseball players have an unbelievable amount of strength. Basketball is more about fluency of muscles. I never had the chance to make that transition."

And, typically, he had a shot for his doubters. "When I left the game of basketball," he said, "one of the reasons I left is that [critics] couldn't say anything about my game. Well, I came back to basketball, and when my game was not the same, that's the first thing they jumped on. So it's a challenge to get them out of my game."

Get the critics out of his game. Whoa, baby, the pride and nasty fire of this guy.

So the Bulls head west on their Circus Tour, and the teams fall before them one after the other. First to go are the 6–4 Dallas Mavericks. Jordan leads the Bulls back from 9 points down late in the fourth quarter to send the game into overtime, then scores 6 of his game-high 36 points in the 108–102 win. Jordan, who is being used to cover the other team's smaller, younger, and faster point guards, has some trouble with the Mavs' Jason Kidd, who collects a triple double with 25 points, 15 rebounds, and 11 assists. But no matter—Jordan has 8 rebounds, 5 assists, and 2 steals to go with the most important stat, the W.

Next up are the 6–2 San Antonio Spurs. Rodman would like to be playing in this game for revenge, so strong is his disgust with his former team, which he felt did him dirt. His contempt for the Spurs front office and for last season's MVP of the league, Spurs center David Robinson, is unconcealed. In his book—and, yes, that is a later story, too—Worm will describe Robinson as being a soft player with a rubber spine; before the 1995 playoff games against Houston and Hakeem Olajuwon, Robinson, according to Worm, "looked so fucking scared in the locker room, he couldn't stop shaking."

But Rodman is not playing tonight in front of the crowd of 35,888 at the Alamodome, and of course there are two sides to the Spurs–Worm story, anyway. In what could have been a transcendent season for the Spurs, Rodman missed 33 regular-season games due to suspension or injury (he hurt his shoulder falling off his motorcycle) in 1994–95, and then was late for practice and benched for a spell in the playoffs, before the Spurs collapsed. Rodman seldom attended team functions all year or spoke to teammates or did much at all except act like a moody, misunderstood child. "Last year was an experience in managing a distraction day to day for all of us," Spurs coach Bob Hill told reporters after the trade. "I saw eleven guys band together trying to keep another one in line." No Spurs were sorry to see Rodman leave. The team was "a zoo" last season, said Robinson himself. Now, he said, it is sane.

But it is still no match for the Bulls, who coast behind Jordan's game-high 38 points, 9 rebounds, and 4 steals for a 103–94 win. Critics had said Jordan couldn't do it on back-to-back nights. His 74 points in 24 hours say otherwise.

There is more on tap two nights later in Salt Lake City, where Jordan scores a game-high 34 points to lead his team over the Utah Jazz, 90–85, before a capacity Delta Center crowd of nearly 20,000. As the Jazz stormed back from an 8-point deficit in the fourth quarter to close to 76–75, Jordan stepped a little harder on his accelerator; in the final 3:37 he scored 15 of the Bulls' last 16 points. He also finished with 8 rebounds, 6 assists, and 2 steals. "The man is just one great basketball player—what more can you say?" gushes Jazz point guard John Stockton. Before the Bulls arrived, the Jazz had been 6–0 at home and had a six-game winning steak going.

Oddly, the Bulls are doing fine on rebounds without ball magnet Rodman. Jordan, Pippen, and Longley have picked up the slack, and the Bulls have outrebounded almost every team they have played since Worm went on the injured list. Also helping out on the boards are the young power forward duo of Dickey Simpkins and Jason Caffey. Against the Jazz they combine for 13 rebounds, playing 46 minutes between them. On the downside is the fact that neither has shown much scoring ability (3 points between them in this contest) or drop-dead defensive skill. Jazz All-Star power forward Karl Malone scores only 19 points in the game, but that is mainly because Simpkins and Caffey get lots of help. The young pair does know how to hack, however, picking up 11 fouls total against the Jazz.

Rodman, it becomes clear, is an interesting strategic addition to whatever team he joins. When he is not playing, many of the rebounds that would have been his are invariably snared by his teammates. The difference he brings is the defense he plays and the kamikaze hustle that unfailingly garners him two or three boards that no replacement player would ever touch. Still, the Bulls are very good without him, and it's possible that he, too, notices this and is filing it away as motivation for his return.

The Bulls slip up against the Seattle SuperSonics two nights later, losing 97–92. They cruise to a 70–54 third-quarter lead, then suddenly fall apart. Their offense vanishes. Jordan looks tired, making just 6 of 19 shots. And those young power forwards Simpkins and Caffey are badly outplayed by superstud Shawn Kemp. In 32 combined minutes they contribute just 4 points, 6 rebounds, and the usual 11 fouls. Amazingly, Caffey has now fouled out of two consecutive games in just 34 minutes of play. Well, okay, maybe Karl Malone and Kemp had *something* to do with it.

I am reminded of Jerry Krause's reaction simply to seeing the 6'10" and muscular Kemp boarding a plane—we were all heading to the 1990 All-Star Game in Miami—during Kemp's rookie season. Krause stopped dead in his tracks. His jaw had dropped onto his chest. He may have gone pale. I thought he might faint. While staring at Kemp's back, which was departing down the gangway, Krause said, I suppose to me, "There is a manchild. *There* is a manchild. There is a *manchild*!" Krause has a tendency to say important things again and again.

There was one other telling failure in the Bulls' collapse against the Sonics: Pippen made just 2 of his 11 free throws. It was a percentage so miserable that it forced observers to recognize that with his incredibly long, sinewy arms and immense hands, Pippen could sometimes have such bad control, loft, and spin problems that he might actually shoot just 18 percent on free shots from 15 feet away, and this would have to be factored into any assessment of the Bulls' chances to go all the way. For instance, as good a ball handler as Pippen is—and he is truly gifted in that area—could the Bulls afford to have the ball in his hands while protecting a slim lead at crunch time?

No matter. The Bulls are right back in the saddle against the Portland Trail Blazers the next night, using a 35–20 third-quarter blitz to propel them to a 107–104 win. Jordan has 33 points, Pippen 21, and the team moves on to Vancouver, British Columbia, for its first game ever against the Grizzlies.

On this tour, the Bulls pull into each town as visiting dignitaries. Or perhaps as visiting soap opera stars. Everybody, of course, wants to see Michael, and all the media hounds ask him the same thing: "Are you the best player in the NBA?" Routinely, he has been saying that no, he is not; Scottie Pippen is the best player, and this is Scottie's team. It's a nice gesture, a nice statement, and it seems sincere enough. But it's not true.

Insiders know this. Opponents know this. Scottie never ran the Bulls. He was the best player when Jordan was gone, sure. But he was never a leader. The 12th of 12 children, Pippen does not have the natural makeup of a leader. He is not glib or demonstrative or persuasive. He is a basically nice person. But at one time he was the manager of his high school basketball team. Michael Jordan was never a manager. Scottie always thought it would be easy to be Jordan, to play the top game, take the heat, make the big shots, handle the tough questions, deflect the off-court scrutiny, take the world by the horns, be the man—until he got the chance. When he refused to play the final 1.8 seconds of a critical 1994 playoff game because he felt slighted that the last shot was not his to take, everyone knew. They knew that Scottie was No. 2. A great No. 2, probably the best in the game. But not the lead dog. Not a numero uno. "He's the vice president," is how Seattle SuperSonics guard Gary Payton puts it. "Not the president." It took Jordan's departure to prove the point, and now Pippen seems quite comfortable in his role as an all-around player, a magnificent and necessary sidekick. But a sidekick. He'd seen the white lights, and they'd done him in.

"He's just trying to show respect," said Pippen of Jordan's bouquets. "It's also him being modest in some way."

Correct.

Coming into Vancouver, Jordan is mobbed by fans and a press that treats him like royalty. The reason, Jordan tries to explain to all, is that he hasn't been to the West Coast in three years. But his mere absence is not enough to explain why tickets to the game are being scalped for as much as $2,500 Canadian. He understands the passion people have simply to *see* him. But it shocks him. "I'm coming back and playing the game of basketball, not like I was dead and being reborn," he says. "I love the game, but it's still a game. Others give much more to society, yet here I am being viewed as a religious cult figure."

On Thursday night, November 30, people throughout Chicago and eastern Bulls country generally begin shutting off their TV sets in disgust as the Bulls stink up the joint against the Grizzlies. It's late, there's work the next day, and here are the Bulls scoring a pathetic 18 points in the third quarter to fall behind, 64–62, to an expansion team that started five unknowns: Chris King, Antonio Harvey, Bryant Reeves, Blue Edwards, and Greg Anthony. Gag. But it gets worse. The Bulls fall behind by 8 points in the fourth quarter, until finally Jordan alone has had enough. He simply takes over, pouring in 19 points in the final 6 minutes to pull out a 94–88 win. He makes drives, fallaways, 3-pointers, and free throws, finishing with a game-high 29 points. Even in the annals of last-minute Jordan heroics, the effort is so unusual and uplifting that as his teammates parade off the court and into the tunnel to the locker room, they begin singing "(I Wanna) Be Like Mike," the happy, reggae-style Gatorade commercial.

Coincidentally, at just this time, noted basketball writer Terry Pluto has come out with a book titled *Falling from Grace: Can Pro Basketball Be Saved?* He argues that the NBA is in grievous trouble from money-grubbing, shallow, thuggish players following the directions of dull, uninspired coaches who think an isolation play is the zenith of offensive creativity. In a column written for the *Sun-Times,* Pluto states: "The NBA is in a crisis, not of the bankbook but of the heart." He explains how the league is ready to go straight down the pipe because of its venality and sameness. But then he notes an exception.

"Because you have Jordan, Chicago, every Bulls game is a snowflake—there is something different and special each time he steps on the court."

He's right about Chicagoans having access to rare entertainment, thanks to Jordan. But he's wrong about the degeneration of the league. All successful sports leagues—the NFL, NHL, and major league baseball prime among them—begin to look like stages for the repetitious enactments of the same mundane contest. A high skill level lops off dissimilarities between teams. Think how many 2–1 hockey games you have seen, or 27–17 NFL games, or 4–2 baseball games. That's how it goes. Pursuit of television and marketing money makes all modern athletes seem greedy. But then check the olden days: Babe Ruth chased money like a pig after corn. Jordan's rare gifts raise the level of the sea upon which all the NBA boats float. If he weren't around, the league wouldn't glitter the way it does. But it would shine from time to time. In any event, Jordan is here now—so why worry?

One more road game; one more victory.

The Bulls polish off the Los Angeles Clippers 104–98, with—who else?—Jordan scoring a game-high 37, including 7 crucial points down the stretch. Pippen has 21 points and a season-high 13 rebounds, and Jordan yanks down 11 rebounds of his own. There is a moment in the game, when the Clippers have cut a 14-point Bulls lead to 3 on a series of steals and baskets that included a breakaway jam by guard Brent Barry off a bad pass by Pippen, when you can just see Jordan boiling.

He takes the ball and, in the midst of the Bulls' halfcourt offense, simply drives in and dunks over the top of defender Terry Dehere. Just out of orneriness. Because he can, and because he's mad.

Luc Longley seems stuck in low gear, and that frustrates Jordan. Jordan gets out of low and sometimes gets so far into high that he forgets basketball is a team game. He just lets his ego spread over the floor like a drum of spilled paint. Such was the case in his 19-point outburst against the Grizzlies. That occurred because, among other things, Vancouver rookie guard Derrick Martin dared to talk some bland garbage to Jordan as the game wore down. Martin knew Jordan from playing with him at Jordan's backlot gym in L.A., so his chatter could be excused as playful buddy banter. But not by Jordan. "It took someone talking trash to me to get my game together," Jordan explained matter-of-factly.

The Bulls have wrapped their Circus Tour 6–1, and at 13–2 to date they are off to their best start ever. Their record is tops in the league, ahead of the 12–4 Rockets, the 12–4 Jazz, the 13–4 Magic, the 12–4 Knicks, the 9–4 Spurs, and the 10–6 SuperSonics. When the Bulls do well on the Circus Tour, they do well all year. And that's putting it mildly: Each time since 1989 that they have finished the trip over .500, they have gone on to win the NBA championship.

Then why is there this lingering worry that something bad is going to happen to the Bulls? Something that will cause all the momentum to dissipate?

The Bulls seem to have so much going for them. They are 6–0 at the United Center, where they will be playing 12 of their next 17 games. They have the leading scorer in the league (now with a 30-point average). They have all-around guy Scottie Pippen averaging 19 points, 7 rebounds, and 7 assists per game. They have the highest differential, 8.5, between their scoring average per game and their opponents' (103.5 to 95). And they have the world's greatest rebounder just hanging out, nursing his calf, not playing, bursting at the seams.

Things can't be this easy. Rodman is going to blow. Worse injuries are going to pop up. Shaq will be back. Dissension will bloom. How much more of this Michael, Michael, Michael stuff can the team take, anyway? The *Forbes* magazine list of the highest-paid athletes just came out, and for the fourth straight year Jordan tops everybody in the world. "There is Michael," says Bob Williams, president of the sports marketing firm Burns Sports, "and then there are the rest."

It just can't last. Can it?

┌─────┐
│ 9 │
└─────┘

IT IS NOW DECEMBER, AND I GUESS I AM AMONG THE GROWING ranks of people who are saying to themselves, Isn't it about time Dennis Rodman did something for this team besides color his hair? How long does a calf muscle take to heal, anyway? So here he is at last, answering all of us, getting ready to start Game 16 against the hated Knicks, who are despised here because of their rough play and their past antics under former coach Pat Riley and, quite simply, because they are from New York.

I have brought my parents to this contest, as a present to my mom for her birthday. After seeing them to their seats on the second level, I walk down to the main floor of the vast and shining United Center during early warmups and take my front-row press seat to the left of the Knicks basket. I don't want to say this is a painless job, this sportswriting gig, but, boy, you do get some fair seats to games.

I sit next to Bob Scarpetti, one of the off-duty Chicago policemen who works security at the arena, and also does private security work for Jordan. Along with fellow cops Gus Lett, Clarence Travis, Joey Rocas, John Michael Wozniak, and Calvin Holiday, Scarpetti tries to keep things safe and sane for Jordan and his wife Juanita whenever they venture into public or into any situation that seems potentially troublesome.

Jordan pays all his guards monthly—but then he bills the Bulls for the expense, an arrangement he worked out with management before he returned to the game. The cops travel with Jordan wherever he goes; not all of them, unless it's a big event, but somebody always comes along. They accompany him on his private airplane, they walk with him through the city, they surround him en route to press conferences or charity appearances. They even at times form a box around him as he walks to and from the court, setting him hopelessly apart from teammates such as Randy Brown and Jud Buechler, men who walk and act and are treated by crowds as essentially normal people.

Pippen often uses off-duty police sergeant Jimmy Gorman for protection, and the two sometimes hang out on Pippen's boat in Diversey Harbor. Rodman moves with his two guards, cops George Triantafillo and Kelly Davis, when he goes out partying, which is often. And none of it, truly, is done out of vanity. These three players need cops running interference for them. But Jordan needs it most of all.

As the arena fills to its capacity of 24,000, Scarpetti's eyes never stop scanning the crowd, back and forth like radar, looking for nut cases. Even as we talk, he never focuses on me for more than an instant. "Michael can't really get out and enjoy himself," he says. "He'd *like* to. He'd like to just sit down and have a drink. But people will not leave him alone. Even in Vancouver, he just tried to shoot some pool one night and in seconds the place was asshole-to-belly button with people. It's crazy."

The cop turns completely around, looking at faces, postures.

"He watches first-run movies at home. But he does go out sometimes. And when he goes out, he *has* to drive himself. He's got two or three Ferraris, a Corvette, a Blazer, a couple of Mercedes, a Jeep. His house will hold thirteen cars inside the two garages."

The personal-bodyguard setup has worked quite well for Jordan. Since his return to basketball, the only scary time came on the Bulls' recent November trip to San Antonio. The occasion was the celebration of James Edwards's 40th birthday on the night the Bulls whipped the Spurs. The venerable Buddha had played a grand 4 minutes in the game, picking up 2 points, 2 turnovers, and 3 fouls. It was a fitting performance by a man old enough to be Jason Caffey's dad. The team dressed and then went out en masse to toast the ancient center.

The problem was that the ever-so-helpful Jack Haley, who had spent plenty of time in San Antonio, appointed himself tour guide. He insisted that they all zip off to the Riverwalk, the yuppie nightspot area along the meandering San Antonio River in the rehabbed center of town not far from the Alamo. "I can get us all into the Hard Rock, no problem," he said. So the team barged into the franchise nightclub and ate some food and sang "Happy Birthday" to Buddha. But management had seated the Bulls in an elevated area so they were on display. "It was like a show," says Scarpetti. "Very uncomfortable."

So Haley suggested they all head to Fat Tuesdays.

"I said that it would be a problem, but Jack insisted," Scarpetti recalls. "George Koehler, Michael's driver, was along, and so was Tim Grover, his trainer. Michael wanted to go. I said, 'It's a messed-up place, Mike,' but he wanted to check it out. He never gets out."

So the group headed out once more, walking through the district. Within yards, Jordan got mobbed by star-gazers. Fortunately, some uniformed San Antonio police came to the rescue and helped clear a path so the Bulls could travel the final hundred yards to Fat Tuesdays. Inside was more chaos, and nothing worth staying for. Scarpetti told Haley that this was not a good idea. Haley had one more brainstorm. "Let's go to Dick's Last Resort," he said.

Dick's is a rollicking, profane place, with a main entrance directly off the narrow and always crowded walkway that follows the edge of the river. I had been there myself with Rodman two years earlier after a Spurs game, and I still sometimes wear the T-shirt he had bought for me as we left. Actually, typical of Worm, he had returned to Dick's after he and I and his girlfriend Kim had left, and then he came back out and caught up with the two of us and said, "Here, I bought you this." He knew I liked T-shirts, especially the semi-obscene ones they sold at Dick's, and this was his reticent gesture of friendliness.

At any rate, the Bulls entered Dick's, and as soon as they did, insanity ruled. "We gotta go!" Scarpetti yelled to fellow bodyguard Gus Lett. But it was too late; the group moved slowly forward, and the crowd closed behind it. Two burly bouncers helped them along, pushing patrons out of the way, but everyone wanted to see Michael. "People just wanted to touch him," Scarpetti says. "Feel him, grab him, make contact. Especially the women."

Scarpetti and Lett, a black, balding crime lab sergeant in his late fifties, kept scanning the crowd, looking for trouble. "I see a woman all googly-eyed," says Scarpetti. "She's with a guy, and he looks bad. He's like, 'Who the fuck is *he?* Who the fuck is *he?*' 'Let's go,' I'm saying to Gus. It's real tense now; you can feel it. Michael can sense it. We're on the second floor, and there's two guys fighting on the third floor, and all of a sudden they come down the stairs headfirst, beating the hell out of each other. The two bouncers go to the fight, and now we're getting pushed over the banister almost into the river.

"In the midst of all this I see the guy who was with the girl, and he's big enough, and he's coming forward, and I know he wants to hit Michael. He's coming, saying, 'Fuck Michael Jordan! You ain't shit!' He gets close enough, and he doesn't even know I'm there, because I'm in plain clothes, and I grab his hand in a 'come along,' and bend his arm and say, 'You better get the fuck out of here.' He almost pissed his pants, because it shocked him. So then we literally *pushed* our way down the stairs, through people. We went to the street and grabbed some cabs and got out of there. I'm telling you, they would have hurt Michael bad."

But tonight, we hope, nobody is going to get hurt. Worm is starting for the first time in 13 games. His hair is green. I ask Scarpetti if he knows why.

"Obvious," he says. "Christmas."

The Knicks are big and strong and surly, but the Bulls prevail, 101–94. The biggest problem in the game is the continued presence of the replacement referees, who will soon be replaced by the real refs, once their new contract is signed. Though the Bulls are somewhat out of sync with Rodman suddenly back in the mix, and fall behind 56–43 at half, it is the Knicks' brutish Charles Oakley who almost brings matters to a head. Whether the replacement refs are incompetent or not is debatable, but they are perceived to be by the players and coaches. After Oakley fouls Worm very hard, the Bulls come to the bench.

"Kick his *ass!*" says Haley to Worm. Haley, of course, is in his usual dress slacks, black shoes, black dickey, and sportcoat (usual because he will probably never be activated), and he constantly runs onto the floor to cheer the players on, and then stands with the coaches during time-outs as though he has something to contribute. But his enthusiasm right now could get somebody maimed. To his credit, Rodman plays hard but doesn't explode. Not for a while.

Pippen gets flattened by Oakley when the Knicks forward drives to the hole. No call. "Bullshit!" Pippen yells almost into the ref's ear. "Bullshit!"

Then Phil Jackson gets into it. "Do you know what an illegal defense is?" he screams in an incredibly hoarse voice at ref No. 7. "You *don't* know, do you?"

Movie director and head Knicks cheerleader Spike Lee is in the front row of seats near the halfcourt line. He is four seats down from movie critic and major Bulls enthusiast Gene Siskel, and they alternately leap frenziedly into the air and shout and clap, depending on the fortunes of their respective teams. The whole place is sort of goofy, with much of the venom being directed at the inept officials.

Jordan screams at ref No. 21, a man named John Heatly, roaring and swearing that Oakley threw him bodily out of the way. The ref actually seems to be considering doing what clearly should be done: give Jordan the T he richly deserves. But the Bulls call time out. Haley rushes between Jordan and the ref. Things calm. At the next free throw opportunity, Jordan, the master manipulator and considerate soul, sidles up to Heatly and out of the side of his mouth, in a voice almost no one can hear, says, "I'm sorry." Heatly stands impassive. But he hears.

Rodman finally gets *his* technical foul, but so does Knicks center Patrick Ewing—for ramming into each other. But the most telling episode of the night occurs when Rodman has the ball at the point, late in the third quarter with the Bulls rallying furiously. He motions for Jordan to move down low, but Jordan yells, "No, no!"

Rodman holds the ball, and Jordan comes out to the top of the key, and Worm hands him the ball. Jordan surveys the defense. He drives, loses his defender, rises into the air and shimmies left and right, prepares to shoot, and then deals a perfect pass to Rodman for a reverse layup and a foul. The crowd goes wild. Rodman and Jordan high-ten each other and seem, briefly, to bond, for the first time in history.

Worm steps to the free throw line. He holds the ball and raises one hand. The crowd increases its fevered screaming. He drops his hand. He pauses. Then he raises it again. The crowd screams louder in a deafening wave. Rodman shoots, misses. He gets his own rebound. Oh boy, the noise. Oh boy, the show biz.

Rodman finished with 20 rebounds and just 6 points. But then, he doesn't particularly want to score, and scoring is a hard thing to do when he incessantly breaks early from his position in the triangle and begins carving out rebounding position. But the "garbage" sates the Worm.

"It's great to be back," he says. "The teammates are great; they respect me for who I am."

He is still on court as he says this, and when done, he whips off his jersey. (His number is 91, which, when the two digits are added together, equals 10, the number he wanted but couldn't have. That is because 10 was former Bulls star forward Bob Love's numeral, now retired and hanging in the rafters.) Rodman hands the jersey to a disbelieving little kid and walks barechested through the crowd to the locker room. As he goes, I observe some of his newer tattoos: the large dice, the zigzag lines, the blue-tinged dolphin. It strikes me that so many players in the league have tattoos now (Shaq with his Superman logo, Dennis Scott with a likeness of his dad, Damon Stoudamire with "Damon" in Gothic script on his shoulder, John Salley with his Chinese stuff) that Rodman is not so much different as ahead of the game, a fashion pioneer.

And even at that, his trailblazing is new only in the staid world of sport. I used to live in Key West in the late '70s and early '80s, and at every Fantasy Fest I attended in that sweltering outpost I saw thousands of people dressed a whole lot weirder than Worm. Wearing a T-shirt, as he sometimes does, that reads I DON'T MIND STRAIGHT PEOPLE, AS LONG AS THEY ACT GAY IN PUBLIC can only be shocking to general managers, gee-whiz sports anchors, and the Christian right. The Worm has done nothing the rock world hasn't done long before. Indeed, he would be *undertattooed* were he a member of the Red Hot Chili Peppers, understudded in Psychic TV, and under-androgynous next to Boy George. But it's a good show in the button-down NBA.

I retrieve my parents, and as we walk to the Stadium Club on the 200 level, my dad says, not completely thrilled, "It's like a three-ring circus." He has not been to a game since Chicago Stadium was demolished. "Noise, video stuff, giant slingshots, little kids in cars. Things going on everywhere."

We sit in the restaurant and order some wings and beers. We talk about the game and the players. I tell my mom that Rodman has just appeared in the buff in the January *Playboy*. I tell her about all his tattoos and body rings.

"I heard," Mom says, "that he had his scrotum pierced."

Whoa.

"But it got infected," I reply. "So I've heard he's having it redone."

As we leave, the United Center is almost empty. Mom brings up Worm again, saying she likes him. "I even like some of his offcourt actions," she says. "I think it's good he's an individual and that he's fitting in with the team. And I think red lights in his hair would be wonderful."

We walk down the stairs to ground level.

"He wants to have control over his life," she reasons. "And who doesn't?"

There, walking up the hallway, is a short, heavyset man wearing a trenchcoat and a hat pulled down hard on his round head. Next to him is a man in a similar trenchcoat, only this man is over 7-feet tall. It's the Sleuth and Sam Bowie, the retired center Krause has been trying to entice out of retirement to join the Bulls. Bowie, of course, is famous mostly for being one of the two players taken before Jordan in the 1984 draft, and never panning out. The other player was Hakeem Olajuwon. He panned out.

"Hi, Jerry," I say. "What's Sam doing here?"

Walking together, the GM and former player looked like a bat and ball.

"He's visiting relatives," the Sleuth answers quickly, somberly.

I almost fall over laughing.

I see Bill Smith, the photographer, and we talk for a while. Ten minutes later, up the stairs comes Rodman. It's an hour and a half after the game. Rodman picks up a little girl and holds her high. She looks at his face, at the various rings, and says, "What are those things?"

After setting her down, he walks over and we chat. I tell him I think he embarrassed sports radio hosts Dick Versace and Peter Brown in their first WMVP interview with him, when he started talking about masturbation on the road and how he had named his right hand Rosie or Lucy or whatever.

"I'm gonna say what I gotta say," he replies.

"Will you say hi to my mom?" I ask. "It's her birthday."

"Happy birthday, Jeanne," he says graciously.

As we leave the building my mother says, "He's much better-looking in person."

■ ■ ■

Two nights later the Bulls whip up on the visiting Spurs, 106–87. Rodman yanks down 21 rebounds, marking the first time a Bull has gotten 20 or more in consecutive games since Charles Oakley did it eight years ago. Almost as important, Worm stays calm against his old teammates. This is good, since a couple years ago in his first game against the Pistons after he was traded from them, he skirmished with old friend Bill Laimbeer and got ejected.

Scottie Pippen, who has been in the slow process of re-creating himself as a solid and caring citizen and a steady team player, had a bit of a backslide today. His attorney went to court for him and settled Scottie's paternity of two babies, born just seven months apart, to two separate mothers. Pippen has had other image problems in the past—a gun possession difficulty, a domestic dispute with a gold-digging girlfriend, and, of course, the 1.8-second sit-down. But, if he can get this recent stuff behind him and stay out of the public doghouse, it seems the world of advertising and promotion is ready to jump on his bandwagon and help him make up for his woefully bad seven-year Bulls contract (averaging a little less than $3 million per season).

It seems that all the Bulls stand to benefit hugely from the vapor trail Jordan and Pippen and Rodman are leaving behind them. Only Scottie and Michael have won NBA titles with the Bulls, and so the rest of the gang (except for Rodman, who won two titles with Detroit, and Buddha, who has been with so many teams—nine—he can't even remember what he has won) are tiptoeing toward a rare reward. Things are meshing for the Bulls in a way that has to be frightening to the rest of the league.

"There are no jealousies on this team," Jordan says of the Bulls' progress. "No individual goals, only team goals. We do have lapses, but why do they occur? Human nature. It's hard not to have them, but we try to minimize them. We maintain our focus, and that goes back to Phil."

Jordan has said that Jackson, the former Knick wildman and now an active practitioner of his own eclectic brand of Zen Christianity, which mandates effort, responsibility, selflessness, tolerance, and a bit of hippie happiness, is the "ultimate leader." Just Jordan saying that brings greater harmony to this amazingly disparate team. How rare it is in this league of malcontents to hear any star praising his coach. When it's Jordan who's doing it, it is very hard for, say, Toni Kukoc to offer an opinion to the contrary.

One of the motivating factors for Jordan is his delight in bringing new guests to the party. "So many guys have never been in this position before," he says. "That's what makes me feel good. Steve Kerr, Randy Brown, Luc, Jud. It's great for them."

■ ■ ■

Snow is lightly falling outside the Berto Center windows as the Bulls finish practice and head for the locker room. In the press room and now spilling onto the court—opened to us, as always, precisely when the players are leaving—is the usual horde of newspaper and TV and radio reporters, as well as at least a dozen Japanese television people. The Japanese folks are always around. They wander about, filming everything, as Longley talks to an interviewer and Otis, equipment man John Ligmanowski's big dog, scurries about, gnawing on an official NBA basketball. "You need a passport to get in," says assistant PR man Tom Smithburg.

One of the foreigners is an attractive and model-tall young woman. It's clear she must be the "talent" for whatever production is taking place. The building was partly designed by the master of evasiveness and secrecy, Jerry Krause. It was his particular devious genius to build a press room that has a full Plexiglas-windowed view of the playing court, and then to install a mechanized blind on the other side, a blind that is always down when there is action acourt and then rises when the players have left. Moreover, just to get into the press room one must be buzzed through a front door after being appraised by an outdoor surveillance camera. Then there is another door that also requires being buzzed through, the one that leads around the corner to the court. Where the players almost never are.

But Longley is captive just now, giving an interview, and we grill him about the upcoming Orlando rematch. He acts as if it's no big deal.

In time Phil Jackson comes out and he, too, speaks of the impending match as just another game on the long journey to something else.

"You want to win," Jackson explains, "but you want to see growth of the ball club. And sometimes when you win, you don't see growth. So it distorts the necessity to improve. I can say, Yes, I'm happy with our record, but, no, I'm not so happy with the way we're playing. Our energy and defense and overall team play could be a lot better. Sometimes you need to have a loss maybe to change it up, make you more coachable."

The Bulls are 16–2, but they should be better, is what he's saying. But I'm confused. So a loss is tolerable?

"Sure." The man who increasingly looks like a lean, 6'8" edition of the late Jerry Garcia shrugs. "Losses are always tolerable. Except at the end of the season, because you can't go back and play anymore."

Jordan, it dawns on me after a spell, has taken this exact moment to sneak out the side door and slip silently away. The timing is perfect. Pippen makes the same getaway. It's a technique they have perfected.

It follows in a long tradition that Jordan established when the Bulls practiced at the nearby health club known as the Multiplex. The setup there was comical, and it shows how far the NBA has progressed in just a few years. The players were supposed to, and generally did, shower in the club members' locker room, right along side Sig from Northbrook and Skeeter from Buffalo Grove. Jordan would sometimes linger, maybe watch the tube in the lounge for a while, but he never showered at the place. And by the end, when people from all over were mobbing the place to check out the Bulls and MJ, he often would burst right through the fire doors at the end of the gym, setting off the alarm, take two steps, and be in his Corvette and gone before anybody could pursue him. He didn't do it in anger; he often winked and waved bye-bye. But he was gone just the same.

I look over now by the main exit at Lacy Banks, one of the *Sun-Times*'s two fulltime NBA guys. He's wearing a green army jacket and stocking cap, leaning against the wall, seemingly asleep. He's been waiting for Jordan for a long time. He'll have to wait longer.

Jackson rambles on with his esoterica. He is right; this is just one game out of 82. But it means a lot, too. The Magic have beaten the Bulls six of their last eight games since Jordan returned. People have been talking about Penny Hardaway being the new "man." And in their last meeting this season in Orlando, Hardaway scored 36 points to Jordan's 23. Shaq is still out with his big bad thumb, but the Bulls need to show they can at least whip this young team that seems to have supplanted them as the team of tomorrow. Indeed, the Magic have won 16 in a row without their gigantic center.

The media pack leaves, but I hang around for no reason I can discern. Sometimes I get into these moods I can barely describe. Stasis, perhaps. Alpha waves. Just sit and stare blankly out the window, caught between doing and drifting, no place to be, everything to do, no desire to start.

I look up. A pretty young woman stands nearby. It is Lindsey Buechler. Her husband Jud finally comes out, the last guy in the place. He must have been lifting weights or something. I like Jud. So does everybody, if they have an opinion about him at all.

He's wearing jeans and when it gets warmer, he'll break out the beach garb, the Red Sand gear, the T-shirts that say "Longboard Magazine" on them. That's longboard as in long surfboard, as opposed to shortboard. Shortboarders are "aggro"—that's "aggressive" in surfspeak: the shortboarding hotdogs are "too on edge, too competitive," says Buechler, the San Diego native who now calls the beach at Del Mar home—or rather, "the office." He is a longboard surfer. That means he is one of the laid-back, retro dudes with a 10-footer who appreciates surfing the way it was supposed to be. "Longboarders are the good guys," he has told me. "They take it back to when you surfed just to surf."

There are not a lot of surfers in the NBA. Not a lot of white guys, either. But the Bulls are different. Despite the trend toward absolute black dominance in the league—the Utah Jazz's 34-year-old John Stockton, for instance, will be the only white player on the 12-man USA "Dream Team" in the 1996 Summer Olympics—the Bulls have a prominent pallid streak. This year's team has five white faces: Buechler, Longley, Kukoc, Kerr, and Wennington. Six, if you count pep squad leader Haley. Last season there were six white players—seven for a time, but Larry Krystkowiak was on the injured list. Why the Bulls have so many whites, no one knows. Most of them are big guys, on whom there is a premium regardless of race. "You can't have too many big men," Krause always says. "You can't teach height."

But the main reason seems to be that with great athletic talents like Jordan and Pippen and now Rodman on the floor, the Bulls function quite smoothly with role players whose skills are more common filling in the gaps. Two or three chiefs are plenty. Let the white guys do what they can. If there is another reason for the makeup of the team, nobody is saying. Or, for the most part, caring.

Still, the 27-year-old Buechler is the only surfer on the squad (though he tried unsuccessfully to introduce Longley to the joys of hanging ten last offseason). He is also its premier beach volleyball enthusiast; indeed, he is good enough that he may try to join the pro circuit when his basketball days are over. "Most of the best volleyball players were former basketball stars," he explains. "Karch Kiraly is a great athlete—I mean really good. He's like, like . . . Michael Jordan, in a way. All those guys have forty-inch verticals."

Drafted out of the University of Arizona by Seattle in 1990 and quickly dealt to the New Jersey Nets, the 6'6", 220-pound Californian arrived in the Garden State aghast at what he saw. "Culture shock," he says. "I mean, I thought *Arizona* was east. But New Jersey? You arrive at Newark Airport and everybody is depressed, looking down, their body language is terrible."

To counteract his gloom, Buechler finally, on one of the Nets' off days, drove a couple of hours to the Jersey shore. "Just to see the water," he recalls. "The wind was blowing, it was freezing cold, it was gray out. I took my shoes and socks off and put my feet in the water and waded. I had a parka on, the hood was up." He shakes his head at the image. "It wasn't the same."

Lindsey, who is a few months pregnant, was actually Jud's savior with regard to his beloved beach pastimes. His father, an ocean-loving high school teacher in La Jolla whose nickname was "Beachcomber Buechler," had seen the way the beach life could ruin promising high school athletes, so he wouldn't let Jud surf as a boy. Jud played basketball and baseball instead. It wasn't until four years ago that Lindsey, a former beach girl who grew up on the strand at Hermosa Beach, showed Jud the ins and outs of shooting the curls and wiping out.

"Now," says Buechler, "I'm almost thankful my dad wouldn't let me surf. Because it is so wonderful. A lot of guys had that feeling back at age fifteen. I have it now. I can't tell you—it is *the* most addictive thing I've ever done. There is nothing better. Sun, water, buddies. All the guys live in San Diego and work for companies like Oakley or Red Sand. They are people who *have* to be around the ocean. The thought of moving to some place like Palm Springs terrifies them."

Yet here is the beach dude, who is averaging 5 points and usually one impressive dunk or 3-pointer per game, landlocked in the Midwest in the dead of winter. He can handle it. When he gets down, he just thinks about the title shimmering ahead. "Michael has said he wants to get us a ring," says Buechler, who along with Steve Kerr helped Arizona make it to the NCAA Final Four in 1988. "People like me and Randy Brown and Steve. And I think it's great."

To sustain him he also has memories of a perfect day at "the office," a day that begins with arrival at the Del Mar beach at 10 A.M., surfing till lunch with the gang (subs from the Board & Brew sandwich shop), volleyball till "cocktail hour," when everybody plays a game called "Ace," in which beer-chugging is the penalty for bad play, then home at 7 to shower and prepare for dinner. Before doing it again the next day.

As he is leaving, Buechler is approached by the still-present Japanese film crew. They must have been hiding in a corner of the gym. The tall, pretty woman shakes hands with Jud. A translator tells him, "This woman was on the national volleyball team in Japan." Buechler nods and chats. Ah, the beach life—it translates everywhere.

10

JORDAN BLOCKS PENNY HARDAWAY'S FIRST SHOT, AND THAT'S about all anybody needs to know.

This Bulls–Magic rematch is in the bag. Jordan outscores the young guard, 36–26, with almost half of Hardaway's points coming at the end of the game, when the Bulls' 112–103 victory is guaranteed.

Toni Kukoc comes off the bench to have one of his slick, graceful games, picking up 21 points on a variety of inside moves in 30 minutes of play. At 6'11" he has the size of a forward or even a slender center but the deft touch of a point guard; when he is "on," few can match up against him. Big men are too slow, little men are too little. Still, Kukoc is always an unknown. It is never certain who will show up for each game, or each half: Toni the Timid or Toni the Tiger. Kukoc knows how he is perceived, and he admits that he needs to be tougher and less sensitive day in and day out. As he says of Rodman and his act, "He does his special thing. If I did that, people would say, 'What is he, on drugs?'" They probably would. There is always a certain pall of sadness, of uncertainty, around Kukoc, part of it because everyone knows how troubled Croatia, his embattled homeland, is and the tumult that has touched his relatives there. But people also see in Toni a petulant, very intimidated, and immature young boy, a nice kid who just isn't hard enough for this cruel world.

He is smiling a bit against the Magic, which he later admits is unusual. "When you see me laughing on the court, it means I'm having fun," he explains, as if that were necessary. "Usually I'm not."

There is an interesting moment toward the end of the game. The Bulls have been way ahead, but Orlando makes a mini-run at them. The Magic's Nick Anderson hits a 3 to make the score 96–87 Bulls, with about 3 minutes to go. This was precipitated by a bad pass from Jordan, a one-hander that sailed over Kerr's head and out of bounds. Phil Jackson looked at Jordan in disgust. No tolerance or cosmic flow here, just the nauseated grimace of a ticked-off dictator.

"Two hands!" Jackson yelled, then he raised both his hands as though showing a child how to pass. Jordan nodded. Jackson looked away and rolled his eyes. There will never be a perfect player, there will never be a satisfied coach.

With the score 100–91 Bulls, and less than 2 minutes to go, Kerr nails a 3-pointer, and now it is truly over. Kerr is an interesting guy that way. He looks harmless, but he just kills opponents when they leave him alone in order to concentrate on Michael, Scottie, Harper, or even big Luc. He is so self-deprecating that you wonder after talking to him how he even made his high school team. (He seems to sincerely wonder the same thing.) But then the daggers come out of the blue eyes, and you know there's something going on inside.

Against the Spurs a week ago Kerr was cracked in the jaw by the much bigger Chuck Person. It was a quick, hard, purposeful elbow, unseen by the refs, that could have done some real damage. Moments later Kerr got the ball and angrily hit a 3-pointer, then walked past Person and yelled, "You fucker!" He looked like a beagle with fangs.

After tonight's game, one of the biggest men in the league sits in the Magic locker room, fully clothed, mumbling answers to reporters' questions in a voice so low that whispering would be louder. Shaq didn't play; his postoperative thumb is still keeping him out. It's been weeks now. It seems so silly, like a busted machine gun keeping a battleship in drydock. Maybe they should just amputate the stupid thing—that would at least give him an excuse for being such a pathetic free throw shooter. I ask him, in a voice that seems to boom through the silence, whether he'll be even worse on free throws when he comes back. This gets him to raise his head slowly and eye me with slight interest and maybe a dab of world-weary contempt.

"It's gonna be the same old missing-free-throws, leading-my-team-to-the-finals, never-hit-the-big-shot-free-throw Shaq," he replies in a near-rap.

I make my way back to the Bulls locker room. Jordan, dressed in his Bigsby & Kruthers finest, is receiving a diamond-shaped framed cloth print of a dragon from the Japanese people who are still hanging around. All of them are bowing, taking pictures, doing voice-overs in their native tongue. I turn away, smiling. Then I feel a big hand clapping me on the shoulder. It's Jordan, smiling at me.

"I have to take my kite and go," he says to me. The Japanese are following, but they can't hear.

"That's not a kite, is it?" I ask of the multihued cloth about 6 feet square. To me it looks like the pattern for a new Rodman tattoo.

"Yes, it is," says Jordan, smirking slyly, fairly certain the foreigners have no idea of his boundless joy.

■ ■ ■

People are still talking about Scottie Pippen as the prime candidate for MVP of the league. Certainly the sheer number of things he can do well, from rebounding, dribbling, dunking, shooting, and passing to swarming his opponent defensively like some kind of four-limbed octopus, makes him the most *versatile* player in the league. He can play any position from point guard to power forward if need be. But in truth, he plays no position at all. The Bulls do not start a 1-guard, 2-guard, 3-forward; they start Jordan, Pippen, and Harper and say *Sic 'em*. It is the beauty of the Bulls' attack that the role of each starter is to *play basketball*: If you can do it, do it. Longley can't do much more than be the big galoot in the middle, and Worm prefers to attack the boards, but if either showed the inclination and ability to bring the ball upcourt or shoot deadly 3s, Jackson would probably say, Make it happen.

Pippen *can* do it all, and as an all-around force, he is throwing out enough sparks to actually out-flash Jordan at times. With the season now in its seventh week, Pippen has just become the first Bull to win the NBA's Player of the Week award. Does he deserve it?

You bet. His three-game stats for the judging period average out to a league-high 29.7 points, 9.7 rebounds, and 6.7 assists per game. He shot 58 percent from the field and 53 percent from 3-point range. He also had 4 blocked shots and 5 steals during the period. And that's not even counting the most recent game against the Celtics, when he had a season-high 37 points on 65 percent shooting, 12 assists, 9 rebounds, and 2 blocked shots.

Still, MVP for the whole league, for the whole year? I wrack my brain and darned if I can think of a game Pippen has won by himself, carrying everybody on his back, doing it all in the last minutes, in his entire career. I know there must have been *some* games like that for Pippen. But Jordan eats big games like cashews. He won three games by himself on this year's Circus Trip alone. Doesn't an MVP have to slay the enemy single-handed?

"He's got to be one of the best players in the game," says Jordan of Pippen. "If not the best."

But Ron Harper, who was once a high-flying star with Cleveland and San Diego and is now a quiet worker bee, knows the bad side to fame.

"In this business, everybody would like to be top dog," he told me when I asked him whether Scottie could handle top dog-ness. "But the top dog is not all it's made out to be."

No sirree. "He's learned how to motivate himself every night," says Jordan, continuing his Pippen promotion. "When one phase isn't on key for him, he contributes in other areas. And I think that's the sign of greatness."

Pippen smiles. It's cool. His free throw percentage right now is 65, compared to Jordan's 85. Drive, and get fouled in the last seconds, when you're down by 1, and make the free ones? To win it all? Enough said.

"He was just being kind to me," Pippen states of his leader. "Everybody knows that Jordan is still the best player in the game."

Or at least they should.

■ ■ ■

I take a hoops break and head to Los Angeles for the Rose Bowl where, for reasons beyond my ken, my alma mater Northwestern's Wildcats will be representing the Big Ten against PAC-Ten champion Southern California. It's been a mere half century since the Cats made it this far. A quarter century since they had a winning season. What's that saying? Anything can happen in sport? Just the other day somebody floated the crazy notion that the Bulls, now 23–2, might win 70 games this season.

"That's outrageous," Steve Kerr responded. "That's crazy."

Probably. But they *have* won 13 straight. And Jordan, who won seven straight scoring titles from 1987 to 1993, is way in the lead again. His 30-point average is 3.5 points higher than runner-up David Robinson's. That is a greater margin than in five of his previous title wins. What does it mean? Maybe nothing. Maybe a lot.

With my mind on football, I go down to the pool at my hotel in Santa Monica, and who should I see but Rodman trade-bait Will Perdue. He's playing Ping-Pong with his new San Antonio buddy Vinny Del Negro. The Spurs are here waiting to play the Lakers at the Great Western Forum tonight.

Perdue is a cheerful enough big guy, with feet the size of attaché cases. I make a mental note to myself to be sure to watch any game the Spurs might play against the Magic, to check the shoes flopping around when Perdue guards Shaq. We start shooting the breeze and end up talk-ing for an hour. Both he and Del Negro see Rodman's good behavior now as simply contract-drive smarts. "I've heard he doesn't have much money left," Perdue says. That, of course, is true. Rodman's new agent, Dwight Manley, explained to me that just a few months ago Rodman had what could euphemistically be called "a negative net worth." Man-ley is a piece of work, a shrewd and brilliant hustler who has made it his pet project to turn Rodman into a media superstar. Way in the black.

Perdue, who started almost every game for the Bulls the previous year, plans to keep his house in suburban Chicago, but he's glad to be away from Jerry Krause. The Sleuth apparently never forgave Perdue for, among other things, telling me about the secret tryout Krause had put Perdue through when the 7-foot Vanderbilt center was a rookie-to-be. The story is worth retelling.

Projected as a backup center, Perdue was brought to Chicago before the 1988 draft and picked up at O'Hare by Billy McKinney, then a Bulls scout, who called Krause on his car phone and said, "This is Agent Blue calling Agent Orange. The package has been picked up and is being de-livered." Perdue was then transported to a hotel, where he was later picked up by Krause for a late-night workout at the Multiplex gym. As soon as Krause pulled into the Multiplex parking lot, he slammed on the brakes and threw the car into reverse, terrifying Perdue, and sped off the lot because he had seen a sportswriter leaving the building. Krause drove around the Multiplex a few times until he was sure it was closed. He then took Perdue in for his test. After that he drove Perdue back to the hotel, where the center was registered under a fake name and told him to leave the next morning without checking out; a cab would be sent for him. Unfortunately, Perdue forgot he was using an alias and watched in bewilderment the next morning as a cabbie wandered the lobby, yelling for his fictional customer. "It was quite an ordeal," Perdue recalled. "I thought this was normal in the NBA, but then I went to other teams and realized it wasn't. The last thing Krause had said to me was, 'Don't tell anybody anything.'"

Perdue smiles at the memory. "He's still doing them," he says of the secret workouts.

"B. J. Armstrong and I are pretty close," Perdue says of the former

Bulls guard whom Krause released after last season. "And when he went to Golden State after the Raptors traded him, he said, 'Will, something is going on here. They're too nice!' He couldn't believe it. The owner had taken him out for dinner. Everybody was friendly and open. It's just not like that with the Bulls. You're supposed to feel it's enough just to be on the team."

11

JUNE JACKSON, THE WOMAN WHOM PHIL JACKSON COURTED years ago by inviting her to climb on the back of his motorcycle for a summer-long trip through the West, walks straight up to me and says: "I have a bone to pick with you."

Well, okay. What might it be?

"You wrote in your column that I was a 'restrictive wife,'" she states.

"I did?"

"Yes, a friend called me and read it to me. How could you call me restrictive? I'm not restrictive."

I thought back. Hmm. "I think I said Phil's *father's* wife was restrictive," I said.

"That's not how it read," she said, giving me the evil eye.

I went home and dug out the offending piece. Jeez, it wasn't like I had written that she was an embezzler or something. Even if I had said she was restrictive. Which I hadn't.

Here's what I wrote: *People have laughed mightily at Jackson's Zen folderol. You know, he's just this ex-hippie son of a Pentecostal minister and his restrictive wife, and all this Eastern mysticism stuff is simply rebellion against the irritants of a highly structured upbringing.*

If you analyze the sentence you see that the word "his" has as its antecedent "minister," thus the wife in question belongs to Phil's father, not Phil. And besides, how could Phil be the son of his wife? I make mistakes all the time when I write, grammatical, factual, and otherwise. But not this time. The sentence might be unclear, but it's not incestuous.

So now I see June again after the Bulls have walloped the Rockets, 100–86, at the United Center. I have put out of my mind the fact that the Rockets were the winners of the last two NBA championships (having taken advantage of Michael Jordan's hiatus), and that the Bulls are now 26–3. What I want to do is explain my words to June. So I point out the antecedents in the column, and the fact that Phil couldn't be her son.

"No, I wouldn't have a six-eight son," she muses. Then she looks at me quizzically. "You're not still thinking about that, are you?"

Well, yes, I tell her.

"Hey," she laughs. "Just let it go. I'd already forgotten."

I tell her I'll remember that the next time I offend the Jacksons in print. Then, out of curiosity, I ask her how she would want to be described.

"Permissive," she says. Then she shakes her head. "No. I don't want my teenage kids reading that."

■ ■ ■

On the plane to San Antonio for the 1996 All-Star game, I shoot the breeze for a bit with Bulls PR man Tim Hallam, a longtime friend. Hallam was the Bulls' assistant publicity guy under former head Brian McIntyre, until McIntyre went off to be the head media man for the league in 1981.

I used to enjoy having a postgame beer with Hallam in the press room or sometimes just in the hallway under the old Stadium. I vividly remember one playoff game against the Knicks in the early '90s. The game actually got boring, so I went down the rickety back stairs behind the court to the tiled corridor that connected the locker rooms and other odd subterranean spaces in that creaky place. I stood down there with Hallam and James Jordan, all of us drinking—Tim and I working on beers, James drinking rum and Cokes with lime—and just jawboning. Waitresses came and went, carrying orders up to patrons in the expensive seats. The Lovabulls also passed through, rushing to make costume changes. We could hear the game, but this was more fun than watching.

Tim and James had seen enough basketball in their lifetimes. I wasn't a columnist yet, so I had no deadline to meet.

Tim smoked cigarettes, and James talked to the girls, kidding with them and asking them to go out with him. He told one to look him up in New York when the series moved there. It was just happy, wise-guy talk, and nobody cared. It was fun, but James Jordan is gone now, and I don't do things like that with Hallam anymore, either.

In September 1994, Tim was arrested in his Chicago apartment after he signed for a postal package that allegedly contained four grams of cocaine. Police also found marijuana and a .357 Magnum in his place, and that was that. Handcuffs, jail, humiliation. The Bulls issued one statement: "We regret the unfortunate incident. In America there is a presumption of innocence. We are hopeful that when all the facts are known, Tim Hallam will be vindicated." After that there was silence.

For Hallam it all led to court, drug and alcohol rehab, and ultimately— and remarkably—his job back as PR man. People can say what they will about bottom-line Jerry Reinsdorf, but somewhere in his business-man's heart is a charitable chamber. Hallam shakes his head over the arrest incident each time he thinks back. Ruin him? "Hell," he says, "it saved my life."

Now he has cut out every bad habit except cigarettes. I usually ask him whether he'd like some illegal drugs or a shot of Jack Daniel's. "Got any pot?" he'll ask. "Quaaludes?" We laugh, but I know it is hard for him still. "Day to day," he says when we're done joking. It was trouble in Hallam's personal life that got him to his worst stage, but no doubt being on the Bulls merry-go-round didn't help his equilibrium much, either. Attending to Michael Jordan is a round-the-clock occupation in itself, one that Hallam has pretty much given up since making his own comeback. "Michael does what he's going to do," says Hallam. "I tell everybody that."

I reread parts of Phil Jackson's book *Sacred Hoops: Spiritual Lessons of a Hardwood Warrior* while the plane is en route. I linger over the section where he discusses assessing blame in a game, how pointing the finger at anyone can be counterproductive. When he was head coach of the Albany Patroons in the CBA, Jackson writes, "I was more interested in the quality of the team's energy as it ebbed and flowed, and figuring out what lessons could be learned when disaster struck." Such thoughtfulness led him to be voted CBA Coach of the Year in 1985. I ponder the quotation from author Ursula K. LeGuin that he cites: "It is good to have an end to journey toward; but it is the journey that matters in the end." Phil has used that mantra often.

Before the Bulls went on a six-game road trip out west at the start of February, he said: "I expect to lose two or three games on this road trip. I'm just being honest with you. I can't see us playing at this level against teams that are very good. We're going to have to work hard just to come out .500 on this trip."

The Bulls went 4–2 on the swing, and a critic could say such frank talk by the head man probably preordained the losses. But Jackson has come by his philosophy rationally; to say you're going to win them all is just coach-blabber, and setting the team free of expectations is as liberating as setting it free of both praise and blame. As Jackson has explained, it allows the team to grow and become what it may without being stifled. "This team has a great appetite," Phil had said earlier in the week. "It's a team that never needs prodding. What they need is to be informed."

Two weeks ago the Bulls showed the effect of being focused and informed but not burdened with tension or false agendas. Down 85–83 to the Raptors in Toronto, they rallied for a 92–89 win, largely on the strength of Jordan's offense, with MJ scoring 15 of his 38 points in the fourth quarter. But Longley was fouled with 6 seconds remaining, and despite hitting almost 80 percent from the free throw line for the season, he missed both attempts.

Now the young Raptors, who had recently knocked off the Magic, could tie the game on a 3-pointer, send it into overtime, and maybe win. But because of wise foul management the Bulls were not in the penalty situation; they were able to apply fierce pressure to the Raptors' inbounds play. Damon Stoudamire had to go to midcourt to get the pass, and Steve Kerr promptly fouled him. No free throws. On the next inbounds play the Bulls again smothered the Raptors. Toronto center Oliver Miller could only heave the ball from way outside as time expired. The shot didn't draw iron.

I read on. Phil talks about his ability to see good in lousy situations. "As my wife likes to say, I can 'smell a rose in a pile of manure.'"

I take the book and walk up to the first-class cabin where assistant coach Jim Cleamons and his wife and the other coaches' wives are sitting. I find June Jackson and read her the passage.

"True?" I say.

She nods. "Except I said 'pile of shit.'"

June is a pistol, and it had to take a restless, searching, and freethinking soul to marry her. She has said that she hopes Phil goes into college coaching sometime, because she likes the collegiate atmosphere and because she wants to pursue a Ph.D. in psychology. For years, to get away from it all, Phil, June, and their five kids have retreated to Montana for the summers. There they live the rustic life without TV or a lot of amenities. Phil's mother lives nearby. "She's eighty-eight and she still chops wood," June marvels. Phil's father died years ago.

Even in the early days of their relationship, when Phil was a Knick, he and June went to Montana. While other NBA players stayed near city gyms or played in summer leagues to get in shape for the approaching season, Phil communed with the great outdoors.

"Phil did nothing until going back for training camp," June says. "Sometimes he'd shoot at the basket we had in the yard, while I stood in front of him holding up a tennis racket. But really all he did was skip rope."

Of course, Phil was a bit of a rebel back then, in the countercultural late '60s and early '70s, and indulged in the recreational drugs of the period. Indeed, his old Knicks road roommate Bill Bradley, now a U.S. senator from New Jersey, admitted recently that he and Phil smoked some marijuana in those days. Just to get it on the table, in case Bradley runs for president some day, so he doesn't have to do Clinton's "I didn't inhale" tap dance.

Whatever enlightenment Phil found he gradually translated into a life vision and a plan that would become the foundation of his coaching technique. A lot of people, including me, have joked about the Zen weirdo's outlook, his use of Indian symbols to help explain proper behavior—the Lakota Sioux wooden arrow, the bear claw, the middle feather of an owl (all of which hang in the team room at the Berto Center)—and his declared belief that much about competition, including the enemy, is sacred.

But there is nothing silly about his interests or his vision or the credo he coaches by. Western culture has long ignored even the most obvious beneficial tenets of Eastern philosophy and Native American teachings, things that can help one live day to day, find peace, and even attain great success. The notion of acceptance alone is mind-blowing. *You mean there are cultures where egocentricity, resistance, denial, and guilt are not all?*

Jackson knows I enjoyed *Sacred Hoops*. Often I'll toss back to him a phrase or lesson from it to see how he'll respond to the message. "One finger can't lift a pebble," I once said.

He had smiled and said, "Teamwork, all five fingers."

Another time I repeated, "For the raindrop, joy is entering the river."

"Isn't that pretty?" he said. I wondered whether Jordan could appreciate the concept of release, of being absorbed into the great liquid sea of life.

Jackson grew up in the strictest of Christian homes in rural North Dakota, without a TV set, learning always from his preacher father's stern example. His life and coaching philosophies would spring from his own ferocious desire to win at everything he played, and from his ultimate realization that such single-mindedness led always to failure of some sort or another.

"Losing made me feel humiliated and worthless, as if I didn't exist," he wrote in *Sacred Hoops*. "My obsession with winning was often my undoing. I would push so hard when things weren't going my way it would hurt my performance."

Thus he developed—through failure and reading and introspection and not a little bit of sheer contrariness—the Zen–Christian amalgam that answered his biggest questions and resolved his biggest fears about simply living this life, and coaching others within it. What he teaches his players is not all that far out. It is like deep breathing: rational, calming, liberating. It is not even new to coaching, nor is it some kind of cultish theory of submission to a superior. Consider this passage written by a former coach in the foreword to a 1995 book titled *Beyond Success:*

> It is my feeling that real success is not the accumulation of material possessions or the attainment of a position of power or prestige.

Rather, it is the peace of mind that is attained only by making the effort to do the best you are capable of doing at any task in which you are engaged. When you embrace this fundamental idea—that your success is determined not by what others think but rather by what you know in your own heart—you have the opportunity to make each day your masterpiece.

As a boy growing up on an Indiana farm, I learned a great lesson from my father: Never compare yourself to others. By understanding this principle I was able to feel successful at times when others saw only defeat, and to increase focus and concentration when others became complacent or self-aggrandizing because they felt victory was assured. Success is not trying to be better than someone else—which may be impossible . . . Never permit yourself to become too involved with things you cannot control, as that will adversely affect the things you can control.

The author is John Wooden, considered by many to be the greatest basketball coach of all time. Compare his words to those of Jackson in *Sacred Hoops:*

What pollutes the mind in the Buddhist view is our desire to get life to conform to our peculiar notion of how things *should* be, as opposed to how they really are. In the course of everyday life, we spend the majority of our time immersed in self-centered thoughts. *Why did this happen to me? What would make* me *feel better? If only I could make more money, win her heart, make my boss appreciate me.* The thoughts themselves are not the problem; it's our desperate clinging to them and our resistance to what's actually happening that causes us so much anguish. . . .

It's not uncommon for basketball players, especially young ones, to expend a great deal of energy trying to be somebody they're not. But once you get caught up in that game, it's a losing battle. I discovered that I was far more effective when I became completely immersed in the action, rather than trying to control it and fill my mind with unrealistic expectations.

The same notes ring from each bell.

■ ■ ■

When Donna Rodgers, Bulls assistant coach Jimmy Rodgers's wife gets up to walk around, I sit on the armrest of her seat across the aisle from June and we continue on.

"I can't imagine what it's going to get like," says June of the hoopla that surrounds the Bulls at the midway point in the season. "It seems like the playoffs already."

And how about the craziness of the trial of James Jordan's killer going on right now? Defendant Daniel Green, who recently changed his name to Lord D. As-saddiq Al-amin Sallam U'allah, previously liked to go by the name of Billy the Kid and spin a gun on his finger, according to testimony from his fellow assailant, Larry Demery. A home video has been introduced showing Green dancing and performing a rap song about murder while wearing James Jordan's trousers, rings, watch, and eyeglasses. Green also allegedly took the dead man's shoes before dumping the body off a bridge, saying, according to pal Demery, "he liked them and this man wasn't going to need them anymore."

In late December, Robeson County District Attorney Johnson Britt had flown from North Carolina to Chicago to show Michael Jordan a frame from the home video, and Jordan had identified the jewelry and glasses as belonging to his dad. June is amazed, as am I, at Michael's equanimity in the storm.

"Can you believe the guy was wearing Michael's dad's *pants*?" says June.

As the head coach's wife, she is thrilled with the success of the Bulls, but it is the individuals on the team that are more important to her.

"I wanted to meet Dennis," she says. "And somebody said, 'He'll be rude,' and then I met him and he was so polite. He and my daughter and I are going out sometime to a nightclub called the . . ."

"Baton?" I offer.

She says that's it. "Isn't it near Harry Caray's?"

"Yes," I reply. "Featuring 'The World's Most Beautiful and Professional Female Impersonators.'"

She laughs. "He's so nice. 'Worm' is an awful name for him."

I head back to my seat. Tim Hallam is having a minor nicotine fit. He jokes about it, but the Marlboros are in the breast pocket of his shirt, ready to be fired up at the first possible moment.

"Why don't you just dip?" I ask.

"Why don't I just quit?" he says.

12

FOR THE SECOND TIME, PHIL JACKSON IS THE COACH OF THE East squad in the All-Star game, an honor bestowed on the leader of the team with the best record at the break. Michael Jordan and Scottie Pippen join him as members of the East team, and Steve Kerr has qualified for the AT&T Long Distance Shootout Contest, hereafter known as the 3-point contest (at least in this book). A lot of people thought Dennis Rodman should have been voted to the team, since he leads the league in rebounding, but the NBA coaches did not give him the nod.

No mystery there. Except, it seems, to Worm.

"What do I have to do in this league to be respected by people?" he asked after learning he hadn't made the team. "The coaches who did the voting are hypocrites when they want to put players in the All-Star game who don't deserve to be there."

Obviously, Rodman is unaware that manners still count, even with coaches. On January 10 against the SuperSonics Rodman was ejected for the first time as a Bull after picking up two technical fouls for, among other things, getting locked up with the Sonics' hatchet man, Frank Brickowski. "I'm getting screwed out there so much, I need a chastity belt," he complained. In a sympathy endorsement, Nike took out a full-page ad in *USA Today* two days before the All-Star game. The entire page was blank, except for a tiny black swoosh centered at the bottom and in small type the question "Where's Dennis?"

But no matter. Rodman is off to gamble—"Viva Las Vegas!" he said before the break—and the Bulls are sailing through the league like a clipper through a park lagoon. Until they lost two games on their recent road trip they had a 41–3 record, the most wins ever by a team with just 3 losses, which broke the record belonging to the 1971–72 Lakers, who made it to 39–3 before losing their fourth game. The Bulls were 14–0 in January, making them just the ninth team in NBA history to go undefeated for a month. Phil Jackson was named the NBA Coach of the Month, and Jordan was named NBA Player of the Month. The recent Bulls–Lakers telecast by TNT was the highest-rated NBA game ever on cable, viewed in an average 4.75 million homes, by 7.27 million people. That broke the record set when Chicago played the Knicks in March 1995.

That Lakers game, by the way, featured the return of Magic Johnson (just back from an HIV-induced hiatus) against Jordan, for the first time since Game 5 of the 1991 finals. The unsentimental Bulls roasted the Lakers 99–84, and after the game Johnson said of the Bulls, "Best team I've ever seen. They're as good as our championship teams were. They're better than their three title teams. They're scary, man."

These Bulls have made the United Center the most profitable real estate in sports. With all seats sold and all 216 luxury skyboxes leased for five to eight years at an average price of $110,000 a season, the Bulls pull in about $50 million in ticket and skybox revenue each season. Not to mention parking, concessions, etc. And all seats have been sold out now for over 400 consecutive games, dating back to November 1987.

And the Bulls' big draw announced during the team's recent trip to play the Raptors that he and a group of businessmen will be opening a new Michael Jordan's Restaurant not far from Toronto's SkyDome to compete against Wayne Gretzky's nightspot. After all, Jordan doesn't have his finger in enough pies, and his net worth is estimated at only $200 million.

And the hype just grows. "With Jordan, Scottie Pippen, and Dennis Rodman, the Bulls are the Beatles of today," says former player turned TNT analyst Danny Ainge.

February 10, the day before the game, I decide to go check up on the biggest present-day Beatle at a huge auditorium called the Lila Cockrell

Theater for, as the personal invitation states, the "Unveiling of the New Michael Jordan Gatorade Commercial." Why? As the invitation states, "Because Life Is a Sport. Drink It Up."

I enter the auditorium a little late, but still I look around for some free liquids to drink up, or at least take home. Nothing. In fact, there are only about 30 people in this place that could seat thousands. But there are half a dozen TV cameras, which is key. This thing is all about a silly, but technologically amusing, video that shows various athletes running, jumping, biking, and rappelling across Jordan's bald head. We watch the video, then a man goes to the rostrum and says that Jordan himself will now answer questions from the media. But only about the commercial. Ring-a-ding-ding. Who cares? Nobody, obviously, because there is not a peep from us scribes. What should we ask—what's the makeup chair like?

So the Gatorade honcho himself poses some questions to Michael, resplendent in a fine Italian suit. Blah, blah, blah. Then the honcho says we'll see the spot one more time, so everybody sticks around, figuring when it's over maybe we can grill Jordan a little about something other than corporate sales. The lights go down. The video runs. And when the lights come up, guess who has vanished.

■ ■ ■

Steve Kerr makes it to the semifinals of the 3-point contest, tying for third with George McCloud of the Dallas Mavericks. The Magic's Dennis Scott takes second. First place goes to 29-year-old journeyman Tim Legler of the Washington Bullets, a man who has played for six NBA teams (Phoenix, Denver, Utah, Dallas, and Golden State are the others), two CBA teams (Rochester and Omaha), and both the USBL and the WBL.

As Kerr stands next to the bleachers at the Alamodome watching the slam-dunkers—or rather, the participants in the 1996 Nestlé's Crunch Slam-Dunk Contest—warm up, he thinks about the Bulls and their good fortune.

"We're real happy as a team," he says. "Are we happy because we're winning, or are we winning because we're happy? I don't know. It's the old chicken-or-the-egg question. But I know that when you do play well, you do stay content. Troubles on teams usually come from the bench; that's where you have to look for that stuff—guys sitting way at the end who are pissed off over one thing or another. But we don't have guys like that. Randy, Jud, Bill, and the younger guys, Dickey and Jason, are happy-to-be-here guys. Toni, he's disappointed at times. But there's a big difference between being disappointed and being disruptive. And the bench is playing pretty well; of course, when we go in we're usually playing with Michael or Scottie."

Kerr signs a couple of autographs, something that still seems to alternately delight and embarrass him. He is making more than half his 3-point attempts this season, and he is proof that there is still room in the game for somebody who can just plain drill it from downtown. A man walks up, an NBA official, and hands Kerr a check. Kerr looks at it: $4,000. His winnings. "Oh, thank you!" he says, genuinely delighted. When he's done pondering his good fortune, Kerr thinks about Jordan for a moment, his old sparring partner. Four grand for Jordan would be tissue paper, nuisance change.

"Michael has mellowed a little bit," says Kerr. "He's pretty much at peace with his game now. Through all that pressure, he's proven that he's still Michael. He doesn't drive as much, but now he's got that fallaway. It's an unbelievably difficult shot to make, but you can't guard it, either." On some of his fallaways, Jordan actually lands 4 or 5 feet in back of where he started. It's a shot no coach teaches; in fact, it's one that would get most high school or college kids put on the bench just for attempting.

"We all love Phil," Kerr continues as he walks to the locker room. "He's awesome. He's as honest as they come. The Zen stuff, he practices it—but not always during games." Kerr looks at me like he's revealed a secret. "I shouldn't say that." Not to worry. We writers have observed Jackson losing it occasionally during games and calling his own players "idiots" or worse. Confucius never recommended screaming until your voice gave out, but Confucius didn't coach in the cutthroat NBA. Sporadic failure to heed his own advice does not mean Jackson is a fraud.

"He doesn't call many timeouts, and he doesn't panic," says Kerr. "That's part of what he practices. He talks about 'mindfulness.' It's a word he uses all the time. We actually met with a teacher of his in

Boston, to work on mindfulness, the quieting of the mind. Michael and Scottie are very accepting of what Phil says. And if the stars are accepting, the rest of us fall into line."

Kerr stands now with a towel around his waist, watching the dunkfest on the locker room TV monitor. The room is deserted; all the other 3-point shooters have gone.

"I really want to see Brent Barry," says Kerr of the 6'6", 185-pound Los Angeles Clippers rookie guard. Pasty-faced, chicken-chested, skinny as a broom, Barry is entered in this contest that always features sinuous, high-flying black players. It is, indeed, the contest a young and springy Jordan won twice, in 1987 and 1988, recording a total of five perfect scores on individual dunks. In 12 years no white player has even come close to winning the event.

But here goes the sunken-eyed, stoop-shouldered Barry, son of Hall of Famer Rick Barry, running the length of the court and then taking off from the free throw line, for God's sake, launching his gangly form into space, still clad in his warmup top—he was cold, he would say later— absolutely no muscle definition anywhere, sprawling through the air like a stork launched from a crossbow, and *jamming the ball home.* To win the contest.

Kerr cracks up. What will crazy white boys do next?

Still trying to think of hidden reasons why the Bulls are doing so well, Kerr shakes his head. "Front office?" he asks. "Reinsdorf? We never even see him. Krause? Aw, you've heard a million Krause stories." He shakes his head again. "There's nothing, really."

Dressed now, he starts to leave. Then he doubles back to pick up his check, which is sitting in his locker. Last year at the 3-point contest in Phoenix he got $1,000 for finishing in a tie for fifth place. He went out to dinner with wife Margot that night; the next day, after the two had driven to Tucson, he received a call from the restaurant. "Mr. Kerr, you left a check for a thousand dollars lying on the table," the man said. This time Kerr plans to be a little more responsible.

13

THE BULLS AND THE WORM TRAVEL TO THE PALACE OF Auburn Hills in mid-February for their second road match against the Detroit Pistons. So many players and coaches from Rodman's old days with the Pistons are gone that there is no personal vendetta left for him. Isiah Thomas, Vinnie Johnson, Bill Laimbeer, Rick Mahorn, and, of course, father-figure coach Chuck Daly have all departed; the only player left from Worm's salad days is veteran guard Joe Dumars, who is such a decent and nonconfrontational soul that even Rodman can't work up any animosity toward him.

The only tension here is caused by the coaching matchup of Phil Jackson and Doug Collins. Collins was the Bulls' head coach from 1986 to 1989, and Jackson was his assistant for the final two seasons. Collins was fired in the spring of 1989 after leading the Bulls to a 47–35 regular-season record and then defeating both Cleveland and New York in the playoffs before losing 4–2 to the eventual champions, the Pistons. Chicagoans were stunned when Collins was canned not long after the last game—the playoff march was the Bulls' best in 14 years—and even more amazed when Phil Jackson was promoted to head coach. Jackson's coaching experience consisted of five seasons as a head coach in the CBA and the two years as an assistant under Collins. Though many reasons were floated for the enthusiastic and sometimes frighteningly intense Collins's firing, Krause steadfastly maintained it was because Collins was the man to get the team from point A to point B, and that Jackson was the man to get it from point B to point C. Point C, of course, was the NBA title.

Collins has never forgiven Jackson for the treachery and backroom whispering he feels must have led to his downfall. One day I simply asked Jackson whether Collins blamed him for the firing. "Yes," said Phil. The two men put on business faces when they meet each other, but it is obvious there is still, and will probably always be, bad blood between them. At least on Collins's side.

The Pistons, now at 24–22, are building around young players Grant

Hill, Allan Houston, and Theo Ratliff, with veterans such as Dumars and Otis Thorpe helping with stability. But they have somebody named Don Reid at center, weaknesses at many spots, and a long way to go before they reach the Bulls' level of performance. Still, there is that fire and hope that springs from Collins's eternal fervor. To beat the Bulls— just once, anywhere, any way—would mean much to the Detroit club and would be a great burden lifted from Collins's weary shoulders. He has made peace with Reinsdorf, who gave him a championship watch after the Bulls won without him at the helm; he has reached a truce with Krause, who was the man who gave him his first head-coaching job. But with Jackson the wound festers.

After leaving the Bulls Collins worked as a game analyst for TNT, becoming, through his intelligent and graceful commentary, perhaps the best NBA color man ever. He turned down many head-coaching opportunities to stay in the booth, preferring to watch his son Chris play hoops at Duke and his daughter Kelly play sports in high school. Still, he itched to lead a basketball team once more, to prove himself where he had failed, to show everyone that he could, indeed, get a team from point B to point C. And when the Pistons job came up last year, he snatched it.

In his first season Collins has done a good job with an erratic team, but the toll is already showing on him. The former college All-American and first pick in the 1973 NBA draft (by the Philadelphia 76ers) is as gaunt as ever, and he starts his day with caffé latte, then works through can after can of Diet Pepsi, until by sundown he is a mop of jangling nerves. "He doesn't look good," his old pal John Paxson, now a bench coach for the Bulls, noted. Of the special rivalry with the Bulls and himself, Phil Jackson says: "I have a feeling it's hard for him to get over it. It's eating at him. He had a good career as a color man, and we had a lot of concern about him coming back to coaching."

Now, as the game progresses, it is easy to see why coaching at this level, at any level, can drive men batty. The Pistons scrape along, never letting the Bulls get a comfortable lead, but seemingly incapable of taking command themselves. Collins can barely stay in his chair. Jordan snares a rebound, Detroit bodies go flying, and no call is made on the superstar.

"Hey, Greg!" Collins screams at ref Greg Willard. "When you go up this way and you end up going *this* way, physics says you were *fouled*!" Late in the third quarter he will get hit with a technical for bitching about another call.

The Bulls looked exhausted. Particularly Jordan. He, along with his mates, has hit the proverbial wall, the brick edifice that rises up and makes the final 30 or so games of every season a brutal test of endurance. Before the game, Jordan had elected not to take shooting practice. Jackson had asked him if he wasn't going out on the floor soon.

"Nah," Jordan said. "We won championships without me going out to shoot."

Jackson considered that. "You were younger then," he said finally.

"I knew that was coming," Jordan said.

With 5 minutes to go in the game, the Bulls have a 91–84 lead and a victory seemingly in the bag. But Jordan is pooped, and the Pistons mount a comeback. They take a 94–93 lead with less than 3 minutes to go on 2 free throws by Thorpe, a 96–94 lead on a running shot by Houston, and then a commanding 101–96 lead when Dumars hits a 3-pointer from 24 feet out with just 37 seconds left.

The Bulls call time out. There is no way they can win, but Jackson puts Kukoc in for Caffey, to see if Toni can possibly hit a long one. On the Detroit bench, Collins is daring to think the impossible: *We can beat this club and I can be reborn.* The game is in the bag. The knot is all but tied.

Action starts and Jordan feeds Kukoc. The Pink Panther, as he is sometimes called, launches one of his slow-spinning, high-arcing 3s. Swish. Thirty-two seconds remaining, 101–99 Pistons. If the Pistons can run the 24-second clock down and score again, the game will be theirs.

But they bring the ball up, miss a shot, and the Bulls get it back and call time out with 7 seconds remaining. The Bulls inbound the ball, shoot, miss, the ball caroms . . . and . . . and Rodman gets the rebound and throws in a garbage layup to tie the score at 101. Collins looks as though a spigot in his chest has just been opened, draining all his blood.

In overtime the Bulls surge to a 106–101 lead, but again the Pistons come back, tying the game at 106 on a layup by Ratliff with 1:30 to go.

Rodman has just fouled out, and things are looking up for Detroit once more. There is hope again for Collins's dream.

But now it's Jordan time. Now a thin dagger is slid into Collins's bloodless heart. Done in by his old player, the one he used to hand the ball to and just say, *Kill those guys.*

Jordan makes two quick jump shots. Though Detroit comes within a point at 110–109 with 9 seconds remaining, they are forced to foul Jordan, who coldly buries both free throws. The Bulls win, 112–109, with Jordan scoring 8 of the team's 11 points in overtime.

In the Detroit locker room Collins smashes a marker board and rages at Theo Ratliff for not preventing Rodman's last rebound. Pistons PR man Matt Dobek closes every door he can to prevent the coach's voice from reaching the outside world. Time goes by. I talk to the Bulls in their locker room, and then just hang out for awhile.

Collins is a friend of mine, a man of quick wit and keen insight on many subjects; we first met back in 1984 aboard the *Sports Illustrated* ocean liner docked at Long Beach harbor for the Los Angeles Olympics. I was there staying with the rest of my *SI* workers, and he was there as a guest of the magazine. Through the years our paths have crossed many times, and I have always enjoyed his company. I decide to visit Collins in the Detroit locker room as a courtesy, and because he was a possible subject for my next day's column.

I see him in his office and he motions me in. I immediately offer words of solace. His face looks shocking. He's been growing a beard for a few days and the whiskers, many of them gray, lend a pallor to his cheeks. But underneath the growth his face is blotched with irregular red spots. They were not there before the game.

Collins is furious, about everything. His lip quivers as he speaks. "Fucking Phil!" he says bitterly. "All that flower-power, Zen-love, peace-and-love bullshit. You know why he wins? Because he's got the best team! He's got the best player! Michael Jordan. Michael Jordan. Let's see him take that stuff and try to win with Minnesota or the Clippers. Let him coach [Isaiah] Rider or [Christian] Laettner and see how far he goes!"

One of his assistants says to me, "This is off the record," looking at me with a somber, imploring face. But Collins has made no such demand. Rick Sund, the Pistons' Vice President of Player Personnel, sits on a couch to my right. Doug sits behind his desk. To my left stands Brian James, a Pistons assistant coach, whom Collins lured away from Glenbrook North High School in suburban Chicago. Everyone is nervous. Nobody knows what to do. I try to soothe Collins, but he is in that place where he just has to vent.

"Phil was on record the last time we played as saying he wanted to embarrass me," Collins snaps. Jackson has denied that, though he remembers Collins talking to John Paxson in their first game. "He told John, 'Next time Phil wants to screw me, tell him to use Vaseline,'" Jackson said. "He knew it would get back to me."

That first game four weeks ago was a rout in which the Bulls were ahead 54–39 at the half, 85–65 at three quarters, and ended up winning 111–96. Jordan played 43 minutes, more than any Detroit player. Jackson justified his tactics in that game by saying, "I was looking down the bench, wondering if he [Collins] was going to pull his starters, you know." Collins saw the entire blowout as bullying.

"Rodman is so overrated!" Collins continues, still livid. "He plays no defense. And Phil sees it in the papers how the Bulls can win seventy, and he wants it. Believe me. Jerry West told me his old Lakers team could have won *seventy-five,* if they'd wanted to!"

Collins looks at the stat sheet.

"The Bulls are *not* gonna do it like this. Look at that." He points to the "MIN" column after each player's name. "Pippen and Jordan played forty-nine minutes! They're not kids with legs like Grant Hill and Allan Houston."

The room feels crowded—there must be five other coaches and assistants in it now—and I feel uncomfortable. I'd like to offer Doug more words of condolence and good cheer, but I know nothing can work at this moment.

This is what the Bulls can do to a man.

14

THE CLEVELAND CAVALIERS ARE A PRETTY GOOD TEAM, BUT like all the other pretty good teams in the league, they are no match for the Bulls. Cavaliers coach Mike Fratello has taught his men to be methodical and calculating, and to play defense-minded, low-scoring half-court ball. This works fairly well against lesser teams; Fratello's discipline enables his average group of players—Chris Mills, Michael Cage, Danny Ferry, Bobby Phills, Terrell Brandon, and top reserves Dan Majerle and Tyrone Hill—to outlast and outdefend less patient teams. The Cavs have a respectable 30–20 record because of it, and Fratello has already been named NBA Coach of the Month as reward.

But against the Bulls the slowdown stuff only slows the rate of death. Playing almost listlessly, the Bulls somewhat haphazardly out-talent the Cavs. Only two things of note occur in the uninspired 102–76 wipeout that makes the Bulls 47–5 on the season: Luc Longley returns from a spell of knee tendinitis that had put him on the injured list, and Jordan makes a simple statement about the importance of respect in the NBA.

Midway through the fourth quarter, in an interesting and naive display of rookie arrogance, first-year Cavs reserve guard Bob Sura tries to steal the ball from Jordan while Jordan holds it high after getting a rebound under the Cleveland basket. The rest of the players have retreated back to the Bulls' end of the floor. Jordan sees the pesky Sura and lifts his elbows higher to protect the ball even more, and to remind Sura that these are, indeed, elbows. Sura continues to give the old 110 percent—collegiate effort. He doesn't know or doesn't care that you don't steal the ball from Jordan in any one-on-one situation, particularly when you're just a baby-faced kid out of Florida State.

Jordan is as annoyed with the guard's persistence as he is surprised. So he carefully, deliberately, and quickly swings his left elbow sideways and hits the aggressive Sura square in the mouth. Sura jerks away, rubbing his bloody lip.

"I told you to get back," says Jordan in a low, firm voice.

The game prior to this one, against the Indiana Pacers, was the one that established for good the rare convergence of the Bulls' three stars, Jordan, Pippen, and Rodman. Worm had 23 rebounds in the 110–102 win, while the man covering him, Dale Davis, had 9. But it was the duo of Jordan and Pippen that took everyone's breath away. Together they ran circles around the Pacers' small men, Reggie Miller, Mark Jackson, and Derrick McKey. For the afternoon at Market Square Arena the pair totaled 84 points, 15 rebounds, 9 assists, 8 steals, and 2 blocked shots. They made 30 of their combined 55 shot attempts, including 7 of 11 from 3-point range.

Jordan had 44 points and Pippen had 40, and it marked the first time in Bulls history and only the sixth time in the NBA's 50-year history that teammates scored 40 or more points in the same game. Indeed, only five other pairs had done it in non-overtime games: Adrian Dantley and John Drew for Detroit, Paul Westphal and Walter Davis for Phoenix, Pete Maravich and Nate Williams for the New Orleans Jazz, Elgin Baylor and Jerry West for the Los Angeles Lakers, and Gus Johnson and Walt Bellamy for the Baltimore Bullets. Of that group only Baylor and West were both superstars of the magnitude of Jordan and Pippen.

Besides Baylor and West, great combos in history include the Milwaukee Bucks' Kareem Abdul-Jabbar and Oscar Robertson, the Celtics' John Havlicek and Bill Russell or Russell and Bob Cousy, Larry Bird and Kevin McHale, the Lakers' Magic Johnson and James Worthy or Johnson and Abdul-Jabbar, the 76ers' Julius Erving and Moses Malone, the Bullets' Wes Unseld and Elvin Hayes. You can debate the merits of each pair ad nauseam, but if you consider overall skills, including ball handling, defensive abilities, and general floor game, you might not find anybody to top Jordan and Pippen.

My colleague John Jackson at the *Sun-Times,* a basically levelheaded man, just took the plunge and wrote it: "As the years pass, the very good become great and the great become legends. But I'm ready to say right here, right now, that Michael Jordan and Scottie Pippen are the best tandem in NBA history."

Then there is the team debate. The talk has become serious that not only are Jordan and Pippen perhaps the best duo in league history, the Bulls just might be heading toward best-NBA-team-ever status. The Bulls are on pace to shatter the league record of 69 wins in a regular season set by the 1971–72 Lakers. Starters on that team were West, Gail Goodrich, Jim McMillian, Happy Hairston, and Wilt Chamberlain. If the Bulls win 70 or more games, does that make them the best? Start the debate machine. Still, in *USA Today,* NBA writer David DuPree argued that, position by position, the Bulls would win three of the five matchups with that Lakers team, losing only the Longley–Chamberlain and Harper–Goodrich battles. I might debate the Harper–Goodrich ruling, pointing out that Goodrich, though high-scoring, was only 6'1" to Harper's 6'6", and no match for Harper on defense.

One person who has an opinion on the matter, an opinion that might count, is former New York Knick and Hall of Famer Bill Bradley, with whom I had a long talk recently when he passed through town promoting his new book, *Time Present, Time Past.*

Bradley is nothing if not a deep thinker, a perfectionist, and a tireless, even humorless, worker. As his former coach at Princeton, Butch van Breda Kolff, once marveled of his great All-America, "Basketball is a game. It's not an ordeal. I think Bradley's happiest whenever he can deny himself pleasure." And so when the senator says the Bulls of today remind him of the selfless Knicks of the early '70s, a team that, but for badly timed injuries, might have won four NBA titles instead of two, you know it is a parallel that has been reached after much weighing, sifting, and reflection.

"I think we played the game the way it should be played," he said. "We moved the ball, we hit the open man, we played tough defense. And I think the recognition that no one of us could be as good as all of us working together is what *allowed* us our success. The Bulls remind me of the Knicks. I mean, Phil is the coach, and he played on those teams. But then you have Michael Jordan, who has reached a level of the game, of his game, that allows him to make the worst player on the Bulls good."

In his foreword to *Sacred Hoops* Bradley wrote, "Here's another comment I have heard: 'Anybody can coach a team led by Michael Jordan to the World Championship.' This comment signifies both an unfamiliarity with Phil Jackson and with the game of basketball. . . . When Phil first took over the Bulls in 1989, many of his players had a tendency to stand around and admire Michael Jordan and his creativity, which limited their impact as a team. Phil changed that."

One of the things Bradley likes about the Bulls is a subtle one, something only a player who has felt the proper flow of action in the heat of a big game could know. "The Bulls will make two or three passes before a basket," he noted, "hitting the right man at the right time. When he's *ready* to do something. Getting the ball to someone who is not prepared leads to nothing."

But are the Bulls the best ever?

"I don't think there's any question about that," he replied. "People say, 'Oh, the league is a lot weaker, with expansion teams and all that.' That's baloney. I mean, it is true in that there are expansion teams, but the players on this team can match up against anybody who ever played the game, and do it man for man. Take our Knicks team. I always think of myself. *Who* on the Bulls am I guarding? Everybody on our team supposedly matched up pretty well—until Rodman came along. But even before, when it came to me and I was guarding Pippen, all I thought was, 'Help!'"

I find myself drifting back to the evening of October 30, before the season had started, when the Bulls hosted, of all things, a bowling party for players, coaches, front office people, and even us lowly media wretches. It was held at the Deerbrook Lanes in a suburban mall in Deerfield, and beforehand PR assistant Tom Smithburg had told me it would be a good event to attend because it was a time "when everybody's in a good mood and optimistic."

Outside the place a two-story inflatable red bull marked the way. Inside it was a good time a-happenin'. The sound of pins crashing and balls rolling down alleys and forcefully into gutters filled the air. As did the sounds of clapping, groaning, and gleeful yelling, depending on the fate of those launched orbs. I was late, and all the available lanes were filled. So I moved past the Halloween decorations toward the area I suspected must house the bar.

As I walked, I observed various members of the Bulls attempting to control these odd balls that neither bounced nor flew through the air, and it did my heart good to see the players were so ungainly at such a simple sport. I saw Jordan bowling a little, then sitting down at a table behind the lane and working the small group with stories about who knows what. In the bar the Monday Night Football game was getting set to go, and the place was empty except for one person, Phil Jackson.

He sat at the bar, a beer in front of him, eating pretzels. He was wearing jeans and an authentic, oh-so-tacky bowling shirt. As usual, he reminded me of a skinny, elongated version of Jerry Garcia.

I sat down beside him, ordered a beer, and asked him how he felt about Garcia's recent passing, knowing that Phil was a bit of a Deadhead and a former counterculture freethinker who had only recently turned 50. He said that, indeed, the summer past had been a very reflective one for him, what with the deaths of two of his heroes, Garcia and Mickey Mantle, in the same week. Both of them from abusing their bodies for years and years.

"I went to the Dead's last concert here," he said. "And people told me Jerry wasn't going to last too long. It was sad, and it's something to realize your contemporaries are dying and it's not that unusual."

The football game came on and we occasionally looked up at it. As a big media star himself, Jackson found that he now was often lumped in with people who had consciously sought fame, even though he had not. Each year he turned down all endorsements and promotions, deals that could make him hundreds of thousands, if not millions, of dollars. This, no doubt, was a habit he picked up from old roomie Bradley, who likewise shunned all advertising riches, on principle, so as to not let commercialism get inside his head and corrupt his essence. Or at least to remain on the outside looking in at mainstream America.

Still, there were benefits to being known, and one was that Phil got to meet and chat with the creative genius Garcia before he died. Jackson spoke now of how making spontaneous music the way the Dead did was almost akin to the action of a great basketball game. The notes, the moves, came out of instant inspiration, and then they were gone; the moments of creativity could never be recaptured.

"When I talked to Jerry, he said. 'Doing an album is like building a miniature ship in a bottle,'" said the coach. "'But a concert is like being on a raft in an ocean.'"

Fellow free spirit Dennis Rodman had been with the team only a few weeks, and his immersion into the Bulls mix was still the hot topic in town. I asked Jackson how he thought Worm would fly, or crawl.

"A lot depends on how comfortable Dennis feels on the floor, with the referees, with the whole atmosphere here," he replied.

I asked the coach whether Rodman still had that nose ring.

"Yes."

"Can he play with it in?" I asked.

"No."

"How about the earrings?"

"No."

"The navel ring?"

"Yes."

He paused for a moment, then added, "And you can play with a foreskin ring in."

The thought occurred to me, as it must occur to all parents, teachers, managers, and coaches at some time: If you don't try to get somebody to conform to arbitrary, established rules or do things to make *you* feel comfortable, you probably can handle just about anyone. I wondered whether Jackson could hold his temper with a guy whose major purpose was to resist normal behavior.

I asked Jackson about his seeming nemesis, Pat Riley, the former Knicks coach now in charge of the Miami Heat, a willful and dynamic man with whom he had often clashed. What was Pat after, now that he had a $3 million–a-year deal?

"Money and power," said Jackson. "I think he wants a franchise."

"You?"

He snorted, looking at me with a wry, get-real grin, an old hippie's grin. Montana is what he wanted.

I went to the restroom, and when I came back, I saw Rodman himself meandering up to Phil. They were the same height, but so different in so many ways. And yet there was a part of them that was so alike. Did anybody remember that when Jackson played for the Knicks, he was a ferocious wild man on the floor?

The two talked, man to man. Not for long, and not about anything important. But they talked.

Back out in the bowling area, I saw that most of the people were gone, including all of the Bulls. Except Jordan. He was still bowling. I thought about challenging him to a game, betting on it, because he can't turn down a bet. That is what makes all the hundred-thousand-dollar golfing wagers he supposedly rang up plausible. Jordan can't stand losing, or not competing. And a shrewd, hustling man could always get Jordan to believe he was better than he really was at some game. And take his money. At any game. Except basketball.

Once I played 8-ball against him in the basement of his townhouse in Deerfield. This was way back, around 1985, when he was single and not yet a god. The table was little, and 8-ball is a stupid game on any size table. But I had all but one ball in the pocket and he had none in. I started taunting him a little, I suppose, and I could see his dander rise. "The house wins," he said. "The house always wins." And sure enough, he made most of his balls, I missed, and he sank the 8-ball to win. I would have challenged him at bowling, except for the fact I stink at bowling.

So I ran a few frames with my sportswriter buddies John Jackson of the *Sun-Times* and Steve Rosenbloom and Terry Armour of the *Tribune*. The Bears were leading the Vikings 14–6 on TV, and the place was about empty. It was close to 10 P.M., and I rolled a hideous ball that left one of those splits even the pros can't pick up.

"Rick!" I heard a voice ring out. "I thought you were a better athlete." I turned around. It was Jordan, in a sweatsuit and stocking cap, leaving. Coward.

15

OLD LUC IS NOT OLD. BUT HE SHOULD BE.

It is my opinion he will make a marvelous old man, sitting on a porch somewhere in the Australian outback, a sweat-stained Digger's hat on his large head, his red-tinged hair mostly white, dingo boots caked with dust, jeans faded, cotton shirt open at the chest, cold quart of Foster's in hand, explaining to the half-dozen children gathered on his massive lap just how crazy things got one year in Chicago, way up there in the bloody U.S.A.

The 26-year-old big man came to the Bulls from the Minnesota Timberwolves two years earlier in a trade for Stacey King. King was a left-handed inside player from Oklahoma who had never panned out for the Bulls. Thus unloading him to get Luc Longley has to be tallied as yet another steal for the Sleuth.

In truth, in his first two seasons with the Timberwolves Longley himself looked like an egregious blunder. He signed late in his rookie season (out of the University of New Mexico) and averaged just 4 points and 4 rebounds for the Wolves that year. The next season, 1992–93, was not much better. As part of a terrible team with bad coaching, bad personalities, and bad chemistry, he was just a very large and quiet nonfactor. His average zoomed all the way to 5.8 points and 4.4 rebounds per game.

But the Sleuth covets big men, scouts them, studies them, hoards them the way a hamster does seeds, and he saw in Luc a solid block of flesh that could simply stand in the center of the Bulls' game as Jordan, Pippen, Harper, and friends whirred past. Plus Luc had always had a nice touch with the ball; his jump shot was that of a much smaller man, and though his footwork and offensive trick bag were marginal, he could learn. He was, after all, from Perth, where men and boys in short pants play Aussie Rules Football or maybe even rugby, and only, ahem, sissies dabble in basketball. He could probably learn more in a month by osmosis from being on the Bulls than he had in his previous two decades.

In his first full season with the Bulls, 1994–95, Longley increased his averages slightly, while missing 22 games with a stress fracture in his left leg. He was a sub behind Will Perdue, playing 18 minutes per contest, averaging 6.5 points and 4.8 rebounds. But this year, with the departure of Perdue and the addition of Worm, Luc became, as United Center announcer Ray Clay always bellows before games, "The Man in the Middle." He now is averaging 9.2 points and 5 boards per game, and there are times, such as when he hits a soft 10-foot jumper or dunks off a nice feed, that one can envision the day Luc Longley blossoms into an NBA force.

But if he never does, he will always be one of the most entertaining and linguistically amusing players in an NBA locker room. He uses words such as "keen" instead of "eager," as in "I'm keen to have a go at it," and "quite" rather than "really," as in, "They're quite good, actually." And of course, he uses "mate" for pal, buddy, guy, dude, friend. All of it, too, with the sweet Aussie accent that makes a bloke think right off of boomerangs and wallabies.

In the preseason, when Longley slugged Chris Webber, he told reporters that the fisticuffs were not sparked by Worm's urging him to be more aggressive. (Worm was the guy who later on would say, "People have labeled Luc a soft pussycat for so long. I told him, 'You're seven-two and three hundred pounds. If you have a guy who is smaller than you, take him to the basket and dunk on him.'") You could hear the civility in Longley's response to the Webber brawl query: "It was simply a coincidence, really, that the fight occurred a few days after Rodman said those things. But I was not thinking of Rodman or anything he said during the incident." You gotta love "incident." And there is a perceptiveness and precision to his speech that one might expect from a player who was set to become a marine biologist, as Luc was, had basketball not panned out. Who else but old Luc would look at the Bulls' dynamite starting lineup during the preseason, analyze it, and state, "I'm a scab, and people will pick at that. But like all scabs, I'll come back."

He has risen well to the esoterica espoused by Phil Jackson, and indeed the two often have long discussions about things far removed from sport.

One day we were sitting around (which is always the easiest way to talk to him—I'm 6'1" and I've sometimes developed a cramp in my neck standing in a mob interviewing him after games) and I asked him about the Outback Steakhouse franchises in the United States, the restaurants with the quasi-Australian motif. I wondered if he had been to one, and if so, did he find it a comforting experience.

He considered the question seriously, then said, "I don't think they did their homework. I *have* been to them, and it's kind of a joke, some of the dishes they have. I mean, they have koala stew. And koalas are extinct, or just about." Luc looked at me with that bemused look he sometimes has when the ref has just called the fifth foul on him and there is still a quarter to play in the game.

Well, but didn't it provide some of the Down Under ambiance he must be missing? The main problem for him, he said, was that by playing in the NBA and before that attending school in the States, and then returning to Australia every June, he was actually experiencing one winter after another, "twenty-one in a row," he mourned. "When it's summer there, we come here. My wife finally said, 'I can't take it.' She's staying there for the season."

But back to that animal topic. Since I have always enjoyed the study of nature, I asked him about some of the unusual marsupials down there in his part of the world. Of course, there are kangaroos and wallabies, but a lot of the stranger ones, such as the platypus, live in New Zealand, he reminded me. But what about rabbits, I asked. They're not marsupials, but I know they're a problem. I've read about rabbit drives in the outback, mass clubbings and the like, to get rid of the pests.

"Yes," he acknowledged. "They were introduced by settlers for food, and then, of course, the rabbits just took off. So the people introduced foxes. The foxes ate some rabbits, and then wiped out most of the marsupials."

■ ■ ■

Phil Jackson, who often gives individual books to various team members, depending on that person's taste, sensitivity, and needs, has handed out his first group offering. The other day, every Bull found in his locker a signed copy of Bill Bradley's *Time Present, Time Past.* Jackson has already hinted that if the day comes and he's tired of coaching, say, in a year or so, after Jordan has left the game, he would like to work on Bradley's oft-hinted-at presidential campaign.

One of the books Jackson gave to the never-activated Jack Haley was *Dirty White Boys,* by Stephen Hunter. "About a prison break, by two bad guys," says Haley. Any good? Haley shrugs. "Haven't finished it." He's had it for months, though.

But then, he's had his knee injury for years. Which is beautiful for the Bulls. The whole injury list procedure is somewhat manipulative and suspect; players such as Caffey and Simpkins and Wennington and Edwards go on and off it depending on game situations rather than actual hurts. Haley has a damaged knee that doesn't prevent him from practicing but that structurally will never get any better.

"It can look fishy," Jackson admits with a small grin. "I have to be careful what I say. But the league looked into it, they flew in a doctor to look at Haley's knee, and the guy said, 'Oh yeah, it's a wreck.' He's got one that will always show up that way. I think it's his left."

Lucky for Haley, because he is not good enough to actually play for the Bulls. But he does work out hard, at times, with Rodman. And he praises Worm's work ethic.

"You'd never know he was almost thirty-five," says Haley. "His body looks like a guy's who's eighteen. The day we played Indiana at noon? We got back at five, and we were in the gym by five-thirty. Lifting weights. Shoulders, arms and back, all upper body. Then thirty minutes on the Stairmaster. We didn't leave until eight."

■ ■ ■

Tonight later hours are in effect. I'm having dinner with Bill Wennington, his wife, Anne, WSCR Sports Radio host Mike North, and his producer Jesse Rogers after a late-February home game. We're at Gibson's Steak House on Rush Street, and Wennington, who was playing a substantial amount while Longley was out with a leg injury, is a little disgruntled that he only got in for 7 minutes in tonight's game. Aw, it's cool, it's cool, says Wen. But it still hurts, and in case anyone isn't aware of it, Phil Jackson does have a hefty ego. He does do some messing with guys' minds. But harmony rules.

Bill and Anne have a son, Robbie, who is only four but, like so many basketball players' sons, is so tall that people mistake him for an immature-acting seven-year-old. Wennington is a loving dad, and a funny guy. And it's certain Robbie, who probably will make it to 7 feet, will be a funny guy, too.

Wennington regales us with tales of his teen years in a part of Long Island where all the good hoops games were in the all-black section of town. Bill and a buddy or two of his would walk the many blocks to the black park just to get in some good runs. Trouble was, it wasn't always the safest thing to do. But Wennington's gift for gab always saved them.

One day, however, his lone buddy got so scared just seeing black men across the street watching them walk that he turned and ran all the way home. "I kept walking," Bill notes. "And I survived."

■ ■ ■

The Bulls have their team picture taken today, and then they do their own little workouts at the end of practice. Most of them practice free throws. Kerr shoots at a hoop with a bounce-back net under it. Buechler runs sprints the length of the floor. Rodman rides his stationary bike. A group of players shoots at a rim that is only 16½ inches in diameter instead of the regulation 18. For accuracy. Through it all Otis, the dog, snorts around with another large dog, a big red one named Bo, whose full name is Bo Jackson. He belongs to Phil.

There are not many media members here, perhaps 25, a small group for this team. Included in the crew is Phil Taylor, *Sports Illustrated*'s main NBA writer. He's working on a Rodman piece, a cover story. Right over the magazine's logo and photo of Worm yanking down a ball a question will be posed: "The Best Rebounder Ever?" The subhead will read, "Dennis Rodman reveals the secrets of his inside game."

Well, this is partly true. He'll tell Taylor about angles and trajectories and positioning. But then he'll note that there are some other little things he does that will remain secret. "I could tell you," he says to Taylor. "But then I'd have to kill you."

■ ■ ■

Atlanta is torn up, a concrete snarl, a nervous city preparing feverishly for the Summer Olympics. The Bulls' bus leaves the Swissotel in Buckhead and crawls to the Omni, arriving a half hour later than it should for this game against the Hawks.

Perhaps the delayed arrival contributes to the sluggish start for the Bulls against this team that is in utter disarray. The Hawks have just been involved in a trade with the Timberwolves, sending Spud Webb and Andrew Lang to Minnesota for Sean Rooks and spoiled brat Christian Laettner. But the new players are not here yet, so the Hawks play with seven players, starting frail 6'9" Alan Henderson at center. There isn't anybody even listed on the Hawks roster as a center except for someone named Todd Mundt, and he is nursing a leg injury.

To his credit, Luc Longley stands solid in the middle, making his first 7 shots, and looking like an office building in a subdivision. But the Bulls nevertheless go in at halftime down 54–41. They seem cranky and far less brotherly to each other than they have been in recent weeks. Jordan gives Harper the evil eye after Harper fails to get a shot off before time expires in the first quarter. But Harper only had the ball because Jordan did *not* shoot with 3 seconds remaining, passing to his startled teammate instead.

Kerr misses all five of his shots and yammers at Kukoc at one point in the second half. Coach Jackson has some choice words for Longley, and Rodman rags incessantly at the refs.

The relationships between team members, part of what media people refer to with that old cliché "chemistry," are always the most fascinating aspect of any team. So many disparate personalities. So many different backgrounds, ages, sensitivities. So many agendas. When all the differences are put aside and the individuals focus on a team goal, on group success, that is when great things happen. That is the burden of every coach, general manager, and owner: to somehow get talented individuals working as one. It's to be expected that even cohesive units sometimes, momentarily, unravel.

Kukoc seems to be in one of his fragile fogs. When he makes an excellent feed to Jordan for an easy dunk, the two players do not even make eye contact afterward, eye contact being the nontactile equivalent in the NBA of a handshake.

"Do those guys seem crabby?" I ask Arthur Triche, the Hawks' PR man.

"Yes," he says. "I had a hard time just getting them to sign a ball before the game."

But it's Jordan, inevitably, who shines through on a night like this. Though he is 33, his will is that of a kid's. He finishes with a game-high 34 points, on 15 of 26 shooting, and the Bulls win, 96–91. But it wasn't so much how many he scored as *when* he scored them. He had 10 points in the second quarter when Pippen was going 0 for 3. It was a moment when it was clear that if Jordan didn't score, nobody else on the Bulls was capable of it.

The Bulls seem like a bunch of campers with cabin fever. So it goes. They are now 48–5, and it is far easier to remember specifics of their losses than of any of their myriad victories. But it is also easier to think of the good times to come than of that dark day back in 1993 when Jordan, in front of hundreds of assembled media members, announced that he was quitting the game. There was bitterness and aloofness in his tone, as he referred often to how little he would miss "you guys," meaning us, me and my pals and scribes everywhere.

But as Greg Boeck wrote in today's *USA Today*, "In a remarkable comeback . . . Jordan [has] dusted off his old skills to produce MVP numbers for himself and a run at history and another ring for the Bulls, and has painted a new smile on his once-dour countenance."

Boeck was speaking in general terms, not of the Atlanta squeaker. I could only hope he remained right, that the smile stayed on Jordan's face. It is the darnedest thing about this man, this mere athlete, that he affects people so much that they want *him*, this incredibly rich, necessarily selfish, often capricious and superficial jock, to be happy. Reporters who like to be contrarians or who are not around Jordan (the New York and Los Angeles press, particularly) will often trash him for his obvious defects. The *New York Times* rightfully took him to task this spring for the questionable performance of his charitable, nonprofit, Jordan Foundation, noting that "the lack of Mr. Jordan's own contributions" to his own fund was "striking." Chicago TV station WMAQ had already ripped Jordan for the fact that only 33 percent of the foundation's funds went directly to charitable causes. So Jordan shuttered the whole thing, realizing he was in danger of creating a big mess, directing his attention instead to the James H. Jordan Boys & Girls Club. To improve appearances, he wrote that foundation a check for $2 million.

Continuing the fashionable chipping away at Jordan's reputation were two other *New York Times* writers. William C. Rhoden, in a column titled "The N.B.A. Is a Stage and Jordan an Actor," took the voice of the Bulls' opponents and stated of Jordan's alleged protection by NBA refs, "When we block Mike's shot, it's a foul; when he blocks ours, it's a great play." Rhoden went on to hypothesize that Jordan came back to basketball because "[b]aseball didn't give him six strikes per at-bat;

when he misplayed a ball, the umpire didn't stop the game and order a
replay. Jordan wasn't given the benefit of the doubt on close plays at first."

Harvey Araton, also of the *Times,* wrote in a May 1995 column titled
"Be Like No. 23, the N.B.A.'s Biggest Brat" that Jordan was one of
those people "who think they are bigger than their teams, travels with a
crack security force and dresses for games . . . in his private room." Araton went on to deride Jordan's "largely adoring news media" and to
state that Jordan has "an attitude, a self-absorbed state of mind. What
Michael wants to do, Michael does. What Michael wants to wear,
Michael wears."

Araton's valid complaints were, however, undermined by the petty
catalyst for their airing: Jordan wearing jersey number 23 against the
Magic instead of number 45. When Araton explained he was only looking out for those "irate parents" who now had to shell out "good
money" for another Jordan jersey for their little kids, the sincerity of his
beef became questionable. When he held up Shaquille O'Neal as a fine
alternative to Jordan because, incredibly (to this reader), Shaq's money-
making rap tunes "revealed an awareness of social issues that Jordan often seems oblivious to," he undermined his case considerably.

Jordan does do what he wants to do, without giving a lot of thought
sometimes to the consequences. And he doesn't speak out on social issues the way he could or, maybe, should. I talked to pro football Hall of
Famer and social activist Jim Brown not long ago, and he savaged Jordan for being such a know-nothing capitalist, angrily stating that if Jordan spoke out, for instance, on gun control or gang violence or racism,
"He could do *so* much."

The real reason he doesn't, obviously, is that he doesn't want to. Jordan is an athlete, a businessman, and that's it. His role model status simply comes with the territory.

"Michael's humanness is what makes him so popular," his agent
David Falk says in defense. "Like anyone else, he has his flaws." As far
as being a spoiled bad guy, Falk says, "He has the standing to be a brat,
but he doesn't have the personality or values to be a brat."

That's why criticisms of Jordan don't stick. It is why years of losing
to Jordan and the Bulls must be quite nettlesome to many irritated journalists in other NBA cities.

It is also why even fellow celebs turn all gooey when they are in Jordan's presence. When actor Eriq LaSalle of the popular TV series *ER* got to narrate a video about Jordan called *Michael Jordan: Above and Beyond,* he gushed of the experience, "Narrating for Jordan is like being a tenor sax player in God's jazz band." I later asked Jordan about LaSalle. He wrinkled his brow a moment, then said, "I've never met him."

When Chris Wallace of television's *Prime Time Live* did a piece on the Bulls, but mostly on Jordan, he said: "I've covered presidential summits. I've reported from the floor of national conventions. I've been at space shots. This is the most fun I've ever had reporting a story." Even Mark Heisler, a gritty sportswriter from Los Angeles, admitted in a profile of Jordan for *Esquire* that he had never so dearly wanted an athlete to like him as he did Jordan.

In that same issue of *Esquire* there was a sad, quietly reported tale by Elizabeth Kaye about two Florida teens, a boy and a girl who were lovers, and how they drowned themselves in the Tamiami Canal because their parents had forbidden them to see each other. Near the end of the tragic tale was a resonant paragraph.

At the funeral for the two 14-year-olds, Chris and Maryling, soon to be buried side by side, friends tossed meaningful mementos onto the caskets. Kaye wrote: "Lester stepped forward. From his pocket, he took the Michael Jordan card that Chris had wanted. He held it, then tossed it over the open grave. The wind bore it upward, then gently set it down on Chris' shiny gray coffin."

That's the kind of thing criticism can't touch.

16

I'M WATCHING MY THREE DAUGHTERS SWIM IN AN AGE-GROUP meet at Deerfield High School on a Saturday afternoon when I decide to take a break and stretch my legs. I walk out of the natatorium and into the gymnasium, where a boys' jayvee basketball game is going on.

As I stand in the doorway watching the action, a woman approaches. It is June Jackson.

Two of her kids, juniors Ben and Charlie, are playing in the game, she says. I hadn't noticed, nor would I have. Charlie is the taller of the two, a forward who is perhaps 6 feet. Ben is the point guard. He's about 5'8". Neither, obviously, is good enough to be playing with the Deerfield varsity, a skilled team ranked near the top of the state.

But then I see the shorter kid, Ben, the point guard, walk off the court during a timeout. He puts his left hand on his hip and tilts his head to the left as he ambles toward the sidelines. It is the spitting image of his dad coming off the floor at Madison Square Garden as a Knick.

"My god," I say to June. "Is that learned or genetic?"

"It's just him," says June, training her video camera at her boys. "He's never even seen film of Phil playing."

She is taking this film, of course, because Phil can't be here—the Bulls are practicing at the Berto Center, just five minutes away. One of the major downsides of being an NBA coach is that during the season your job is all-consuming. Both parents care deeply about their children, however, and one reason Phil wants to re-sign with the Bulls is so he can stay in Chicago and not disrupt his youngest two children's final year in high school. It seems pretty clear that Jerry Reinsdorf knows this as well, and has factored it into all of his strategy for lowballing Jackson in the still-unsettled contract situation.

I ask June, since we're talking about familial walking styles, what she thinks about Phil's increasingly gimpy gait.

"He had his spine fused," she says. I know that it all started with basketball injuries, one thing leading to the next, until now Phil walks like a very old man. "His calf nerves are gone and the muscle just gets smaller and smaller," she goes on. "He'll walk with a cane soon."

I ask her about the outing to the Baton with Worm.

"As soon as my daughter gets back we're going."

Then I ask her whether she remembers the beautiful blond woman from the other night, the one who was at the game as Worm's friend. Of course, she says.

"That was a guy," I tell her.

"Get outta here!"

True, I tell her.

"She was in the wives' lounge," June says thoughtfully. She laughs. She likes that.

As the Deerfield jayvees slaughter Niles North, she continues to talk about basketball and what it means to her and her kids. The boys pick up a lot from their dad, but even more from their own observations. June herself has certain things she does not like about the pro game—mainly rude, selfish players.

Ben was a ballboy at the All-Star game, and all the players were reasonable with him, she says, except for Alonzo Mourning. (He, of course, is the player who just as the season started had left the Charlotte Hornets, which had offered him millions and millions of dollars, for the Miami Heat, which offered him millions and millions of dollars. And probably one dollar more. Then he ripped the Heat fans for not being as loudly supportive of his efforts as the Hornet fans had been.) "He's an ass," says June. "He ordered Ben around. He said, 'Get me a cup and water.' That really isn't a ballboy's duty, but Ben did it. Mourning looked at it and said, 'A cup *and* water!' He needed one to drink out of and one to spit into. Ben was upset about it and thought about it for quite a while."

■ ■ ■

The Sleuth has been active. Not long ago, word was floating about that Krause had been out looking at big men again. Of course, he never truly stops looking for that most prized possession, the big man in the middle, but at times it seems there is no corner left to peer into, no towering human on the face of the earth whom the Sleuth hasn't observed, analyzed, and catalogued. The recent report had it that Krause was actually looking at Darryl Dawkins, ol' Chocolate Thunder himself, now 39 years old and a lumbering load for the CBA Sioux Falls Sky Force. Could the Sleuth truly be considering adding to the Bulls the man who came into the NBA as a spacy teenager straight from high school, and who once claimed to have been born on the planet Lovetron?

"I'm not going to deny that we scouted him or that we'll scout him again," Krause said, much the way an international arms dealer might testify at a Senate subcommittee hearing. "We scout a lot of CBA guys."

Before the big Orlando game on February 25, I spot the Sleuth roaming the hallways beneath the United Center stands like a lab mouse searching for reward pellets. I enjoy messing with Krause so much, doing the old back-and-forth thing, actually having an odd type of fun with him because of the in-depth information and disinformation I get from him in an undifferentiated stream, that I seldom walk past him without popping out a couple of questions.

"Any centers out there anywhere?" I ask tonight.

"Where?" he fires back, stopping in his tracks.

"Anywhere. The globe."

He shrugs.

"Nobody out there seven-foot-six or more that you don't know about?"

"Nope."

"Nobody in China?"

He looks at me.

"Do you know of any centers out there?" he asks.

"No," I say, wishing I did. "So there wouldn't be somebody out there, say, seven-seven, that you don't know about?"

"Nope."

"Okay," I say, and we walk off.

■ ■ ■

The Bulls thump the Magic tonight. Just paste them, 111–91.

Mostly what they do is unleash Toni Kukoc in the fourth quarter and simply watch him rain shots out of the sky. The most graceful tall man in the world scores 15 of the Bulls' 37 points in the period, hitting 3 consecutive 3-point shots in just over a minute to blow the game open. Luc Longley guards the thumb-rehabbed Shaquille O'Neal pretty much man-for-man the whole night, and though Shaq scores 33 points, he gets just 4 in the critical fourth period.

The Bulls have figured out how to play the Magic—not doubling and tripling down on Shaq, and letting them try to figure out how to defend Toni themselves—but they can't take too much credit for this win. The Magic are an atrocious road team. Though they are 28–0 at home, they have lost 15 times on opponents' courts. They are a fluky team, not one that can be depended upon to act in any specific way, and beating them at one's home arena means little.

Plus there is always the fear that the Bulls are getting too big for their britches. They had gone to Miami to play the Heat two nights ago, carrying a seven-game winning streak and a 48–5 record, and had gotten shocked by a team with just eight players, losing 113–104. The Heat had been waiting for new members Tim Hardaway, Tyrone Corbin, Chris Gatling, and Walt Williams to show up, but it was the Bulls in their arrogance who were left somewhere behind. They had partied so hard and late the night before after checking into the sensuous Mayfair House in Coconut Grove that they practically staggered through the first three quarters.

Jackson had made the mistake of telling them that since they had flown in late after their win over Atlanta, there would be no shootaround the next day. Sure, it was late. But it was warm, and it was Miami. Party! "I will never do that again," Jackson admitted. "Even if I'm not having a shootaround, I will not let them know that in advance." At any rate, down 91–68 after three quarters, the Bulls made a furious run at this vastly inferior team. But it was not nearly enough to counteract Heat guard Rex Chapman's career day: 9 for 10 on 3-pointers, 39 total points. And there was the Worm factor. Always the paranoia. "I should put a target on the back of my head and say, 'Here you go, nail me,' " he said of the refs. It didn't dawn on him, of course, that he very nearly does have a target on his colorful dome.

The Bulls are in full sail, naturally, two nights after the Orlando win, against the dreadful Minnesota Timberwolves, whipping them in Chicago, 120–99, for the team's 50th victory.

This is a singular achievement. At 50–6, the Bulls have reached half a hundred wins faster than any team in NBA history. (The 1982–83 Philadelphia 76ers reached 50–7.) Not only that, the Bulls have got their 50 with fewer losses than any team ever in any major North American professional sports league. Baseball's New York Giants went 50–11 back in 1912. The NHL Montreal Canadiens went 50–7, with 10 ties, in 1976–77. The NFL Miami Dolphins went 50–7–1 from 1970 to 1974. The rest is all Bulls.

The Sleuth feels good about what he has put together, but tonight before the Timberwolves game, he is furious.

I run into him in our usual spot in the hallway and he is fairly snorting.

"Frigging John Jackson [of the *Sun-Times*] says we're going after Herb Williams," he snarls. "Wrote it in the goddam paper." Williams is another creaky big man, recently traded by the Knicks to the Raptors, who released him. He's a stiff, but what the heck—must be a few paces ahead of Chocolate Thunder.

"You're not?" I ask.

"*Hell* no."

"Well, I know John doesn't make things up," I offer helpfully. "Where do you think he heard it?"

"Probably got it from [Williams's] agent," Krause snaps. "Did he ask me? No! I could have told him it was bullshit. I'll find him and let him know what I think. Buddha reads the papers. Think how he feels. I gotta go in and straighten him out." The weight of the world is on the Sleuth's shoulders. He heads into the locker room in disgust.

I am left with the image of the venerable James Edwards, who came to the Bulls knowing he might be waived at any moment, who hasn't played a lick in days, and who is, I believe, on the injured list preparing to accept Medicare payments, reading the *Sun-Times,* and having his world collapse around him.

But Krause hates correcting us insects, us press. This man who has spent virtually his entire life assessing baseball and basketball talent feels he has a gift that we don't have. Instinct, he calls it, the ability to identify and evaluate skilled athletic movement. "It's God-given," he says. Thing is, he's probably right. To a point.

"I remember actions, how a guy walks or runs or throws or shoots," he has told me. "If those actions change, I see it. If a hitter is going bad, I see it in two or three swings. If somebody has the goods, I see it right away, basketball or baseball. Swinging a bat and shooting a ball are exactly the same: wrists, hand–eye coordination, recognition of the pitch, how to get the shot off."

Krause is a scout of epic proportions, burning obsession, monumental quirks. He and Stan Kasten of the Atlanta Braves and Hawks are the only men ever to be executives in both major league baseball and the NBA. Kasten is more of a manager, while all of Krause's clout has derived from the simple premise that he can ascertain, better than almost anyone else, who can throw, hit, catch, and shoot well enough to play in the big leagues.

For much of the time between 1961 and 1985, Krause was a scout for the Cleveland Indians, the Oakland A's, the Seattle Mariners, and the Chicago White Sox. And now for 29 years he has worked in the NBA, with the Baltimore Bullets, the Phoenix Suns, the Los Angeles Lakers, and the Bulls, doing double duty with baseball in many of those years. For 11 seasons Krause has been at the helm of Chicago's basketball operations, having been hand-picked by chairman Jerry Reinsdorf, who plucked him from the staff of the White Sox, another club Reinsdorf just happens to own. At 56, Krause has seen so many ball games that he has decided that if he ever writes his autobiography—an act that would clash wildly with his clandestine nature and thus will never happen—he says he will call it *One Million National Anthems.*

Who has heard more? I ask. "Nobody," he says proudly.

Scouting, Krause believes, is the foundation of everything in big league sports, like Atlas holding up the world. Krause scouts athletes, as a writer once put it, "much the way an out-of-control industrial fire scouts all the oxygen in a warehouse." If Krause sees a kid he likes, one who has the stuff, one who—God willing—almost nobody else knows about, he falls in love with him, head over heels. He becomes a stalker tracking a starlet.

When he first saw Scottie Pippen, then a skinny forward from uncharted Central Arkansas, at a postseason tournament for prospective NBA players before the 1987 draft, he became delirious. "I almost had an orgasm looking at him," he says. Even before Pippen had taken off his warmups, Krause hissed to then–Bulls scout Billy McKinney, who had already seen Pippen, "There he is! There he is!"

"How do *you* know?" McKinney wondered.

"Look at his arms!" Krause cried. "You said he had long arms. They're down to freaking *here!*"

Then there is Krause's own body: a golf ball amidst 2-irons. Lithe, lanky greyhounds can't get past it. Nor can the press. Nor, it seems, can the public. "It bothers me that because he's not six-two and good-looking, he doesn't get the respect he deserves," says Reinsdorf.

Indeed, with what he has achieved, Krause in all his disheveled roundness could—should—be seen as a lovable Runyonesque character à la Red Auerbach, particularly in a city that has embraced oddballs like William "The Refrigerator" Perry, Mike Ditka, and oddest, though not heaviest, of them all, Dennis Rodman. But because he is so serious about everything, because he never lets up, because he needs approval so badly and wears that need like a sign on his back, he never strikes a sympathetic chord with observers.

"He says, 'I'm ugly and fat, and that's why people hate me,'" the *Trib*'s Sam Smith, a Krause nemesis, told me once. "But that's not it at all. I have lot of friends who are fat and ugly, and I don't hate *them*."

There is a revelatory sentence in the Bulls' media guide that says more about Krause and his insecurities than intended. Krause, it states, is "responsible for the acquisition of every Bulls player other than Michael Jordan and all the coaching, scouting, and administrative staff that combined to become only the third team in NBA history to win three consecutive championships." Think of that: everyone "other than Michael Jordan." And Thomas Edison's boss did everything to make the light bulb other than invent it.

So Krause carries the burden of blind good luck no matter what he does: He came to his new job, and the best player in history just happened to be sitting on the waiting room couch. Even though Krause built around Jordan, even though he signed free-agent guard John Paxson in 1985 to shoot the wide-open jumpers that came when Jordan was mobbed, then got B. J. Armstrong and finally Steve Kerr to do the same thing, snagged Pippen (draft day trade with Seattle, 1987) and Horace Grant (first-round draft pick, 1987) to complement His Airness, traded Charles Oakley for center Bill Cartwright in the summer of 1988 to keep the big men off Jordan, acquired the role players who efficiently fill the gaps today, and, of course, went way out on a limb to acquire Rodman and all his hangups—even though he did all that, Krause is still seen by many as little more than the tool carrier for the genius inventor.

"That's nonsense!" Reinsdorf has roared at me. "When Jerry came here this was a lousy team. Check it out."

In 1984–85 the Bulls, with Jordan, were 38–44. After Krause arrived in 1985, they went 30–52, 40–42, 50–32, 47–35, 55–27, and then 61–21 and 67–15 in their first two championship seasons. That's almost a straight line upward. They went 57–25 in the third title season, 1992–93, then faltered only a bit when Jordan left, going 55–27 and losing in the second round of the playoffs in 1993–94. Last season, with Jordan there only at the end, they finished 47–35. No matter how you slice it, with Himself aboard or not, Krause has done an outstanding job.

"He had a plan, and he implemented it," Reinsdorf has stated. "The fact is, Michael Jordan *was* here. You can't change that. But if Krause didn't have him, he would have done things differently. The truth is, Michael's presence elevated us to mediocrity much faster than we wanted, and mediocrity is the worst thing. We certainly would have been in some draft lottery without Jordan. Jerry Krause has to be given credit."

But then Reinsdorf casually, unwittingly perhaps, tossed the grenade: "The real test for Krause will be when Jordan is gone."

Jordan doesn't like Krause, can't stand the way he's always hanging around, taking what Jordan believes is too much of the spotlight. Supposedly (though Reinsdorf denies it) Jordan went to the boss in 1991 and said of Krause, "It's either him or me." Reinsdorf supposedly calmed Jordan, but since that time Jordan and Krause have seldom talked.

"I'm here, he's there," Jordan said to me one day in 1993, pointing his finger first to that corner, then to this one. Of Krause's stewardship he said, "The trade of Oakley was good, and the best thing he did was to get Pippen and Grant. That's it. His claim to fame is that he drafted Earl Monroe for the Bullets [in 1967]. And I say to him, 'What pick was that?' He says, 'Two.' And I say, 'Hell! Earl Monroe was a real secret, huh? A real secret? If you hadn't taken him, he'd have gone third!'"

Though their relationship has reached a sort of détente since Jordan's return, the rift itself is so unnecessary and odd that it cries out for deeper explanation.

"I'm the only one who has told him no," Krause said to me before the third title. "When he had that broken foot back in 1985, I told him he couldn't play. If we had let him run rampant, we wouldn't have the two championships.

"This kid has had his butt kissed by everybody in the world except his parents and me. If we listened to him, we'd have [Jordan's former North Carolina teammate] Buzz Peterson on the team! My goal is not to be his friend. My goal is to win titles."

Jordan well remembers that day ten years ago when Krause told him he had to sit out. For Jordan it wasn't just what Krause said (he *did* need to stay off the foot), it was the way he said it: coldly. "He said, 'You're Bulls property now, and we tell you what to do.' I was a young, enthusiastic kid, and that just made me realize this was a business, not a game. We never hit it off after that."

Unlike anyone else in the Bulls hierarchy (and unlike any of the players except for Randy Brown, who attended Collins High School), Jerry Krause was born in Chicago, in the Albany Park section, the only child of gregarious Jewish parents. "We treat everybody the same," Jerry's dad, Paul, would always say. The family name was originally Karbofsky, but Paul changed it to Krause so that his own parents wouldn't know he had pursued an amateur boxing career. "He fought Barney Ross three times and got knocked out three times," says Jerry. "He didn't have a high school diploma, but he was honest and he worked hard."

Paul Krause worked for the Cook County assessor's office for a time, then ran a delicatessen, and finally opened a shoe store in Norwood Park, a northwest neighborhood that was heavily Polish–German and Catholic. "It was very anti-Semitic," Jerry recalls. "They burned out Jews. When I went to Taft High School, you know what the number of Jewish students was? One." Every day Krause felt that he was singled out for contempt. "They'd yell, 'You kike! You sheenie! You Jew bastard!' I had to fight, and I learned about prejudice."

The funny thing about these revelations of victimization was that after I printed them in *Sports Illustrated,* the magazine received letters from several Jewish alumni of Taft High, all of them stating that Krause was full of it. Krause, obviously, had not been the only Jew at Taft, nor were Jews "burned out." Nor, the letter writers claimed, was anti-Semitism rampant in the neighborhood. If Krause had social problems, his former schoolmates stated, they were problems of his own making.

People looking to psychoanalyze Krause don't have far to dig, if they go with the perpetual-outcast theory: the small, athletically average (he was a backup catcher on the Taft baseball team) minority member who immersed himself in observation and analysis of sport so as to beat at their own game those who were athletically gifted, mainstream, and cruel. It's so pat that it's probably nonsense. Except in the Sleuth's mind. Some people *need* enemies. Coaches routinely create them for lethargic teams. What works for the power forward can work for the general manager.

And, clearly, it has.

17

THE WAY YOU WORK THINGS WHEN YOU WANT SOMETHING FROM Michael Jordan, such as a one-on-one interview (if you don't simply stumble into him after a tip from somebody like Wes), is you talk to somebody in an official capacity with the Bulls, say, PR man Tim Hallam, and state your request, then you wait, knowing that none of it makes any difference whatsoever. You have to track down Himself yourself, somehow lure him away from the horde for an instant, plead your case, hope he says, "Yeah, okay, we'll talk," and then you simply wait. Every so often you try to get close to him to remind him. He'll say, "Right, we'll do it." And then you wait some more. Most people—journalists, business folks, deal-makers, groupies, golfers, leeches—get screened out through this somewhat crude but practical and highly effective technique.

It is highly effective because it exhausts all but the hardy. It is practical because even the people who never see Jordan again have been touched by his personal, albeit irrelevant, acceptance. For guys like me, it just means hang in there.

I had started the ball rolling with Jordan at our summer session at the Solheim Center after his workout. "I'd like to see you out there in L.A. when you go back for the movie," I said. "What do you think if I zip out there and maybe check you out in your big Hollywood career?"

He smiled—damn, what a smile—and said, sure, come on out.

So I did. This was in early October. I call George Koehler, Jordan's driver and friend. They're all staying at the Beverly Hills Hotel, the entourage, and Michael is quite busy, George says. But we'll get together sooner or later, he says. Another day goes by. I call George again. Michael is filming constantly and then playing hoops and then working out. But we'd do it sooner or later.

Another day. Man, says George, Michael is on location now, shooting baseball scenes in the stadium at Long Beach State. Why don't you just drive down there and see what you can arrange?

So I do. I go to the university, but the stadium is empty. I drive around. I ask somebody whether there is another baseball stadium anywhere in town. Yeah, the man says, an old one called Blair Field. It's a municipal park where the Los Angeles Rams once trained. Down by the water.

I drive there, and sure enough, there are orange signs on the street nearby saying "Space Jam" in black letters.

I park and follow the crowd of arriving spectators up a ramp and into the small, old-time stadium. A crowd of people is sitting in the stands, arranged in one of those Hollywood clusters that, when properly filmed and edited, would fool movie viewers into thinking the whole place was packed. Which it is not. Is there going to be a game, or what? I know only a little about the plot of the movie: Jordan hangs out with Looney Toons characters and plays a few sports, and it's all supposed to be funny and encourage people to buy movie spin-off stuff.

Assistant directors, junior assistant directors, grips, gaffers, gofers, and other movie people mill about, with no purpose that I can discern. Some baseball players are warming up on the diamond and in the outfield, but I don't recognize the uniforms. And I don't see Jordan anywhere.

I take a seat on the first base line next to a man holding a Birmingham Barons sign. That must be one of the teams—Jordan's minor league club during his excursion into America's Pastime. A woman sitting next to me holds a sign that says "Jordan #1." I study the field and can see that one club is, indeed, the Barons, and the other is, I barely ascertain, the Carolina Mudcats. But still no Michael.

"Okay, we need to take up every seat from here on down," a production assistant barks through a bullhorn. I'm just one of the extras now, so I move with the group.

"People, please!" begs the P.A., who is wearing a *Waterworld* T-shirt and has an annoying whine to his voice. "Quiet!"

So now I'm sitting a few rows behind the dugout, behind a little kid who's practicing his lines to a big man with shoulder-length white hair. That has to be the director, Joe Pytka, famous for making all those Nike Air Jordan spots. I had heard Pytka could be nasty, so I keep quiet, afraid of what he might do if he found out some idiot had wandered onto his set.

Shortly, Michael Jordan comes walking up to the box-seat rail, in front of the little boy. But wait a second. It isn't Jordan. It's a lookalike, dressed in a Barons uniform with number 45 on it. I spy the real Jordan out near the cameras, wearing Bermuda shorts, a golf shirt, and a cap. But wait—that isn't the real Jordan, either. It's *another* lookalike who has the Jordan act down perfect, except for the real man's trademark self-confident, sore-footed, athletic gait.

"Folks," says Waterworld, interrupting my reverie. "You will stand because Michael Jordan has just hit a home run. I'll go 'Bam!' and that's your cue to go bananas." He does, and we do. Again and again. Jordan Fake No. 1 waves to us as though he were the real thing, and we applaud and shower him with love.

"That would be a cut!" Waterworld says. "Your Oscars are in the mail. Now let's all move behind home."

It's 8 P.M., and I'd been here two hours, and I begin asking myself how this is advancing my journalistic career. I ask the guy next to me why he's here. Did he just see the signs and stop by? "Casting," he says. He's getting paid, as is everyone else. "Forty bucks for six hours, then time and a half." And he's been doing this for ten hours already. I calculate. Hundreds of extras at $50, $60 or more a day, plus food and drink—this is an expensive venture, a major film, as they say.

I think about just getting up and finding Michael, doing the interview, and getting the hell out of here. But I can't, because here comes Mr. Jordan now, the real deal, in his Barons uniform, nodding to us, taking his place at the plate, and hacking away at pitch after pitch by former major league pitcher Brad "the Animal" Lesley.

"People, I'm begging you!" Waterworld screeches. "There are six hundred and fifty of you and only a few of us! Shut up!" Boy, this guy is irritating. Taking a few moments to collect himself, he says in a calmer voice, "Mike's at bat. He's the hometown hero. It's a ball game. You know what to do."

And we do it, even as Jordan fouls off lollipops, grounds to third, fans, hits lazy cans of corn to the Mudcats scattered throughout the field. Then, finally he hits an honest home run, and I fear the hirees might bring the bleachers down. It's only 348 feet down the line, but it is out of here. You'd have thought the extras had each been awarded a free Mercedes. I sneak out during a seating shift and walk under the stands and strike up a nice conversation with a group of movie ballplayers, former low-level players in the minors and major leagues who are now actors themselves. They're in baseball uniforms, smoking, drinking coffee, discussing the movie biz. One of the actors is Ernie Banks's son. All of them say how much fun it is actually playing baseball in a film, and all of them say how great it is having Michael around.

"He's like a kid," says the Mudcats shortstop. "Always playing catch, tossing a football around. And somebody's been working on his swing. Last week he couldn't hit at all."

The real Michael walks by, en route to his trailer past left field, but he doesn't see me, and I figure I'll grab him when the shooting is finished. One of the players mentions how Jordan recently ticked off Pytka royally by telling him he was "slower than Sydney Pollack." Some kind of Hollywood in-joke. Pytka had stormed away, and the ballplayers ate it up. And then there was the time, they tell me, during a Nike shoot when Bo Jackson, having taken all he was gonna take from Pytka, allegedly knocked him out with a single punch. Allegedly.

Later I would meet the editor of the film, a veteran movie man named Shelly Kahn, who would tell me about the challenges Pytka always threw at Jordan. Pytka, a fair athlete in his time, wanted to play Jordan one-on-one in basketball. Jordan said no, it would be ridiculous. But he'd play Pytka two-on-two; Pytka could have anybody he wanted and Jordan would take, let's see, uh, he'd take the bespectacled, diminutive

Kahn as his partner. It was just a challenge to shut Pytka up, one that was not going to happen. But when they were alone Jordan said very seriously to Kahn, "We'll beat them. Just get me the ball."

I walk back for my final scene—the one where the flying saucer lands in the outfield and Michael arrives from Mars to hit the final, redemptive tape-measure home run to beat the hated Mudcats.

Huge electric fans have been turned on, simulating the exhaust of the spacecraft, dust is flying, and we all gaze into the turbulence with wonder and awe. The stand-in Michael waves at us, and as soon as I can, I bolt out to Jordan's trailer to do my job.

It shouldn't have surprised me, but it did: Michael was gone for the night. He wouldn't be back here at all. And my plane left in the morning.

■ ■ ■

So Michael felt sort of bad about the mixup. We'd do something, he said, once the season was well underway. It didn't happen. One night in the locker room, he said, "Here, I'll give you my number." He made sure none of the press could see it, then wrote on a corner of my notebook.

"You'll change it before I call," I said. "You probably change it weekly."

"No, I don't change it," he said. "Just call."

So I did. I got Juanita on a recording. I said that I wanted to do this little thing with Michael. Instead of an interview, I had now decided that Michael could help me promote this TV roundtable talk show I participate in for SportsChannel called *The Sportswriters on TV.* Producer John Roach wanted to get film of me playing a silly game of one-on-one against a Bull, and at the end dunking over the top of the player by flying off a trampoline; he'd cut it so I looked like Herman the Helicopter. There would be some punchline at the end, like "Sportswriters can jump," or "Sportswriters talk a good game." Director Bob Albrecht had suggested we use Buddha as the fall guy, or Bill Wennington. I said, nope, let's go for the top draw. I'd get Jordan, I said, because he owed me.

And here he came.

Practice at the Berto Center is over, the gym is empty except for, well, hell, it's not empty. It's never truly empty until He has left the building and every reporter is certain of that and knows he or she can't be scooped on anything possibly having to do with Him. As Jordan walks out in his newest-generation black Air Jordans, red Bulls trunks, and a cut-off black T-shirt over a white Bulls practice jersey, the buzz spreads among the reporters and camera people who are here or in the press room or the hallway, and they start streaming in. Please, I want to tell them, go home.

Jordan looks at me and at Bob Albrecht, SportsChannel producer Nancy Newman, and the SportsChannel camera guys, and says dubiously, "What am I supposed to do? Just stand here?" As Bob and the others wire him with a mike, he looks even more dubious. "What is this for?" he asks.

I'm wearing a *Sportswriters on TV* T-shirt (featuring the show's logo above a cigar billowing smoke out of an ashtray), blue Hawaiian shorts, a salt-crusted baseball cap from the old Chicago Blitz of the USFL, white socks, and some cheapo Avia basketball shoes from the back of my closet. My role model is Woody Harrelson in *White Men Can't Jump.* Or every other badly outfitted sportswriter I have run into. Which is a huge number.

Jordan looks at me in amazement.

"What is *this* for?" he asks, looking at the trampoline.

I've been practicing flying off the thing while Jordan was in the locker room. "That's for you when you dunk over me," I say.

"Nah, nah," he says somberly. I'm amazed he believes me, but what does he know? I had told him this was just a little thing with him and me messing around in front of a camera, but I'm sure he has forgotten. All he remembers is that I'd done my time, showed my perseverance, and, according to his rules, he will reward me for that. I had talked with Mark Vancil, the writer who produced the *Rare Air* books with Jordan, and Vancil said Jordan was now not accepting any major commercial endorsements for less than eight figures. There was no way anybody could get Jordan to do something this stupid or promotional unless he wanted to just for kicks.

Over on the sidelines the reporters who have stuck around are beginning to make wisecracks. Jordan looks over and snarls, "Hey, Lacy!" He looks at the *Sun-Times*'s Lacy Banks, who has been yelling, "Take it to him, Rick! Dunk on him!" "Hey, Lacy," Jordan says, "why don't you write correct stuff in your column?" Banks had written that Jordan lost $10,000 when he was fined that amount by the NBA for not showing up for media day at the All-Star game. Which was true. Jordan had been out playing golf with Charles Barkley. Jordan always skips All-Star media day. But he didn't like people thinking he threw away money like that. "Preacher," he continues (Banks is an ordained minister as well as a sportswriter), "I got twelve thousand dollars for winning the game. And I owe ten thousand. That's a great investment, wouldn't you say?"

"Kill him, Rick!" the Preacher says.

"Who are you?" Jordan says to director Bob Albrecht.

Bob explains who he is and says, "This is a challenge. Rick's going one-on-one with you, and then he's going to dunk on you."

"You'll do that when I'm not here," Jordan says firmly.

"He's going to trash talk a little bit," Albrecht continues, explaining the concept.

"I won't say much," says Jordan.

We get ready, though this is not what I'd had in mind at all. This was supposed to be raw footage of Jordan doing this and that, swatting away my shots, me clanking some jumpers, him scoring at will, that could be pieced together with the trampoline-dunk to tell a story. A silly one, yes, but a story. All the hollering from the sidelines has turned this into something else.

Just before the cameras roll I tell him, "The theme is 'Sportswriters can jump.' *Can* jump. Sort of like the movie. You do know about movies, right?"

He is oddly silent, watching me dribble the ball at the top of the key, up next to me, paying the ball no attention, crouched in an athlete's defensive stance, staring low. A small smile comes across his face.

"You're bowlegged, too, aren't you," he states as if he has just solved a puzzle. He finds this terribly amusing.

"You can't stop a sportswriter," I say, dribbling to my right. "Nobody can."

Jordan looks perplexed. "Come on, man. What kind of shoes you got on? You can't afford Nikes?" he asks. He's looking at my beat-up sneakers, sympathetic. "Oh. Sportswriters don't get paid much. I understand."

I shoot and miss. He gets the ball.

This was not supposed to be a back-and-forth game, or a game at all, but what can I do? Now the other TV stations' news cameras on the sidelines are shooting the stuff. Filming the filming.

"Come on, Mr. Looney Tunes. Mr. Nike. Where you going?" I say, trying to rev things up.

I push hard on his hip. He is wiry and strong, but not nearly as strong as he looks on TV. He is cut so amazingly high that his center of gravity is way above what it would be for a normal 6'6" man. I weigh only about ten pounds less than he, but at 6'1" I could easily get low and block his progress—if he didn't race around me to either side, fall back and nail a shot, or simply sail over me. He has a perfect basketball body. But he would get killed in hockey. Or handball. Or, pointedly, baseball. In fact, I can't think of many disciplines that would be less rewarding to his lean, long-limbed, midair acrobatics and shifty footwork and cutting ability than the close-to-the-dirt, straight-line, precisely routed sport of baseball. I thought at the time that if Michael Jordan needed to take off to explore his skills at another game, he should have chosen beach volleyball or the Olympic sport called team handball, in which sprinting players dribble a palm-size handball, then leap into the air to try to throw it past the goaltender and into the net.

"No hand-checking!" he says, slapping my hand away hard.

He rises up on a jumper, I push him, and he misses. I retrieve the ball, shoot and miss. I swear loudly. He rebounds.

"Whaddayou got?" I say. "Black shoes? Nikes? How much they cost?"

"Don't worry about it."

I lunge for the ball.

"You reach, I teach," he says, dribbling the ball from his right to his left hand, back and forth.

He fakes a shot.

"Where you going? Huh? Open up," he says, shooting from 18 feet. Swish. "Tell me what it tastes like."

He walks to the top of the key, in a rhythm. I hold the ball just in front of him, pulling it back.

"Come on, gimme the ball!" he cries.

"Watch out," I say, bouncing it to him. "I represent all the sportswriters in the whole world."

"Sportswriters," he scoffs. "Look at those pale legs. *Look* at them."

I pull my shorts up even higher. He rises for a jumper, and I jump, too, flicking his right elbow almost imperceptibly, a high school defensive trick that often fools refs at the highest level. The ball misses the rim.

"Well, that's a foul," he states, turning and walking back to the key.

I have the rebound—I keep the ball—and I say, "What do you mean, a foul? It's the NBA."

"Okay," he says, looking nasty for the first time. I dribble and he pushes me hard with one hand. I bounce backward about three feet.

"I go this way, too," I say, heading to my left. I shoot—remember, his defense is still of the casual, there's-no-money-riding-here kind—and I miss. I started for two seasons on my Peoria Richwoods High School varsity team in the late '60s, but I never could shoot—I was a rebounder. At 47 I still can jump up and grab the rim, a fact about which I am quite proud, all things considered, but my shot is, was, and always will be one grain shy of a brick. That is what is so remarkable about Jordan, that fact that he is an unearthly athlete *and* a fabulous shooter.

Years ago I spoke with Connie Hawkins, the original sky-flying playground star from New York City, and asked him if he didn't think jumping ability was the most obviously God-given, genetic skill in basketball. He thought about it and said yes, that might be, but from what he had seen, shooting skill was every bit as God-given. When Jordan first joined the league, people compared him to his obvious stylistic predecessor, Julius "Dr. J" Erving. It was an apt parallel, except for one thing: Erving was an average midrange shooter and a nonexistent long-range shooter. As somebody said back then, "Jordan is Julius with a j."

He has the ball now. "Am I supposed to let you win?" he asks.

I shrug.

He drills a jumper.

"That's one," I say, enjoying the smart talk.

"One?" says Jordan. He looks at me and frowns. Then he looks to the sidelines. "Can we get some oxygen over here?" I am panting hard. Practicing the early dunks had winded me. Plus, talking like this may be natural for Jordan, who said he was going to be quiet, but it's hard for me.

Jordan is goofing off, enjoying himself. On this very day, February 29, 1996, in Lumberton, North Carolina, Daniel Green has been convicted of murdering James Jordan two and a half years ago. In the testimony, accomplice Larry Demery said that after Green pulled the trigger, "we both stood there and watched the man die," and that it wasn't until they rifled through their victim's possessions that they knew precisely what they'd done. As Green then told his pal, "I believe we've killed Michael Jordan's daddy." I find myself wondering whether Michael knows all this. I'm sure he does. But he has an ability to let things go. There is an expression, and variations on it, that his close friends say he often uses when things go wrong for others: "He'll get over it," or "They'll get over it." His friends say he also uses the expression to encourage himself after failure or heartbreak: "I'll get over it." And he does.

"Just (puff) imagine (puff) Shaq's inside," I say.

Jordan looks at Albrecht. "Every shot he takes, you're gonna edit, I know," he says. "Except the next one."

I drive in for a fallaway layup. Jordan bumps me.

"Flagrant foul!" I yell, as the ball rolls out.

"Flagrant, my ass," he says, snatching the ball. He looks at Bob. "Cut that."

He sinks another long shot.

"Hey, Lovabull!" he yells toward the sidelines. "Hey, Preacher, come on out here!"

Lacy Banks continues to heckle and taunt.

I get another rebound. "If a tree falls in the forest," I say, dribbling, "does it make a sound?"

"Yes," says Jordan.

I dribble between my legs, backing up, trying to figure out which part of that epistemological question I got wrong. Jordan looks at me in boredom. He stops guarding me. He puts his hands on his hips.

I fire one up. Wide open, I miss anyway.

"That was in," I say, angry at myself.

Jordan gets the rebound and nods his head. "No wonder you're all writers," he says, very loudly, for all to hear. "You're *terrible* athletes. You're frustrated athletes, that's what you are. All of you. You can't play. You can't do nothing. And you dream all day long."

"Patent leather shoes," I wheeze to interrupt his soliloquy, to no effect.

"You sit behind your typewriters and your pencils all day and you dream. That's all you do!" he says. "You sit there and dream."

He shoots and misses.

"I remember when you weren't afraid to take it inside," I say, dribbling. "When guys like me couldn't score on you." I shoot and miss again. Damn.

"You see? You see?" Jordan sneers. "Tomorrow in your column you can dream you made that shot. Look, come here," he says, gesturing me toward him. "Dream this!"

Yuk, yuk. He misses. I get the ball, palm it, hold it out to him. "Is this it?" I say. "This what you wanted?"

I shoot a long jumper, and—hallelujah!—it hits the rim, bounces off the glass and goes through. I hold up three fingers. A trey. Walk around in celebration.

"My ball?" he says.

"Oh." I had almost forgotten. "No, no."

He gives me the ball, disdain in his face. "What are we playin'?" he says. "In the 'hood we play make-it-take-it."

I dribble. He reaches around me for a steal, hits my arm, misses the ball, and I take off to the right, straight at the basket. He's behind me, and I sense that, and I wonder what he's going to do, how he'll respond. Later, looking at the tape, I would see that I had in fact beaten him, because he was messing around, and that he was pursuing me full-speed and was coiling in that remarkable pantherlike way of his, ready to fly over me and pin the ball on the glass, to cuff it, to crush it, to throw it into the next century. Except that in my excitement, I lost control of the ball, it careened out of bounds, and I went flying after it in desperation.

"Into the Gatorade!" shouted Jordan, who effortlessly uncocked as smoothly as he had cocked.

When I walk back oncourt, I pull the wad of gum from my mouth and hold it out. "Want some gum?" I offer.

"I don't want no gum."

"Cigar?"

"Ready?" he says.

I say nothing.

"Ready?"

"Yeah."

He dribbles the ball between my legs, picks it up, and soars in for a layup, hooting as he goes.

"Look at those pale legs," he marvels.

"It's the middle of winter," I say. "I'm a white guy."

He shoots and misses. I get the ball.

He cocks his head. He looks at me. "Wait," he says, holding up both his hands. He tilts his head, then turns to the spectators. He gets quite serious. "Listen. Listen."

Everything grows quiet. My panting breath is all that can be heard. It is deafening. Jordan cracks up.

Okay. I shoot, run in, get my own rebound, and lay the ball in. Jordan has seen about enough.

"Next basket wins," he states.

I have the ball. Just get a shot off, I'm thinking. Put it in, and it's over. "This is for all the ink-stained (wheeze) wretches," I say, "who have to watch guys like you (pant) not go to the hole."

"You're right, Rick," he says. "You're right." He breathes as hard as he can, his eyes wide in terror.

I actually try to get open on this one. I shoot from way out, off-balance, and he gets part of my wrist. "Get out of there," he says to the ball.

"Huh?" I say, slapping my wrist, looking at him. "Huh?"

"Nah, that was no foul," he snorts.

Booing rises from the sidelines. Loud jeers. Whistles.

"Write it in your columns!" Jordan snaps.

He dribbles up top.

"Come here," he orders. "Come on. How you want it?" This is unmitigated trash now. Finger-pointing. Rec center rubbish. "Move your feet. Move 'em! Oh, don't look at the head."

"Don't try between my legs again," I warn him.

"How you want it? Huh?"

"Come on, Scottie isn't here to help you," I whisper. "Where's Worm?"

He dribbles from one side to the other, his immense hands almost holding the ball still with each change.

"Up shot," he says, rising. "Here it goes!" And his jump shot sinks quietly into the net.

All that's left now is my dunk, and contrary to what he said at the beginning, he obligingly stands under the basket as I launch myself from the trampoline and go soaring awkwardly over his head and almost into the basket myself.

That's it. I pick myself up, shake his hand and thank him. He has a few more words for Banks, then he departs.

Looking at the different rough cuts a few weeks later, I find myself chuckling. In the one that has the No. 2 camera trained solely on him, Jordan talks half to himself, half to somebody unseen on the sidelines as I prepare the mini-tramp for my aerial assault.

"What if I blocked this?" Jordan is saying impishly, looking like a misbehaving kid in school. This is the man, Pulitzer Prize–winning author David Halberstam recently wrote in *World Business* magazine, who is "the most dazzling and most personable athlete of modern time." "Wouldn't that be great?"

18

MARCH 2: THIS IS JUST A SCHEDULED GAME OF NO CONSE-quence, a guaranteed win against a once-proud team that now has no heart, skill, or clear focus, the Boston Celtics. I am here because this is the night Rodman has said we'll go out, maybe take in a show at the Baton.

In the stands at the United Center the signs begging Rodman to throw his jersey this way or that way are waving like wildflowers in the breeze. "Rodman My Parents Met You At The Mirage And They Said You Are A Lovely Young Man. Can I Have Your Jersey?" a typical one says. Buxom young women hold signs full of sexual innuendo; kids hold signs that simply beg. Rodman's routine of giving away his sweaty jersey after each win—or whenever he fouls out or is tossed from a game—is now a vital part of the Bulls circus. Nobody in the building leaves until they see which little boy or girl, or occasional babe, has copped the coveted wet wad of cloth.

The Bulls are just fooling around.

They are up 72–48 toward the end of the third period. And at one point Jordan comes up to Mark Grossman, the statistician at the scorer's table, and says irritably, "I'm trying to get a triple double, but these guys can't hit a damn shot." He'll finish with 21 points, 8 rebounds, and 8 assists in an easy 32 minutes.

But tonight it's Worm's world; in fact, it is Dennis Rodman Hair Color Cup Night at the United Center. The first 20,000 fans received large plastic cups that have two photos of Rodman on them. When cold liquid is poured into the cups, one Worm-do turns pink, the other lime green. It's a pretty slick gimmick, and the cups will go on to become hot items for cold-liquid drinkers everywhere.

I admit that my favorite section in my own paper, the *Sun-Times,* is the box that sports editor Bill Adee puts out after each Bulls game tracking Rodman's dye jobs. The chart, called "Hair It Is," now reads thusly:

Color	*Games*
Blond	20
Blond (red streak)	3
Green	13
Rust-oleum	8
Mango	2

By the end of the season it will include red, flamingo, and cranberry flame (a swirling kaleidoscope of hues similar to what you might get if you handed a child a bunch of primary colors, a yellow canvas, and said

Go to it). Oddly, the only color never represented in Worm's palette will be his natural one, black.

At the end of the third quarter Rodman, obviously feeling frisky on this his special night, attacks the boards with extra fervor, going for one rebound after another. He pursues one all the way to midcourt, snares it, dribbles back down to his end, weaving about, heading toward the right corner. Everyone in the place can sense what is about to happen, and sure enough, it does: Rodman, the man who never shoots, who can't make a free throw, launches a long 3-point shot. There is no teammate under the basket, and the ball misses the rim by a good two feet. On the bench, Pippen, Kukoc, and Buechler almost fall to the floor in hysterics.

Shortly after that, Phil Jackson makes a lineup adjustment: Jordan along with the very white Kukoc, Kerr, Buechler, and Wennington. "The Vanilla Connection," hollers Lacy Banks.

A good time is had by all. When asked postgame what he thought of Rodman's ludicrous 3-point attempt, Jackson grinned and said, "It's high comedy. I enjoyed it. I encouraged him."

So now I'm off for a night on the town with the encouraged Worm. His plans have changed, however; the Baton is too subdued, and he needs action, and so Crobar it is.

Before I set sail, I ask Jackson if he has any advice for me on my maiden voyage to the nightclub. "Hmm," he says. "Keep your zipper up. Make sure you don't get caught in a compromising position, and don't step into dark alleys or dark parts of the bar."

And away we go.

First stop is the usual, Gibson's Steak House, to fuel up. Worm presides over an intimate dinner party that includes his agent, Dwight Manley; five members (including a sleeping four-year-old girl) of the Rich family from Oklahoma, the country-twangin' white people who "adopted" Dennis when he was a lonely student killing time at South-eastern Oklahoma State by shooting hoops alone in the gym with a quarter stuck in each ear; Channel 5 sportscaster Jon Kelly; Bigsby & Kruthers men's store co-owner Gene Silverberg; Shyra, the long-haired dancer from the Hammer video, about whom I would write in my col-umn describing the evening that she was sitting four chairs away from

Rodman, but that it was "pretty clear she'll come into play later"; body-guards Kelly Davis and George Triantafillo; Dick Versace, who has brought along two small boys; and little me.

Rodman is jittery and quiet.

He eats his salad, drinks some iced tea, and gobbles a steak. No fries, onion rings, broccoli, mashed potatoes, steak sauce, ice cream, or anything else that others are eating. No distractions at all.

Aren't your knees sore? I ask Rodman. Don't you just want to take it easy for a while?

"No," he says. "I'm ready to go."

But it's not time yet. People are still eating. And the galley proofs of his soon-to-be-released book, *Bad As I Wanna Be,* are being passed around the table. Nice family fare from Delacorte Press. The proofs get to me, and I flip through them, noticing the hip, oversize print that proclaims such things as, "This was some serious shit," and "Madonna's a connoisseur of bodies," and "She wasn't an acrobat, but she wasn't a dead fish, either."

Manley, wearing a baseball cap and looking like a baby-faced accountant on his day off, looks at me and says sternly, "You can't use any of this. You can't write anything about the book."

It's all top-secret. Trash, but top-secret. Manley is an impresario of the classic variety, manipulating everything, playing it all for maximum effect for his client. As I recall, the book's existence and publishing date have already been announced in the press, but fine, I nod like a good boy and promise not to leak such bombshells as the fact that Rodman likes to "wear different earrings when I wear a halter top."

Rodman is eager to get out of here so he can delve deeper into the nightlife. He is going to party till dawn, he has said, then catch a morning plane to Los Angeles to shoot a TV commercial. This is Saturday. The Bulls don't play again until Tuesday, which leaves lots of time for catching up on anything that might be missing from his agenda, such as sleep.

Our core group, now joined by producers Jacqueline Payson and Barri Chattman of ABC's *PrimeTime Live*—doing camera-less "research" for an upcoming segment—drives off in several cars to the warehouse area where Crobar stands like a bunker in a demilitarized zone.

Inside lasers are flashing so brightly that one hits me in the eyes and I stagger forward, blinded. I don't have to worry about falling down because there isn't enough space between bodies to drop even a hanky to the floor.

Rodman leads the parade, slicing through the dark, flashing sea of humanity like a knife. We establish a beachhead near a corner bar. Overhead is a metal ladder leading to a trapdoor, which occasionally opens from above and disgorges or receives patrons. To our left is an elevated steel cage with two women gyrating in it.

Rodman looks at home.

He drifts into the human ocean. I ask Shyra what one would call this music.

"Techno-house," she screams.

Worm floats back. He comes here sometimes on men's night, meaning when the fellows take over the place, and dances with guys for hours on end. Just now he's feeling tip-top, since this is almost the perfect environment for him: a place of vivid sights, sounds, and activity with little chance for meaningful dialogue or nonphysical communication. People offer him drinks. It's a hoot to see short, scrawny club crawlers in the latest grunge garb straggle past him and say, "Love your game, man." Most of the folks in the crowd simply let him be.

"Didn't you tell me once that Bill Laimbeer taught you a lot of that tiptoe rebounding?" I ask as we stand side by side, braced against the sound.

"I *watched* him and learned it," he yells. "But he didn't teach me, really."

Somebody sends him a shot of something. Rodman waves, leaves it on the bar, drinks his own beer.

"Tipping helps," he continues, "because it's very hard to go up and get a ball with two hands. There isn't room. I learned to tip it to myself, but the main thing is I never give up."

It was just last week that the *Sports Illustrated* with Rodman on the cover hit the stands, the one that asked, "The Best Rebounder Ever?" I can't believe that all that jumping and scrambling and colliding hasn't taken its toll on Rodman's joints, especially his knees.

"Don't your knees *hurt?*" I ask again.

"Not now," he says. "There's nobody in the league my age who keeps themselves in the condition I do. I feel great."

In the wee hours I leave the well-conditioned marvel and his entourage and the decibels and the human tide. I always look for a final frame, and the last I see is of Worm. He's standing above everyone, looking cool and mellow and full of pep, a fur-lined policeman's hat pulled low on his head, shades, his assortment of metal hoops everywhere, disco-era synthetic-fiber shirt buttoned to the top, cigar in hand, standing in a cloud of billowing techno-smoke at a bar presided over by a woman in a bra.

I am totally beat, but I know now that 82 games are not nearly enough for this almost 35-year-old youngster.

19

WHEN THE BULLS PLAY THE PISTONS IN CHICAGO ON MARCH 7, Detroit coach Doug Collins is a different man. Before the game, journalists try to get a rise out of him regarding his rivalry with Jackson, but Doug has let it all slide past, giving calm, short answers that are nothing if not circumspect and gracious.

When the writers are gone, we head to his visitors' office to talk. He has accepted the differences in the two teams, in the capricious workings of fate. He doesn't bring up his tirade of a few weeks ago, but it's plain he knows certain things are beyond his control. He got upset once; there is no percentage in doing so again.

"Michael is unguardable," he says with a smile.

And isn't that the truth. The Bulls win tonight, of course, and Jordan finishes with 53 points, 11 rebounds, 6 steals, and 2 assists. He shot 75 percent from the field, and was, indeed, unguardable.

It should have been an upbeat night all around, but there's trouble waiting for me as I enter the building and walk out onto the floor 90 minutes before game time. I see George Triantafillo, Rodman's bodyguard, and he is looking at me, shaking his head. What's wrong?

"You shouldn't have written that," he says.

"What?"

"About the other night. That was all off the record."

Dennis is very mad, he continues. And I should not have written about the two TV women who came along, the ones from *PrimeTime Live*. There are secret issues going on here, competition with other television shows, and this is all very embarrassing.

"But they gave me their cards," I say. "They're grownups."

"They weren't even with Dennis; it had nothing to do with him," George says. "They were with me."

Yeah, right, I think. If Rodman hadn't been in the group, all these people would have gone to a late-night dance barn with George? Okay, maybe I should have been less flippant about Shyra, and maybe Dwight Manley *had* said, "Don't write about this." But I assumed "this" meant Rodman's book, about which I said nothing in my column that wasn't already public knowledge. I'd figured everybody knew I was along as a journalist and not just as a sidekick. I mean, hanging out in new-wave dance clubs until 3 A.M. is not what I normally do in my spare time.

"What about the book?" says George. "You weren't supposed to write about the book."

"It's public record," I say.

To my left Ron Harper is shooting jump shots by himself. The stands are almost empty and no other players are anywhere in sight.

"You shouldn't have done that," he says, without turning his head from the basket. "The press. You can't trust the press."

Now what in hell has this got to do with *him*?

"They've been talking in the locker room," Harper says.

"Yeah, well, okay," I say, turning to George as Harper dribbles to the other side of the court to continue his warmup. I feel my blood starting to percolate. "You want to find out about real journalism? You want me to *dig*? Want me to write about the parties on the road and the girls and the hookers? I mean, I can do that."

I am steaming. I mean, Rodman posed nude for *Playboy,* flaunting the tattoos and the metal studs, and I might damage his *reputation?*

I go into the press room underneath the stands to eat my dinner. And cool my jets a few degrees.

I'm not even sure about the hookers, but it sure sounded good. You know. Heat of the moment.

■ ■ ■

Just to give you an idea of how difficult it is to read or predict the mood or future of an NBA team, consider that Sam Smith, one of the most knowledgeable NBA writers in the country, has just written, in the March 11 *Tribune,* that there is a good chance Phil Jackson will be the new head coach of the Knicks, and that Michael Jordan may be going with him. This, of course, was scary to all Bulls fans. As time would show, it wouldn't come close to occurring. More noteworthy on an immediate level was Sam's throwaway comment at the end of his piece that even though lots would be going on in the back rooms during the Bulls' upcoming roadtrip to New York and then in the summer, the game itself would be a snore. The Knicks' interim head coach, Jeff Van Gundy, taking over for the canned Don Nelson, would be unable to rouse his mutinous team, and the 54–6 Bulls would have no trouble trouncing the Knicks, who had lost their last four games against Chicago, once again. "The Knicks won't put up much of a fight Sunday," Sam wrote.

Oops. Not only do the Knicks put up a fight against the Bulls, they humble them, 104–72, manhandling them like no one has, holding them to their lowest point total this season while winning by their own largest margin of the year.

Scottie Pippen, who has been struggling since midseason with knee and ankle problems, and hurt his back when he was knocked hard to the floor against the Celtics recently, is now so battered that Jackson is forced to put him on the injured list.

This team has some real concerns despite its stellar record. Sam Smith is correct in a sense: Neither Jackson nor Jordan has a contract for next season, and they could—and probably should—be getting leverage for negotiations now by talking to other teams (technically illegal, but done by agents all the time), and perhaps by making veiled threats of leaving. None of that is good for team unity or focus, but the fact remains that Jordan is the most underpaid—salarywise—player in the history of the game. And Jackson, with his three NBA coaching rings, is the 16th-highest-paid coach, behind Bernie Bickerstaff, P. J. Carlesimo, George Karl, John Lucas, Paul Westphal, and Del Harris, among others. Moreover, Rodman is unsigned, besides always being a threat to explode, and many of the top players are just worn down by the season. Since the All-Star break, which was no break for Jordan, Pippen, Jackson, and Kerr, the Bulls have played 14 games in 27 days (6 on the road), a wearying schedule for a team with the oldest players in the league.

Age means experience and know-how, but it also means age. I find it amazing that the Bulls can, and have, put a starting lineup on the floor of Jordan, Pippen, Harper, Rodman, and Wennington, the average age of which is 33, and which has kicked the butt of much younger squads. If Jackson were feeling particularly contrary and entertaining, he could substitute the 40-year-old Edwards for the 30-year-old Pippen and have a fivesome averaging about 35 years apiece.

"I'm going to try to take advantage of the rest," says Pippen of his time on the injured list. He's basically scheduled to play basketball year-round, what with the preseason, regular season, playoffs, and then the Olympics in July.

Players are getting more and more elusive after practice, sick of the endless grilling by local, national, and international reporters. On this afternoon in mid-March at the Berto Center, even Jack Haley, who still hasn't suited up for a game and takes a pounding as a seeming hanger-on, is playing hard to get.

Dan Bernstein of WSCR Sports Radio ("the Score") scurries up to the edge of the forbidden area—the area beyond which the press may not venture—crying, "Jack! Jack!" Haley, on his way from the weight room, stops. "Can you come on the Score for a minute with Mike North and Dan Jiggetts?" asks Bernstein, microphone and tape deck in hand. "Just to clear the air?"

"No," says Haley, and walks on.

The only dependables are Kerr, Buechler, and Wennington. And you have to snare them whenever they have not slipped away with the rest of the group. Today I spot Wennington in his gaudy Zuba pants, Harley-

Davidson T-shirt, and shades. He knows I like tales of New York City playground basketball, so he tells me another story from his youth.

"So one Saturday morning, oh, maybe ten o'clock—early for a playground, you know—I'm there at the park. I walked three miles from my home. This is an all-black neighborhood, remember, and I'm the only white guy there. Hell, practically the *only* guy there. The only other people who are there are guys who have been out all night, the ones who are half out of it.

"So I'm sixteen, shooting by myself, and these three dudes come walking up to me. A little guy, and two big guys. I knew right away who the boss was, it was the little guy, and he had muscle with him. So they stand there and start working on me: Where am I from, what am I doing here, all that. I tell them I'm just here playing ball. They're drinking Colt .45s, and the little guy says, 'Let me see you dunk.' Okay. So I did. What I did was"—here Wennington demonstrates with an imaginary ball—"is I went up two-hand, behind-the-head, and jammed it, and the ball comes down fast, hits the little guy in the face, knocks his beer all over him, breaks his sunglasses, cuts his nose, and I'm thinking, 'Uh oh.'

"The two muscle guys grab me by each arm and hold me and I'm thinking, 'Yep, I'm done.' The little guy rubs his nose, looks at me, and then he says, 'Well, I *did* ask him to dunk the ball.'"

When Wennington is gone, there is not much else to report at the Bulls camp, so some of the press simply sit around and b.s. for a spell. The topic is injury list manipulation and fake injuries used by coaches to stash players and maneuver lineups. A common practice—one employed this season by the Bulls and their rotating "injured" big men—it has been refined to an art form by the most creative and shameless clubs. Bernstein comes up with the topper, we all agree; it has to do with former scrub center Keith Tower, a redhead out of Notre Dame, who played briefly with the Orlando Magic.

"He sat out a good part of the season with what was described as a 'nonhealing skin lesion,'" says Bernstein. "What happened was, in the preseason he got a bad sunburn."

■ ■ ■

On St. Patrick's Day eve, Rodman detonates. Maybe the thought of all that green coloring soon to be stirred into the Chicago River, coloring that could highlight one of his 'dos, has unhinged him. (Re color: The Bulls are so disgusted with their new black road uniforms that they have voted not to wear them again. Their normal road color is red, but they have worn black 12 times this season, as a sheer money-grab by the organization to sell more replica jerseys to kids. The Bulls are a "mere" 8–4 in the black things, while they are 18–3 in red and 30–0 in their home whites. "Dump 'em," said Steve Kerr, speaking for everyone who had to put them on, and they are being dumped.)

The Bulls had coasted past the Washington Bullets, 103–86, on March 15 in their first game without Pippen, and sailed past Denver, 108–87, in the second game without him. But now in Game 3 of Scottie's absence, at the Continental Airlines Arena (formerly the Meadowlands) against the New Jersey Nets, they witness one of their deepest fears: Rodman coming unglued.

After receiving an early technical foul for smashing the ball to the floor after the Nets' Armon Gilliam beat him for a basket, Rodman is called for a personal foul about 4 minutes later while battling with the Nets' Rick Mahorn, a former Detroit teammate of his. Rodman is discussing the call with ref Paul Mihalik, who had blown the whistle, when ref Ted Bernhardt suddenly slaps the second T, and automatic disqualification, on him. Neither of the technical fouls seemed particularly justified, but then Rodman is Rodman, and his reputation precedes him like a sonic wave. It is my firm belief, after watching Rodman for many years from court level, that most refs—the majority of whom are smallish (particularly when compared to the players around them), authoritarian white males—are terrified of him. Or more to the point, they have no common bond to aid in understanding him, and thus they are nervous as hell—and even physically fearful—when he's on the court.

At any rate, Bernhardt makes the technical sign, and Rodman loses it completely. The reason for this second one may be that Rodman put his hands in his trunks in what was pretty clearly an obscene gesture. But now the heat springs from Worm's basic sense of being wronged.

Rodman screams at Bernhardt as teammates try to stop the rampage, but he leans forward abruptly and sharply headbutts the little man, forehead to forehead. Now he's in big trouble.

He storms away, ripping off his jersey in the process, tossing it, and then knocking over a Gatorade cooler near the Nets' bench before finally leaving the floor.

Watching from the stands is NBA operations director Rod Thorn, the league's top cop, the guy who hands out suspensions and fines. After the game, reporters interview Thorn, who says curtly of the display, "After being ejected, he obviously didn't leave the court in a timely fashion." Of a possible suspension Thorn says, "If you physically make contact with a referee, that's at least a one-game suspension."

Rodman knows what's up. He goes into full world-against-me mode. "It was an accidental headbutt," he says of the blatantly deliberate smack he gave Bernhardt. "I was shocked I was kicked out."

Rodman had just 4 rebounds and no points in his 10 minutes acourt. And his departure could not have come at a worse time for the Bulls, who are already minus Pippen and have reserve power forward Dickey Simpkins legitimately on the injured list. Just a few days ago, Jordan had said that everybody was aware of Rodman's tendency to explode, but observed, "If he was going to go off the deep end, then it would be during the regular season. But I don't see that happening. I think he's very comfortable. He's happy in Chicago and he's respected in Chicago, and I think he sees the success of this team and how he fits in." Just shows that even the World's Best doesn't know everything.

And this all comes after Rodman, the league leader in technicals (now with 25), was tossed from the recent Milwaukee Bucks game for committing a "Type 2" flagrant foul on Bucks guard Sherman Douglas as he attempted a breakaway layup. The *Tribune*'s headline after that game was "Rodman's Blood Boiling." And it comes after he dived for a loose ball that was far out of bounds in a game three days ago against the Bullets, landed on a photographer's camera, and threw an expensive telephoto lens to the floor in outrage. The anger was perhaps understandable, since photographers do work the floor very close to the out-of-bounds line, putting them in the path of a scrambler like Rodman, but, typically, Worm's over-the-top response took him from being a potentially sympathetic character to a juvenile, self-centered one. When asked whether he might buy the photographer a new lens, Rodman scoffed, "Hell no. I ain't buying him nothing."

Phil Jackson talked to Rodman after viewing the tape of that incident and told him, "You know we don't need that. There's no place for it on the court."

Then, too, there was the way he reacted to his embarrassing scene in the Nets game, making it worse by giving vent to angry paranoia rather than expressing remorse. "The referees in this league pick on me," he said. "I'm picked on every game. They're gonna suspend me no matter what. Suspend me. Make an example out of Dennis Rodman. I don't care. It's getting ridiculous, picking on me every damn game."

In a display of off-base bravado, he even trashed Thorn, ripping the man whose empathy he needed most, saying, "Rod Thorn isn't even man enough to talk to me." But the part that had to make everyone question whether Rodman was just clueless or plumb crazy was when he said, "I'm gonna be the guinea pig for everything on the court. Why am I so different than the rest of the league?" Why indeed?

The immediate upshot of the whole mess was that Michael Jordan had to crank up his routine one more notch that night in New Jersey and handle Scottie's and Worm's duties in addition to his own. Which he did, leading the Bulls to a 97–93 victory. He played 43 minutes, more than any of his teammates, and scored a game-high 37 points, yanked down a game-high 16 rebounds, and also had 4 assists, 3 blocked shots, and no turnovers.

I sat in my office on the day after the blowup, Sunday, March 17, and studied a book I had read previously: *Bodies Under Siege: Self-Mutilation in Culture and Psychiatry* by Dr. Armando R. Favazza, professor and associate chairman of the Department of Psychiatry, University of Missouri School of Medicine.

It is not a pleasant tome to digest, and there is no chapter on Dennis Rodman per se, but as I leafed through it again I felt that much within it could be used to shed some light, however refracted, on the unusual and often self-destructive behavior of the Bulls' rebounding prodigy.

Multiple tattoos (particularly those of graphic or antisocial content) and extensive body-piercings are examples of self-mutilation, Favazza writes; self-mutilating acts "are coping mechanisms ultimately adaptive to sustaining life." The people who do these things (or have them done) to themselves are generally people who have had painful upbringings, who received "inadequate supplies of parental love, nurturance, and comforting physical contact," and who as children experienced "a sense of abandonment, of loneliness, and of unlovability." Anyone who has read any of Rodman's biographical material knows that he qualifies on all counts.

The defacing of one's body, Favazza writes, becomes an act that enables one "to gain sympathetic response from other persons, correct negative self-perceptions and alleviate feelings of self-hatred . . . ventilate anger, and provide euphoria and relief from feelings of alienation."

Is all this more insight than we need into a man who is, after all, just a basketball player? No, because Bulls fans want to understand this superlative athlete, this potential world-beater with the long history of self-contempt and self-destruction. His detonation against the Nets came at an unlikely time. And that may have been no accident.

I ask Dwight Manley, Rodman's agent, about all this. He acknowledged that things had never been better for Rodman than they were prior to the headbutt.

"His mom was at the Denver game in Chicago, and he gave his jersey to her," says Manley, who is abandoning a California vacation and flying to the Bulls' next game, in Philadelphia, to help Rodman regain his footing and avoid an even worse tumble. "They posed for a picture for *Life* magazine and it was wonderful. He hasn't been in a better frame of mind since the Pistons won the first championship. I mean, things have never been better."

Which may, I suggest, be why he blew up.

"He apologizes to the fans of Chicago," Manley says. "He boiled over. Perhaps Dennis was making a statement because Rod Thorn was there. I don't know that yet." I tell Manley I'm an eensy little bit skeptical about the happy spin he's putting on everything.

"I'm very aware of the situation," he says. "And that is why I'm going there, because going forward, everything is going to be fine. If I have to be with him every day for the rest of the season, just to deal with the bad stuff and keep him focused, I will. But he knows what he's doing and he's very remorseful right now."

I'm not sure I buy that. But I do know that this is the time Rodman and the Bulls and their Faustian bargain will be put to the test. This is where behavior and ego and tolerance and leadership and embarrassment all converge. How the Bulls and their black sheep handle the stretch run for the NBA title will be something to behold.

■ ■ ■

On Monday March 18 the verdict comes down. Guilty.

Rod Thorn and the NBA nail Rodman with a six-game suspension and a $20,000 fine. He will also be docked $183,000 in pay for the missed games. Rodman now is becoming the homewrecker all his critics said he would become. He is the imp who can't use good manners at the family dinner table, even as the holiday feast is being served. Nor is his victim pose working. As NBC's Bill Walton told *USA Today,* accurately, "Dennis is trying to paint himself as the victim who the league's out to get. The league wants nothing more than for Rodman to be great."

The truth behind what Walton is saying is that the NBA thrives on characters, not necessarily character. Flash and weirdness work well in big arenas and in quick TV bites. Rodman's posturing and appearance are no different from those of many, if not most, rock stars; he can bring a lot of kids and Generation Xers to the game. Total anarchy, though, doesn't work in music or sport.

20

CRAIG SAGER FROM TNT GETS MY ATTENTION. IT'S MARCH 19, Tuesday. We're at the Berto Center after practice, waiting for Rodman or someone—anyone—to come out. Just around the corner from where we're standing, we can hear voices. It's Phil Jackson, Rodman, Dwight Manley, and I suppose Jack Haley, since I saw him duck around the corner.

"I'd like you to see a doctor," Jackson is saying.

"No," says Rodman, who had entered wearing a large Mad Hatter's hat. "It's over and done with."

"The doctor is one of our people," Jackson says. "Whatever happens will remain private."

In time everyone leaves, and no one has anything much to say to the press. Rodman has issued a public apology that reads in part:

> To Chicago Bulls fans and my teammates:
>   I want to apologize publicly for my actions on Saturday, March 16. I was wrong in making contact with any NBA official and I deserved to be punished for my actions, although I do believe they [the penalties] are severe. I realize that the NBA referees are doing their jobs and it's my job to respect them and the rules of the game. . . . Chicago Bulls fans and my teammates have treated me with great warmth and acceptance and I realize I let them down. . . . My sole aim from now until late June will be to help bring the NBA championship back home to Chicago.

Great humility, great damage control, great phoniness; it reeks of Manley the manipulator. Some members of the press cynically were asking whether Rodman could even spell the words used. Making it particularly suspicious is what Rodman had said just a few hours earlier on his paid morning radio show on WMVP, when he was his normal, why-is-everybody-out-to-get-me self: "It's very hard for me to change," he said of his behavior and the league's censorship of it. "It's like saying, You have to change the way you are to be accepted in the league. I haven't done anything different than I've been doing the last ten years. . . . What am I doing in the game that no one else is doing?"

I wait.

In time, Phil Jackson invites me up to his office for a chat. He knows about the book I'm working on, and he seems bemused that someone else is trying to assimilate the unique qualities of this season. I look around his office, which is different from just about any coach's office I have seen. Phil's leather Bulls jacket is on a chair. Books by various new-age philosophers are on the shelves, along with basketballs, one with an Indian headdress on it, photos of a younger Phil with June and the five kids, a photo of Phil with his old high school teammates on a ranch in Montana. There is a Deadhead sticker on a lamp, and in front of me on Phil's desk is a little box of sand with six pebbles in it and a tiny rake. Nearby is a rattlesnake skin, which one of Jackson's buddies acquired when he and Phil encountered its original owner on a hike. The friend killed, slit, and stripped the snake so fast, Jackson remembers, that the white, headless, and skinless body was still breathing on the ground as the men walked away. "My friend cured the skin in antifreeze and sent it to me," Jackson says.

He sits leaning back in his chair in jeans, a cut-off Bulls sweatshirt, white socks and black loafers, glasses, and a baseball cap with a triangle logo. He bounces a small rubber ball on his desk. Behind him is a large window that looks down on the court. As I look at the coach, I see a bird fly past.

"It's a dove," he says, spinning around. "It's been here two days. We're trying to get it out somehow. It's going to die unless it gets out. They partner for life, so its mate is somewhere. It's sad." He explains the different techniques he has been using to get the bird out. Then we turn to Rodman.

"He's waiting for failure, planning failure, because of his personality," Jackson says. "He's got self-worth problems, his image of himself."

So what can a coach do?

"You try to put him in a situation where he can help himself. Clubs have sent him to psychologists and psychiatrists—he went in Detroit, I don't know about San Antonio. These are professional helpers. When we did Dennis's agreement I talked to his therapist, so I'm aware of his problems. And one of his basic characteristics is goodness, the good side to Dennis."

I mention that in certain ways Rodman reminds me of a not malicious but self-centered, insecure, and self-indulgent 13-year-old. Jackson smiles, brings his hand to chest level and points his thumb at the floor.

"Twelve years old?" I ask.

He points downward.

"Eleven? Ten?"

Keep going.

"Eight?" I say. "Six?"

The coach smiles and shakes his head. More, his thumb indicates.

"Five? Four?"

Jackson's smile has always been one that causes his eyes to squint virtually shut.

"Three," I state, refusing to go lower.

He nods. That, says the coach, is the age at which, in certain basic developmental procedures, Rodman is stuck. Could it be he doesn't like himself enough to feel worthy of receiving good things?

"It's a conundrum," Jackson admits. "No doubt about it. Dennis and I have touched on that. I've said, 'I'm not going to pretend to know all this stuff, but I do know that you're waiting for the next shoe to drop. And it doesn't have to drop.'"

"What does he say to that?"

"Dennis doesn't want to show his feelings, and when you force him to make responses, his statements are lucid but jumbled. He says them in a slurring manner. They're kind of offbeat, as you well know. He's much more conversational with reporters than he is with friends or colleagues. Because he doesn't want to look at you when you're addressing him, a lot of times he won't look at you, and what he says is all asides. I think he has come to a point where he at least understands *something* about his nature. It's not like a mystery to him. Having dealt with I don't know how many sessions he's been to, whether it's ten or sixteen or twelve, he's got some appreciation.

"I've introduced him to our [club] therapist. He knows him. I've encouraged him to go see him. Dennis doesn't think there's a need for one."

The phone rings. "This must be the guy," he says, meaning the Bulls' therapist. I had already agreed to wait out in the foyer while Jackson took the call, and that's where I head now. Five minutes later, he calls me back inside.

"This therapist works for our organization, and we have a real good relationship with him," Jackson says. "He understands Dennis very well. He's gotten copies of the stuff from the other therapists. And he says that Dennis can get fixated on one thing, like the persecution thing, and he'll see himself being singled out by the league, and it can start things going the wrong way. He said Dennis does a lot of projecting, like a kid lying in his bed listening to rock music, saying everybody's ignoring him, and yet he's loving it. Dennis does that kind of stuff. Juvenile fixation."

A high that would have to be pursued again: Scottie and Michael with the "3-Peat" trophy in 1993. (Phil Velasquez/*Sun-Times*)

For nearly a year and a half, Jordan tried to make it in a sport ill-suited to his unique skills. (Phil Velasquez/*Sun-Times*)

Jordan's return from his strange baseball journey ended badly when Nick Anderson and the Orlando Magic embarrassed MJ and the Bulls in the 1995 Eastern Conference playoffs. (Phil Velasquez/*Sun-Times*)

Orlando fans didn't know it during the 1995 playoffs, but a taunted Jordan is a *dangerous* Jordan. (Tom Cruze/*Sun-Times*)

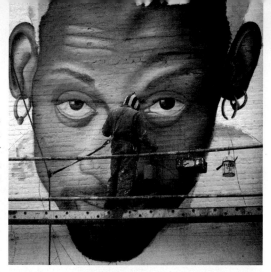

Welcome to Chicago! Dennis Rodman's likeness on the Bigsby & Kruthers billboard was too much for commuters and was quickly taken down. (Phil Velasquez/*Sun-Times*)

Preppyish Dwight Manley met Rodman at a Las Vegas craps table and is now the mastermind behind the Worm's commercial assault on the world. (Phil Velasquez/*Sun-Times*)

The best-dressed cheerleader in town: Jack Haley roots his team-mates on, eagerly awaiting his own seven minutes of playing time that would come at the very end of the 1995–96 season. (Tom Cruze/*Sun-Times*)

NBA coach as Jerry
Garcia lookalike: Phil
Jackson, the perfect
chef for a crazy stew.
(Richard A. Chapman/
Sun-Times)

Zen general Phil Jackson and lieutenants (from left) Cleamons, Rodgers, Paxson. (Phil
Velasquez/*Sun-Times*)

The most unlikely Bull
celebrates a most unlikely
occurrence—a Dennis
Rodman basket. (Phil
Velasquez/*Sun-Times*)

A compassionate warrior no-no: ostentatious display. This chest-thump after a Pippen
halfcourt 3-pointer against the Cavs earned Pippen a team fine. (Phil Velasquez/*Sun-Times*)

Payback: The author (in Hawaiian shorts and cheap shoes) drives past the loud-mouth trash talker in a one-on-one death match. (Taken from a SportsChannel video.)

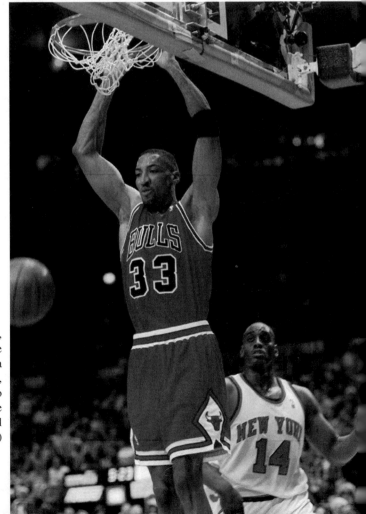

"I'm the Vice President, not the President." The greatest second banana in the game, Pippen, delivers his message to Anthony Mason and the New York Knicks. (Phil Velasquez/*Sun-Times*)

Cake in the mouth, nose, eyes, and ears—Rodman acts the fool and risks tearing apart the stampeding Bulls. (*Sun-Times*)

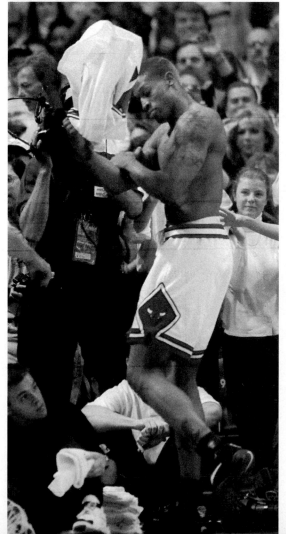

A Rodman jersey give-away provides fans with a chance to read the man's body language. (Tom Cruze/*Sun-Times*)

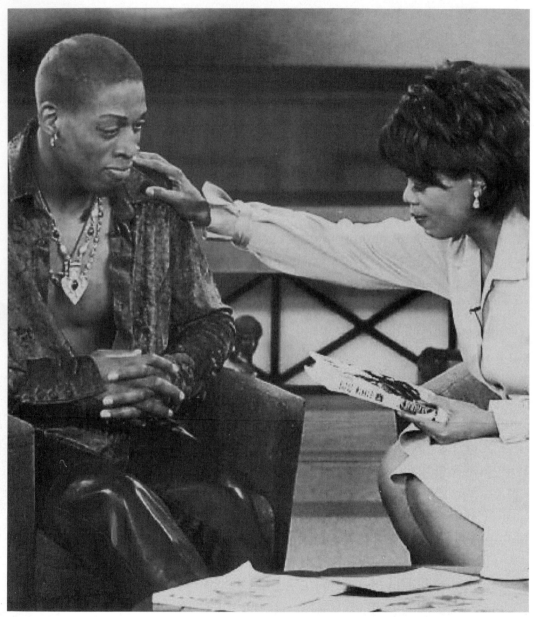

Lights, camera, tear ducts: Oprah squeezes a magic TV moment from the sensitive clown prince. (*Sun-Times*)

Steady, heady Ron Harper battles John Starks of the New York Knicks for a loose ball. (Tom Cruze/*Sun-Times*)

"Produce 'em!" says an angry Patrick Ewing to taunting Bulls assistant coach Jim Cleamons—as a ref, Luc Longley, and Phil Jackson stand in his way. (Bob Ringham/*Sun-Times*)

The Worm displays that special rebounding thing against the hated Knicks. (Phil Velasquez/*Sun-Times*)

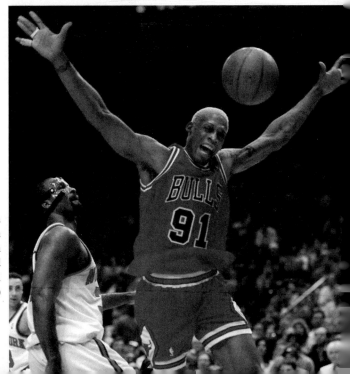

An acting career begins on the court: Rodman flops in horror after a shove from thuggish Knicks forward Charles Oakley. (Phil Velasquez/*Sun-Times*)

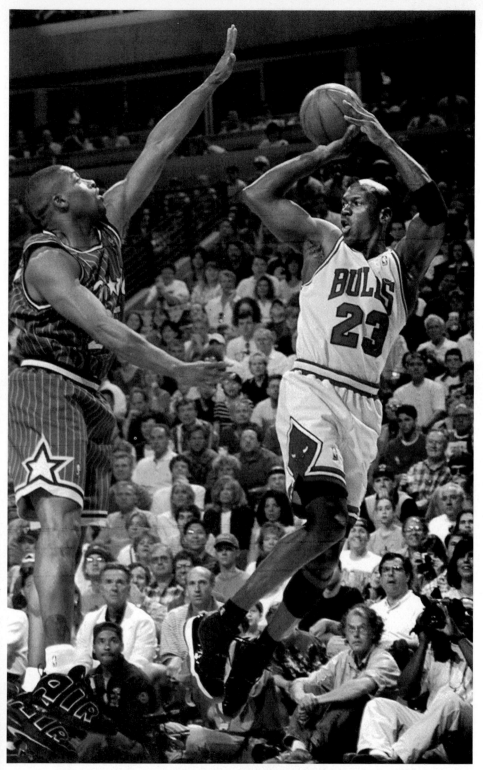
You can't touch this: Jordan's perfected fallaway. (Phil Velasquez/*Sun-Times*)

Jordan receives his fourth MVP Award from NBA Coach of the Year Phil Jackson. (Al Podgorski/*Sun-Times*)

Kukoc bounces back from back pain against the Magic. (Phil Velasquez/*Sun-Times*)

Seattle's Gary Payton, the NBA Defensive Player of the Year, made a mistake when he got in Jordan's face. (Pablo Martinez Monsivais/*Sun-Times*)

Scrub love. Subs James Edwards, Randy Brown, Bill Wennington, and Jud Buechler celebrate their 1996 Eastern Conference championship. (Phil Velasquez/*Sun-Times*)

Jordan works a ref hard. (Phil Velasquez/*Sun-Times*)

Uh-oh. The Sonics show up for Game 4 to spoil the sweep. (Phil Velasquez/*Sun-Times*)

The Cigar Rules. Steve Kerr celebrates fame, fortune, and the return of his shot with a nasty tobacco stick in the Bulls' championship locker room. (Phil Velasquez/*Sun-Times*)

You scratch my back, I'll scratch yours. Jordan and Pippen in ecstasy after clinching title number 4. (*Sun-Times*)

"So what are you supposed to do?" I ask. "Can you give him something, a buzzword, a look, or have something like a dummy on the sidelines and say, when things are going bad, 'Dennis, come here and kick this'?"

"Last week I started this 'Bohica' thing with him," Phil says, nodding. "'Every time you get a bad call, say this to yourself. It's something you can use.'"

I had read about that in the papers, though none of the writers seemed to have any idea what it was all about. My *Sun-Times* colleague Mariotti thought the word was "Mohica" and had something to do with Indians. What it is is an acronym for *Bend Over Here It Comes Again.* Not too highbrow, but it helps Rodman understand that getting screwed is part of life. Or it was supposed to. He had his Bohica mantra before the headbutt.

"It's not working, so I'm going to give him something else. I told him I'd give him a rubber band that he should just snap to get his mind back on track."

The coach bounces his ball a few more times. Right now, he explains, he's just trying to be pragmatic. "I mean, Dennis knows, if he fucks up again, no one's gonna risk another fuck-up chance. If he didn't do it in the best situation possible for him, how's he gonna do it in a tough situation? There's a contract sitting out there waiting for him at the end of the rainbow. If things work out for him, there is so much to be gained. And there's so much to be lost if he screws up. He's never been able to stay focused, ever. He throws it away, because he feels he's not worth it. He shouldn't make more than a plumber, he feels. He feels he's a low-class bum.

"He told me this is the first year he's been able to make money, and he said the endorsements are coming in hand over fist. He said that in the last month alone he's gotten over a million dollars in endorsements. So there's all kinds of pressure on him, on his self-esteem."

"Getting somebody to feel they're worthy of good things sounds so simple," I say, thinking how convoluted the human mind is. "Like telling an anorexic, 'Just eat!'"

Jackson nods. "Very true," he says.

Did he know what he was getting into back in October?

"Oh yeah," he says matter-of-factly. "I had an awareness of it all. I told Dennis, 'There's so much more pressure with playoff games. TV games. We'll work with you, if you work with us. We'll try to get you through this situation.' But we have to provide for the team to play regardless of whether he can contribute or not."

Which brings us to Michael Jordan. How's he handling this confusion, which could be looked at, in a sense, as betrayal?

"Michael's handling it well," Jackson says. "He's taking it all well, including Scottie's demise. He knows that Scottie's gonna give as much as he can. Scottie was shooting fifty percent and averaging twenty-three a game, and since these injuries, he's shooting thirty-eight percent. He's pulling up. He couldn't make a layup. It was all in his feet at first, then it went to his knees and then his back, and then he sprained his ankle. But Michael is just so tough.

"He's—" and here Phil pauses to think. "He's relentless. He wants to play eighty-two games. He wants to be there for every game."

We talk awhile about rebounding, something Jordan must do seriously while Rodman is out. Jackson acknowledges that if he put Jordan at small forward and told him to attack the boards, Jordan would lead the league in rebounding.

"He's the best free-throw-line rebounder I've ever seen. Rebounding our own balls, from the second slot. It's an amazing process, to watch him play. Last night, he had a terrible half [against the 76ers]. He came to the locker room and said, 'I feel pretty good about this game. It's been a struggle, but we're not gonna shoot any worse than we shot in the first half. So we're gonna win.' I said, 'But Mike, you gotta pick your spots.' He said, 'Aw, I can't hit the broad side of a barn. But I'll find a way to get it done.' His third quarter wasn't great, but at some point in the fourth he started going. He wouldn't let me take him out. I said, 'Come on out.' He said, 'No, no, no, I'm fine.'"

This, of course, was another Bulls win, a close one, 98–94, in which Jordan played 47 of 48 minutes, filling in again for both Pippen and Rodman. He finished with 38 points and 11 rebounds. If anyone wanted to know what difference Jordan makes for the team, all they had to do was watch this game.

"I took him out in the first quarter for a minute," Jackson says. "A little more than a minute, figuring I'd give him a little rest. So with him out, we lost six points. In that amount of time. That was his break for the night."

The Bulls have a game tonight, against the Sacramento Kings. Back to back. So Jordan was supposed to rest last night even more than normal. But he wouldn't allow it. Jackson explains how he runs all kinds of substitution patterns and "midrange" timeouts, just to keep Jordan from getting exhausted.

What about conditioning, particularly for Scottie when he returns? "These guys are so amazing, all they need is a day to get their shooting touch," Jackson says. "Sometimes they can step in and be *right there*. Michael doesn't need training camp. Who do we have training camp for? For exhibition games. To make money. I mean, Scottie two or three years ago missed training camp, had an operation on his ankle, missed the first trip west, came back, had one day of practice, and [trainer] Chip Schaefer is saying, 'Wait another week,' and Scottie has thirty-seven against Phoenix in his first game back. The guy hadn't even played."

"What's their body fat?" I ask.

"Michael's is five."

I ponder that awhile. My nose has 5 percent body fat. I switch the topic to Phil's success, telling him I'm amazed that he has 400 wins in just seven years of coaching.

"I am too," he says. "Seems like I just went by three hundred. But we're not making seventy wins our focus, we're just trying to win every game. All of a sudden we're under twenty games till the end of the season. And we're fifty games over .500."

"You go twelve–five and you win seventy," I say.

"Which is reachable, even with an injured team," he says. "These guys come with the attitude of, How do we solve tonight's problem? They're experienced enough that they say, 'Okay, Mitch Richmond is a scorer; who else is going to beat us tonight on this particular ball club?' They make everybody else on that team play above their heads to win."

He does have serious concerns, though, beyond Rodman's mindset. "Luc was playing some really outrageous ball," he praises. "Until

Friday night, when he hit a wall. And he can't react. It's like he's stuck in mud two feet deep."

Phil mentions how he confers with Jordan about everything involving the team, from Rodman's difficulties to "press demands that seem like they might be a problem." But he can't stop thinking about Rodman, even laughing about Worm's singularity.

"That's not a Mad Hatter's hat," he says. "It's a Cat in the Hat hat. In New York he had a court jester's hat on. It was *ridiculous*." He shakes his head. "You just don't give up on him."

21

DWIGHT MANLEY CALLS.

He wants to know what's going on, and I tell him I know Dennis is supposed to see a shrink.

"How do you know that?" he asks, upset.

"I know lots of things."

"You overheard Phil and Dennis and me talking."

I am fascinated by this Manley guy and even, oddly, drawn to him for the remarkable way he has taken his sole client from the outhouse to the penthouse, at least as far as offcourt opportunities are concerned. But I'm not getting bullied by him, because, as I like to say, what has he done for me?

"I don't need to tell you how I found out anything," I say.

Manley says I need to be gentle with his client, that Rodman is fragile and could be easily hurt if I just start blabbing out all the private things I know about him.

I keep thinking back to that very public scrotum ring. And what about the public "apology" Rodman just sent out? "Like he really wrote that, huh, Dwight?" I say.

"That *is* how he feels," says Manley sincerely. "Maybe those aren't his words exactly. But he does think the refs do a great job, and he thinks they're vastly underpaid, too. His questions are directed at the league. If only they knew the real him—he's such a gentle, passive guy."

Stop. I'm starting to melt. I know there is some truth in what Manley is saying. Like the schticks of so many rebellious pop figures who catch our eye, part of Worm's act does spring from true alienation and psychic pain. But part springs from pure manipulation. It all gets blurred as the act progresses, until even the rebel himself has no idea what's what.

But he is gentle. Consider that yesterday, unbeknownst to the world at large, Jerry Krause's beloved dog, Poppy, died. Who was the only Bull to send Krause $100 worth of flowers and a sympathy card? Well, OK, it was Manley who had ordered them, at his client's request. Coincidentally—or perhaps not—Krause received the flowers just as he was talking on the phone to Rodman and Manley, who were on a speaker phone. This was just after the league had informed the Bulls of the impending suspension. Krause, the horned toad with the soft underbelly, was truly touched by the bouquet, and he began crying. "I love you," he said to the Rodman–Manley combo.

"I was crying, Dennis was crying," Manley admits now. "Jerry broke down and we had to discontinue the call."

■ ■ ■

I'm feeling burned out for reasons I can't discern. I'm not depressed, just hopelessly lost in a world I seem to have entered the way a hotel guest on the way to his room accidentally wanders into a wedding reception in the Regency Ballroom and suddenly it's 3 A.M. and he's dazed and dancing with the mother-in-law.

I wander into the Bulls locker room at the United Center on April 4 an hour or so after the Bulls have waxed the Miami Heat by a score the numbers of which I don't recall. They just beat this same Heat team two days ago in Miami in a rout, 110–92, so what difference does it make? They'll probably play the Heat in the first round of the playoffs and thrash them then, too. Isn't 64–8 a ridiculous record? I could swear some of these games were played earlier in the year and are simply being rebroadcast.

I bump into an unusually tall Japanese man. I look at his face. It's Los Angeles Dodgers pitcher Hideo Nomo. Why shouldn't he be in the Bulls locker room? I ask myself. At some point everybody is.

Nomo and Jordan shake hands and, with the aid of an interpreter, a rather plain Japanese woman, the two men discuss baseball and joke about forkballs and Michael's minor league career. Jordan, in a quiet show of kindness and inclusion that is typical of his people skills, has very naturally put his arm around the interpreter, something nobody has noticed but something that she'll remember, perhaps for all time.

Some photos are taken by Bill Smith; Jordan says he'd like one, please, and then he leaves, the jet trail of friends and sycophants and media hopefuls following behind. Nomo stands alone in the locker room for a moment. Nobody cares about him.

In the hallway I run into Philip Knight, the founder and brains and chutzpah of Nike. Between him and Jordan, they have sold so many shoes to so many people that the distinction between sport and fashion has been permanently blurred. I figured something must be up, and when I ask Knight what that might be, he says vaguely that Jordan and the Japanese market are a natural mix. Something about a summer tour to Japan. Nomo, of course, is a Nike guy. So he'll be going along, too.

I look at Knight, a bearded, unobtrusive if nervous-seeming middle-aged man in casual clothes and a pair of beat-up, non–Air Jordan Nike running shoes. Is it possible that Nike, the great, ruthless empire, actually started out with this guy selling his products in the Pacific Northwest from the trunk of his car? "Your shoes look a little battered," I say.

"They're comfortable," he says, smiling but keeping everything else close to the vest.

Then he adds, "We sell the new ones."

■ ■ ■

Rodman is back, and so far so good. He is taking his medicine well, being a good boy oncourt. It is early April. The Bulls are 66–8. Longley is out for a while with his knee tendinitis problem, but the mighty Bulls steamroller rolls on.

One thing you realize after a time as a sportswriter is that the clichés are true. The best teams do play them one game at a time. Why? Because planning too far ahead leads to scattered thinking. Players do need focus; they do need intensity; and they must have team chemistry—that rare blending and sublimation of parts that can lead to an entirely new compound. But most of all they must want it.

Tonight, April 8, against the Charlotte Hornets the Bulls are weary, bored, and seemingly just going through the motions. They beat the Hornets in Charlotte three nights ago, by 34 points, after taking a 73–74 halftime lead. Tonight, they take a 15-point lead, watch the Hornets' best player, Larry Johnson, go out with a wrist injury, and then blow it to go down by 3 at the end of three quarters.

It's one of those nights when you realize that basketball is a funny game, a game of chance, that there are times when a nobody such as the Hornets' Matt Geiger can find the winds of fate blowing his way. The shaved-headed Geiger, looking like a pirate with a murderous attitude, hits two 3-pointers in a row, and suddenly the Bulls are down 84–72, with only part of the fourth quarter left to play. Then they start a comeback. Kerr hits a 3. Kukoc makes a layup off a lob feed. Harper gets a layup. Jordan dunks to cut Charlotte's lead to 84–81.

But here come the Hornets again, behind guard Kenny Anderson. The Bulls miss 5 free throws in a row, Jordan himself missing 4 of them. Finally, he makes a free throw, to make it a 3-point game with 90 seconds to play. He makes another—a 2-point game.

In the big picture, this is a meaningless contest. The Bulls already have everything they need wrapped up. They would *like* to win all 41 home games this season, to beat the Celtics' record of 40–1 in a season, but if they don't, so what? The NBA title is the plum.

However, the Bulls do want this game. Sleepy as they are, they want it. Out of habit. So they give the ball to Jordan and clear out. He scores 2 more free throws, his 39th and 40th points, to tie the game at 96. Harper makes a free throw and the Bulls take a 1-point lead. But the Hornets' Dell Curry gets clobbered and sinks both his free throws for a 98–97 Charlotte lead. The Bulls call time out with 9.8 seconds remaining.

The ball comes in and Kukoc puts up a driving layup that barely rims out. The Bulls are in a frenzy; this is the kind of game that could be a precursor of the playoffs. Lose this, and who knows? Rodman tips the ball. Jordan rises over everyone to grab the rebound, shoots, and misses. Pippen fires and the ball bounces out yet again. It is tracked down by

Kerr, who picks it up and then is clobbered by a Hornet as time expires. Of course no foul is called, although Kerr was crushed. He's Steve Kerr, and he's never going to get that call.

The Bulls lose their ninth game of the season, 98–97. The game was more exciting than most of their wins. But above all, as Jackson says afterward, it was an "okay" game to lose.

■ ■ ■

Randy Brown doesn't play much, but he knows what's up. "We were real frustrated against Charlotte," he says a few days later. The point he's trying to make to me is that no matter what it looks like to spectators, these games are hard. And all of the Bulls' opponents are doing their damnedest to win.

"There are some teams that just aren't that talented, and it looks like they're not trying," he says. "But they are. Like that first game against Charlotte [the blowout win]. Pete Myers is my good friend, and he told me before the game that they wanted it bad, and he said, 'Damn, we need this!' It was a big game for them. There. And we jump out to a twenty-to-nothing lead."

He shrugs. Explain that.

He's part of this team, but it's a mystery to him, too.

"We knew we were good in training camp, but not this good. Who knew Michael was going to have a season like this? And Kukoc and Dennis. And Ron Harper is a guy who has really done well. A lot of people thought he was washed up." This is true. Harper was brought in as a free agent for a lot of money in 1994, after Jordan left, to be the new Jordan. But he couldn't do it. His rebirth as a defensive stalwart and fourth option on offense is one of the surprise stories of the season.

Brown, like at least half a dozen other members of this team, is being pulled along by the inexorable force of good fortune and good timing. He walks down the streets of Chicago, his hometown, like a regular citizen. "Maybe two or three people out of a hundred will notice me," he says. "And a lot of them think I'm Jason Caffey." He often muses about Michael Jordan and his separate world. "I'm sure he would like to be me, just be normal," he says. "I don't ask him, but I'm pretty sure. Just for a day."

■ ■ ■

The Rodman Suspension and Return has had a ripple effect. It has made it possible for the Bulls to keep Kukoc in the starting lineup. He broke in when Pippen was out for five games, then he stayed in all through Worm's headbutting penalty, and in the seven games that Rodman has been back, Kukoc has not been demoted to sixth man, which makes him very happy. The Bulls have done well with Kukoc starting and Rodman's demotion to substitute. And just as important as the way Kukoc has responded to being a starter—with increased productivity (points up from 11 to 20, rebounds from 4 to 5, assists from 3 to 5)—is the way Rodman has handled his reserve role: with almost no complaining.

By returning and not going nuts, and coming off the bench to play an undersize pivotman's position without bitching, by not letting questionable calls against him rattle his cage, he has made his star rise even higher in the Chicago sky. This is a city that loves to embrace misunderstood prodigies, to open its arms to hardworking, two-fisted, lunchbucket-type heroes (even ones in eye shadow). But don't mess with that work ethic. And don't betray that trust.

April 12: The Bulls have just pulverized the 76ers, 112–82, with Rodman, having served his penance, now being allowed to start again because Longley is out with knee tendinitis once more. Rodman's face on the Bigsby & Kruthers billboard, which is actually all three sides of a building along the Kennedy Expressway, was so disconcerting to commuters when it was put up a few days ago that massive traffic jams were occurring on both sides of the highway near Armitage Avenue as people slowed, and even stopped, to gawk at the huge likeness with the bright red dome of hair rising above the building like half a playground ball. Now instead of Rodman in his torn-off-sleeved sportcoat and tie, there is just a white wall with the words "Resume Speed 55" painted on it. It is amazing how far his mere looks can go as an entertainment gimmick.

Tonight he appears in hot pink hair, which has been done, he says, out of sympathy for the cause of the Y-ME foundation, the national breast cancer charity. Now even Worm's hair is rooted in goodness. (Thank you, Mr. Manley.) But in the postgame locker room Rodman is nowhere to be found. And so the throng around Jordan swells to ludicrous proportions.

As I stand listening and asking the usual reporter's questions, I feel a slight pushing at my kidney level. Wedged in, I turn around in place and look down. Three young girls are there. Maybe 10 or 11 years old. All in black Rodman jerseys. What's this? I'm used to the network aggressors and the celebs and the deal-makers pushing to see Michael. But not this. I pivot a bit more, not wanting to lose my spot in the stew, and there I see Jerry Reinsdorf and his fellow White Sox investor Jerry Einhorn and another suit, all of them grinning away. These are their daughters or granddaughters or nieces.

Well, I've heard enough from Michael. He already told me the Bulls will get their 70 wins and then "we'll get some rest from you guys," us media pests. So, okay, let's call it a night. I make a tunnel for the girls by turning sideways and keeping my arm extended with my tape recorder out. The girls step forward toward the altar. Their eyes are huge. They are barely breathing. One has her hands over her face. One of them whispers, "Oh . . . my . . . God." I have seen nothing like this since looking at that 1965 newsreel of girls at Shea Stadium approaching the Fab Four. Danny Ainge is right: The Bulls *are* the Beatles of today.

■ ■ ■

Worm has handled his punishment well, but now he is getting *out there*. On his weekly Channel 5 TV show on Sunday night after NBA-record-tying win number 69, he wears sunglasses, a black pimp hat, a red, iridescent, clingy, long-sleeved disco shirt, and a large black feather boa and minces about like an effeminate pro wrestler. He says he would like to play Miami in the playoffs, rather than Charlotte, because South Beach "makes me feel exuberant, alive, and vibrant."

He watches himself on tape, throwing a long pass to Jordan for a bucket. "Can you say, 'Greg Maddux'?" he asks with a lisp. He pats the boa into place. Kelly asks him about Cleveland, their victim tonight, as a potential playoff foe.

"They suck," says Worm.

22

MILWAUKEE.

Everybody on the planet knows the Bulls are going for their 70th win tonight, April 16.

And what can stop them?

I have driven the 75 miles north to this gritty Wisconsin city, gotten here early, and stopped at a bar on Kilbourne Street to visit with some friends before they and half the city head over to the game. At 6 o'clock, I leave the group and walk over to the Bradley Center, past the mobs, in through the press gate, and then directly into the Bulls locker room, where I stop to talk with the trainer, Chip Schaefer, who is keeping these guys together as best he can. A couple of days before, I'd asked him about the Bulls' overall condition and he had replied, "They're doing pretty good, about what you'd expect for a team after this many games. At other stadiums, I ask ballboys for sixteen bags of ice, and they look at me, and I say, 'We *do* have the oldest team in the league.'"

The security is nothing here. The locker room is small, almost like a high school's. The Bucks are terrible—24–54 coming in—and until tonight, there hasn't been much cause to get excited here in Beer City.

As I walked into the arena I was handed a printout from the Bucks PR staff, advising me of the glut of humanity expected for the game:

Dear Members of the Fourth Estate:

As is readily apparent by a quick look around you, tonight's Bucks/Bulls game is probably the most heavily attended event by media this NBA season outside of the All-Star Weekend.

This game was an announced sellout last October on the opening day of ticket sales. Press credentials issued for this event number between four- and five-hundred. . . . We have worked to accommodate our friends in the media. . . . However, despite our best efforts, it is a physical impossibility to accommodate everyone desiring to cover tonight's game with a seat in the main bowl.

Many of you will have to watch tonight's game from either the press room or the inner west atrium. . . .

Television feeds of both the game and the post game press conference are being made available by satellite as well as a distribution amplifier feed provided by Trio Video. . . . The post game press conference can be accessed on Telstar 401, transponder 21, audio 6.2 and 6.8. The feed time will begin at 9:30 P.M. and conclude at 11:00 P.M. A "pool" camera will cover the press conference.

There was more, but I didn't care. I had my seat.

I walk over to Randy Brown, who is sitting in front of his locker, and say hi to him. I ask him about the homemade tattoos on his arms. The one on his left forearm says "Randy"; another shows a basketball going through a crudely drawn hoop and net. He shrugs sheepishly.

"Did them when I was young," he says.

"But you do love basketball," I respond. "It *is* your profession."

"Yeah," he agrees. "And my name *is* Randy. At least there's no girl's name on there."

He laces up his shiny, black-trimmed Air Jordans. James Edwards is lacing up his Air Jordans. Kukoc and Harper have theirs on already.

"Did Michael give you all Air Jordans?" I ask.

"Yeah," says Brown.

In the entrance area, John Salley is leafing through a book of Chinese proverbs and wisdom. He is in street clothes and he sits like a tutor next to pupil Jason Caffey. Salley has a Chinese tattoo that says something meaningful (to him) on his biceps. Just now he is saying some meaningful stuff to Caffey, whose face is intensely thoughtful. He is showing Caffey the book's instructions and illustrations on the proper way to masturbate.

"Your sperm is your spirit," he says. "Your *power*, you understand."

Caffey nods.

"Rick, could you move?"

It is Chip Schaefer. I am sitting on the taping table, and I quickly get up. Kukoc sits down and extends one bare ankle.

Buddha is resting across the way, eating popcorn. Then, at once, you can almost feel the air charging with voltage. Jordan has walked in. He is dressed all in black: black pants, black shirt, black shoes. He jokes with teammates here and there, gives one of them a backrub, smiling like he's showed up for a ride on the Ferris wheel.

"You're pretty loosey-goosey," I say, feeling like maybe it's time for me to leave the inner sanctum.

"I *am* loose," he says, as I head for the door.

But he doesn't play that well in the game. Typically, the Bulls fall behind early and are down 49–40 at the half. After three they are still trailing, 68–62. But in the fourth quarter the Bulls simply put the defensive hammer down, holding the Bucks to just 12 points, none in the last 4:19, while scoring 24 points themselves and winning 86–80.

The star at the end, at least offensively, is Steve Kerr, who gives the Bulls the lead for good on a 3-pointer and then hits 2 free throws to ice it. It is typical of the Bulls' dramatic sense of timing that their biggest lead of the night, 6 points, occurs as time expires. I know the *Sun-Times* has sent six writers and two photographers to cover this event, so I figure there is nothing worthwhile for me to write about, other than my impressions of the same thing everyone else has just witnessed, which, frankly, were I a reader, I wouldn't spend ten seconds reading.

My *Sun-Times* editor, Bill Adee, had suggested I write about the game from perpetual pine-rider Jack Haley's perspective. I liked that idea, except I didn't want to interrogate Haley, who probably would have been defensive and cliché-spouting, and I knew I'd have to work so hard to make anything he had to say interesting to people who would rather hear from Jordan or Pippen or—what the heck, I just didn't want to talk to him. So I took a prompting from the Li'l Penny Nike commercials, the ones featuring Anfernee Hardaway and his puppet alter ego, Li'l Penny. I laugh every time I see the ads, because they are so screwy and the puppet Penny is such a loud-mouthed moron. I created my own character.

Ta-da, Li'l Haley!

The puppet sat with me during the game, I wrote, because big Jack was mad at him for asking why big Jack always wore a black dickey under his sportcoat and if he ever was going to suit up. I got sick of his blabbering myself and locked him in my briefcase for a while. When I let him out, the Bulls had won, and he promptly started mouthing off about how he and big Jack were going to get endorsements, really cash in. I raised my hand to smack him and he took off across the floor, saying now he wouldn't introduce me to his "special friend."

And who was that, I asked, not caring.

"Li'l Worm," he sneered.

■ ■ ■

On Thursday, April 18, I go to the Berto Center after practice to find all the players gone except for Kerr, who is shooting free throws, using his bounce-back net. I watch for about five minutes and do not see him miss. We're supposed to chat today, and after he dribbles between his legs, left and right, then sinks a 10-footer, he heads toward the locker room.

"I'll be out in about ten minutes," he calls.

"Take your time," I say.

"No, I was talking to my brother up there."

I peer up at the balcony outside Krause's office that looks out over center court. A young man who looks identical to Kerr except with darker hair stands there petting Bo Jackson, the dog.

"Wow, there is a family resemblance," I say.

"The dog or me?" asks the young man.

I laugh and then am interrupted by a harsh voice. "We're trying to do an *interview* here!" says some guy with a British or Australian accent or something. He's standing with his camera crew, holding a mike, preparing to grill Phil Jackson at the far end of the court.

Sorrrry.

So Steve and his younger brother Andrew, visiting from Washington, D.C., and I head off for a sandwich at the local deli. Steve Kerr is such a normal-acting, self-deprecating, witty, and unobtrusive guy that if someone introduced him as a vital member of perhaps the best basketball team of all time, you would laugh and say, "Yeah, sure." Right now, though, he is the only active player in the NBA making more than half his 3-point attempts. Last season he led the league from the 3-point zone with a .524 percentage; it is amazing to think that Kerr shoots better while guarded and hurried from 22 feet or so than a number of NBA players do from the calm of the 15-foot free throw line. Kerr is deadly from there as well, making 93 percent of his free throws this season.

But the thing I'm most interested in is Kerr's stint as one of the co–sports editors of his high school paper back at Palisades High School in Pacific Palisades, outside Los Angeles. His partner in jock journalism, Mike Silver, is now a buddy of mine from our shared time at *Sports Illustrated,* where he is now a senior writer covering the NFL and writing athlete profiles, including the infamous one on Dennis Rodman, the one for which Rodman is dressed like a slut on the cover. One day last year Silver and I had been talking about the Bulls, and he said, "Steve Kerr and I used to write a column called the 'Riptide' back in high school."

Well, I had to see this literature with my own eyes; knowing Silver, I assumed it would have a decidedly "irreverent" quality to it. And the thought of an honest-to-God NBA player as a member of the press, a seemingly impossible marriage of dog and cat, fascinated me. Silver sent me some copies of the *Tideline* from 1982 and 1983 folded open to the "Riptide" column, along with a note that said, "If you can get through these without vomiting, yours is a strong stomach. Forgive us the numerous insider references. I swear they're all hilarious."

Here is a typical Kerr–Silver paragraph: "While we're on the subject of academics, the *Riptide* extends its warmest congratulations to the academically ineligible cheerleaders, led by the girl from Utah, Susan 'Books' Chapmyn. If anybody really believes that a cheerleader's grades reflect the way she shakes, they'll also believe that Jen(ital) Koslofski will be the maid of honor at Nina Jacobson's wedding."

All right. I drop the papers onto our deli table and ask Kerr what this was all about. Somewhat shocked to see the actual columns in black and white, he chuckles in that way people do when photos of themselves in bellbottoms or Nehru jackets suddenly surface. Kerr basically adopts Silver's defense: This stuff was really funny back then; you just had to be there.

"It was," he says, "a completely unveiled attempt at humor. Riptide, you know—to rip people."

"So I'll bet it was the most read column in the paper," I say.

"Among our friends, sure."

Silver also had sent me a piece Kerr wrote for the *Daily Californian,* the student newspaper of the University of California, Berkeley, which appeared February 4, 1988, before Kerr's University of Arizona team played in Berkeley. Again, the column was a little too inside-y for an outsider to fully appreciate, but the timing and the cheekiness were remarkable. Here was a prominent senior basketball player getting ready to play in front of, as he described them, "the most obnoxious fans in the PAC-10," and he's saying to one "earthy-looking girl" who had repeatedly screamed at him during Arizona's last trip to Berkeley, "Kerr, what kind of hairspray do you use?": "Before you ask for advice on hairspray, try . . . the simple basics of personal hygiene—like showering."

He shrugs.

I point out another installment of the "Riptide" in which they suggest a new slogan for the Palisades High volleyball team.

"Oh, the team the year before had a slogan that was 'Let's Go All the Way,'" says the former co–sports editor. "But there were kids on this year's team who were into cocaine, so we said they decided to change their slogan to 'Coke Is It.' Again, an attempt at humor."

I ask him whether his own writings have helped him understand the natural, instinctive cruelty of sportswriters.

"Yeah, I give you guys more leeway, since I was one of you at one time."

Kerr is a smart-alecky but thoughtful and polite kind of guy. After Jud Buechler scored 3 points and had a steal in one minute of play in a late-February game against the Magic, Kerr studied the box score and then defended his buddy: "He'd be averaging a hundred and forty-four points and forty-eight steals if Phil would just let him play."

Part of Kerr's makeup comes from his response to the tragedy of the murder of his father by terrorists while teaching in Lebanon in January of 1984; but much also comes from the fact that he was never a star, and never a bonus-baby star, and never thought of himself that way, either. "In high school I was like a spot-up, stand-still shooter only," he says. "I couldn't even play point guard on my team. How shall I put this? I wasn't equipped. I didn't handle the ball real well. You'll notice my lack of speed now. Well, I'm like a blur compared to then. I look back at tapes even of, say, my freshman year in college and it's embarrassing. I remember my mom saying once, 'Steve is such a modest boy,' and my dad nodded and said, 'Yes, and he has much to be modest about.'"

Kerr learned to rely on his sense of humor because his early basketball career was dotted with letdowns. Barely recruited out of high school, he was invited on just one college trip as a senior, to little Gonzaga University in Spokane, Washington. He wasn't exactly given a hero's welcome even there, and at one point the coach looked at him and, possibly none too impressed with the skinny, innocent-looking kid who somebody had told him could shoot the ball, asked Kerr to scrimmage with the varsity.

"Jay Hillock was the head coach and he said, 'Come on out and play with our guys,'" Kerr recalls with a shrug. "Of course it was illegal. But, okay."

Kerr matched up against another pasty-faced, scrawny, anemic-looking white guy, who proceeded to humiliate the high school senior. "He stole the ball from me, drove around me, scored at will, did it all to me," Kerr says. The fellow's name was John Stockton, but that didn't mean much to anyone at the time. "I didn't know much about Gonzaga," Kerr says, "and Stockton didn't have a big name or anything. I thought to myself, 'This guy is pretty good, and I'm terrible.' It was pretty depressing. Nobody else called. I had no other offers."

Kerr was prepared to give up basketball and maybe rethink things about his life in general. Then, just before school started in the fall, Arizona called and offered him a scholarship. "I guess something fell through for them," he says. "Somebody they were counting on left."

So how did he get to the NBA?

"It's like I went through a metamorphosis or something," he says, without great conviction. "I guess weight training and playing against guys who are a lot faster, and just natural maturity."

In the 1988 NBA draft, Kerr was drafted by the Phoenix Suns, the 50th player taken that year.

To improve his game once he made it to the NBA, Kerr had to reconstruct himself from scratch once more. He was dismayed to see that all the classic basketball moves he had learned were of virtually no value in the big league. "The fundamentals I'd learned at the John Wooden

Basketball Camp didn't work, because everybody in the NBA is so quick," he says. "I'd spot up and take my little shot, and I got sick of seeing it swatted into the tenth row."

So he studied the shots and quick releases of Jeff Hornacek and Mark Price and Craig Hodges and tried to duplicate them. He taught himself to look at the floor, lulling his man into something less than full attention, then to rise quickly, find the basket in midjump, and cut loose with a shot that, while not classic in form, was unvarying in its precision.

I mention that he picked some fairly earthbound players to pattern his game after.

He takes another bite of his sandwich. "Who would you want me to pattern myself after? Scottie?"

And, of course, he shoots and shoots and shoots. I ask him how many total shots he thinks he's sent toward a basket.

"Lifetime?" he says. "Oh man."

"Don't forget all the shots you took before age three," says Andrew, helping.

"Whew," Kerr says after a time. "Over a million."

One would figure, then, that Kerr must have a good time shooting against Jordan in practice, because Jordan can be baited by just about anybody, and if you throw some money on the bet, or some manhood, you can really get him to bite.

"No," Kerr says. "For some reason, we never shoot together in practice. He's always shooting with Harp and Scottie—they shoot for money, and he always wins. So maybe that's why he doesn't shoot with me."

"With your shot, you could really work him," I say, promoting the idea.

"Yeah, but he can shoot, too," Kerr says. "I mean, he's an incredible shooter. What he does, I've never seen anyone do. He can shoot going in any direction, he can shoot on his way up, on his way down, falling backwards fifteen feet, leaning forward, just hanging. It's ridiculous. It's amazing, because he'll be falling to the right and backwards and his mind will process those forces and tell him how far he's gone, how much spin to put on the ball, how much leverage to put into it.

"I mean, most guys don't even have the opportunity to try what he does, because they're not athletic enough. Guys like me. I've never seen Oscar Robertson play, but somebody told me he could shoot falling in any direction, too. The thing about Michael is that he has the base of fundamentals, so that even when he's flailing and his legs are scissored and all that, his shoulders and his elbows will end up square to the basket and his upper body will be in perfect shooting position."

Kerr, on the other hand, simply tries to control the small forces of his small game. He was disgusted with himself last season for shooting only 78 percent from the free throw line, so he vowed to work at that stationary part. "It was the worst I've ever shot," he says. "And one of the problems last year, and every year, is that I don't go to the line enough in games to feel comfortable. I'll go four or five games without even shooting a free throw, then all of a sudden I'm at the line four times in a game. So I decided I would shoot a hundred free throws a day, every day, just to feel comfortable. Get that little toss-back and do it. Takes about fifteen minutes."

"Every day?"

"Yep."

Structured practice of that nature simply forces bad habits into the background. It's as simple as that. Well, not always.

Kerr was in a slump earlier in the year; his shot was off and no amount of practice would correct it. So he tried another method of breaking the spell, one that had been effective for him once at Arizona: He went out and got drunk. Actually, he didn't go out and get drunk, he went up on the Bulls' airplane to Orlando before a Magic game the next day and proceeded to alter his state of consciousness with alcohol.

"Luc helped me," he says. "You know, it's not something to brag about or anything, but I started drinking on the plane, some beers and stuff, and then when we got to the hotel some of the other guys took care of me. I know mothers probably don't want to hear this stuff, but it's not like I'm endorsing it. I just had to do something."

The bigger Bulls players—and who isn't bigger than Kerr?—thought it was pretty funny. That night at the hotel golf course the players ran around in the dark, and Wennington and Longley held Kerr over a sprinkler, and generally acted like ten-year-olds. Jackson found out about the escapade and told the players they were idiots and to keep the story away from the press. And did getting drunk work this time too? Basically, yes. It was almost like a self-imposed erasing of bad formulas on the blackboard. "You feel so awful afterwards that you're not thinking about all the details and trying so damn hard," Kerr says. His shooting did, indeed, pick up. And at the very least, the event effectively put a line of demarcation between then and now.

We drive to Kerr's rented house in Lake Forest, where he will demonstrate some of his shooting skills for me in his driveway, so I can analyze this proficient long-range bomber and see just what it is he does that is so above the norm. There is a "For Sale" sign in the yard, and a wagon on the sidewalk. Wife Margot drives up. A babysitter walks up the street with the Kerrs' son Nicholas and daughter Madeleine.

Brother Andrew stands downcourt as Kerr gets a half-deflated ball from the garage and tries a long shot at the 9-foot, bent-rimmed, netless hoop that wavers in the 20-mile-per-hour breeze.

Kerr lets fly and the ball . . . misses everything. He shoots again. Same result.

"Tough court," he says.

"I'm far from a textbook shooter," he continues. "My left hand is more on the ball than maybe it should be. I wouldn't pick my shot to show to kids. There are guys with beautiful shots. Eddie Johnson. Mark Price. Dell Curry. Sometimes I shoot almost a knuckleball."

He misses again.

"My fundamentals are not picturesque. But my shot is the same, every time, like tying my shoe."

He is now 1 for 12.

"At least you're consistent," says Andrew.

Kerr is laughing now. The slope, the wind, the rim. It's hopeless.

"It's all in the legs," he says. "I've done a lot of squats to help with my leg strength. The legs are where you get your touch; the rest is just a flick of the wrist. That old three-point line, I had to be real loose and warm just to get the ball to the rim. It was almost a heave for me. Now a lot of times I don't even know I'm at three-point distance. It's very comfortable for me."

Just the 21 inches the line was moved in before the 1994–95 season made such a difference to Kerr that his 3-point shooting percentage went from 42 to 52 in one year. But he doesn't like to talk about his stats or his status as perhaps the best 3-point shooter in the league.

"Stats do mean a lot," he says, giving up and tossing the ball to Andrew, who dunks it. "Because that's all management talks about. But I've turned down all kinds of incentives from Jerry Krause, because I don't want to be thinking about any of that with a game on the line. I like not knowing, not thinking. I mean, taking a shot and knowing twenty thousand dollars is riding on it? You know those million-dollar shots they have at halftimes? I feel sorry for those poor people. They're not going to make those shots, just from thinking about them. NBA players couldn't, either. It's too much."

He looks at his rusted, junky hoop in this peaceful subdivision.

"As Phil says, you need mindfulness." He grins. "But you also need mind*less*ness."

23

APRIL 18: THE BULLS PLAY THE PISTONS ONE MORE TIME IN Chicago, looking for win number 71.

It should be harder to achieve than this, that extraordinary number, but it's oh-so-simple because neither Joe Dumars nor Grant Hill is in the Detroit lineup tonight. Dumars has an upper respiratory infection and Hill a sore left foot, and you have to wonder whether their teammates or Doug Collins really feel the urge to put it all on the line for this contest. There is even some whispering that the 45–35 Pistons wouldn't mind losing this game so that in the first round of the playoffs they could meet the Indiana Pacers (whose star, Reggie Miller, is out with an eye injury) rather than a lesser-ranked but full-strength team.

None of it matters anyway. The Pistons are a Bulls-whipped team, with or without their ailing stars. The Bulls lead from beginning to end, with the only problem occurring when Ron Harper sprains his left ankle early in the game.

In the locker room after the 110–79 charade, Jackson says that the goal now is to stay loose and prepared for the big dance. "Seventy-three is the number that sticks out there," he says of the Bulls' potential to go 73–9 in the regular season. "We want to win. But we're trying to play with mindfulness, concentration, and focus, and without brain-rattle."

I'm pleased to find out that my Li'l Haley creation has made it into the Bulls locker room, has made it, indeed, into Jordan's locker, where the little fictional creature seems to have filled some need in the mischievous Jordan's arsenal. Equipment man John Ligmanowski gave the column to Chip Schaefer, who showed it to Jordan, and that was all she wrote. Once Jordan got it, the cracking on Haley, who is often ragged by the Bulls' regulars as it is, began in earnest. A while ago Jordan had told the new Bulls mascot, Da Bull, a dumb-looking creature who cavorts during games with the original Benny the Bull, that if he didn't get his act together Jordan would have Da Bull and Haley traded for the Phoenix Gorilla.

The real Haley seems impervious to such onslaughts. He looks dapper tonight, anyway, in his fancy street clothes, and is as hyperactive as ever. He cheers on Rodman, who has started wearing some particularly unusual get-ups himself offcourt. In Milwaukee, Worm sported a large yellow "cheesehead" hat, and before that he had sported a black-leather bondage mask of the type worn by the Gimp in the movie *Pulp Fiction*. And his pink hairdo is gone, replaced by a yellow-orange flamelike pattern that resembles the hood of a greaser's '57 Chevy.

Basically, the Bulls are in a carefree and lighthearted mood. Michael Jordan even turned to the media gang during the game and gestured to where four fans with pink hair were sitting in a row. "They're from Hamburg, Arkansas," said Jordan wickedly—that being Scottie Pippen's home town.

On Sunday, April 20, in the second-to-last game of the regular season, against the Pacers, the Bulls fiddle around until the end, then go on a furious 8–0 run to tie the game at 99 with just seconds remaining. Jordan, of course, is instrumental in the run. Then, as the Pacers' Eddie Johnson attempts a long, off-balance jump shot that has almost no chance of going in, Jordan leaps and gets a piece of the ball. Ref Hue Hollins, the Bulls' nemesis through the years, mostly with questionable calls against Pippen, does it to the Bulls again. He whistles Jordan for a foul with just half a second remaining on the clock. It is a questionable call at best, one that is seldom made at this point in any close game, and Jordan goes ballistic. Johnson makes one of his free throws, the horn sounds, and the Pacers win, 100–99.

Jordan stayed angry about the call. "It was a call all right," he said derisively of Hollins's whistle. "I understand why those guys get bumped in the head."

In a sense, the game was a meaningless one: Neither the Bulls nor the Pacers could improve their playoff positions. With Harper on the injured list because of his ankle, Jackson went so far as to activate Jack Haley for the first time all year, making the game a mirthful event right there. The players had decorated Haley's locker with cobwebs and chanted "Rudy!" in reference to the corny movie about a Notre Dame football scrub, as Haley dressed for warmups. But the loss means the Bulls can't tie the NBA record for home victories in a season, 40, set by the 1985–86 Celtics, and that was one of those little marks Jordan and the others had hoped to attain in this special season. "That was important to us," Jordan said, "and I wanted it. It would have been something else for our team to be proud of."

Jackson had rested his regulars quite a bit, however, and Harper's absence meant the defense wasn't as ferocious as usual. And it wasn't clear whether Phil really directed this game properly in any sense; by the time he reinserted Jordan for the comeback, it was too late except to make the loss frustrating. It's obvious the playoffs will be simpler for the Bulls to deal with: Just beat the hell out of everybody any way you can.

The final game, against the Washington Bullets, is pretty much a waste of everybody's time, except for one remarkable occurrence: Jack Haley dresses in a Bulls uniform once more, and this time . . . he actually plays!

He confidently—or is it shamelessly?—throws up 6 shots (making 2) in his 7 quality minutes of the 103–93 victory, and afterward he talks about his game plan and his value to this club. "I think I was real aggressive, almost a shot a minute," he says. "Not to have gotten in would have been a monumental letdown. I've been here all year, and I've been a big part of this team." Actually, apart from hanging with Dennis, Haley's major effect on the team this year was colliding with Jason Caffey in practice and putting the first-year man on the injured list.

One other notable thing: Buddha Edwards got into a tiff with the Bullets' Ledell Eackles late in the fourth quarter and was knocked to the floor. He got up and was going to slug Eackles, but Pippen grabbed him, shouting, "Playoffs! Playoffs!"

Edwards calmed down, and Eackles would end up getting a $7,500 fine from the league and a one-game suspension to start off the 1996–97 season. It was a measure of the Bulls' and Pippen's maturity, if not the ancient Edwards's, that the team did not enter the playoffs with one of its own players suspended. Then too, Buddha got in the best blow in the spat, saying afterward that yes indeed, Eackles had tried to punch him, but "he scratched me. Like a girl."

■■■

72–10.

That's the final tally for the Bulls.

It is something to look at.

Oh, how nice 73–9 would have been, with the single digit in the loss column. And how many of the Bulls' losses were close ones like that Pacers 1-pointer, or the Charlotte 1-pointer, games that could have gone the other way? But why be greedy? How about some of those wins that Jordan seemed to have willed into existence? Or Worm's critical rebounds? No, 72–10 is pretty darn good, and pretty darn fair. Are the Bulls the best team ever? Who knows? They have a long way to go to win the title that would seem a necessity to make such a claim. But they have by far the best regular-season record ever. Surely, that must count for something.

And then there are the individual achievements.

Jordan played in all 82 regular-season games and averaged 30.4 points per, making almost 50 percent of his shots. This has earned him his eighth scoring title, an NBA record. Kerr went 1 for 1 from the 3-point line against the Bullets and has finished second to the Bullets' injured Tim Legler in 3-point shooting percentage, having made 122 of 237 attempts for a .515 percentage.

Rodman has won his fifth rebounding title, with a 14.9-per-game average. He finished far ahead of old Spurs softie David Robinson, who finished second with a 12.2.

Phil Jackson, with a career 414–160 record, has passed Pat Riley as the NBA coach with the highest winning percentage (.721) of all time.

And the Bulls franchise itself has now had 427 straight home sell-outs.

Since Jordan returned at the end of last season, the Bulls have cranked out a 100–19 record. That is something. They win 10 of every 12 games they play when he's in uniform.

But the journey is still in progress. Jackson has had hats made up for the team, inscribed with a slogan Harper has spread around: "72–10. It Don't Mean A Thing Without The Ring." The coach's countenance and demeanor are the same as ever: Slit-eyed, bearded, hobbling with the bad legs and the bad hip, stern but smiling mysteriously at the simplest of matters, he seems no different than he was at the bowling party many months ago.

"Phil has a calming influence on everybody" is how Jordan puts it. "That's why he's the best."

■ ■ ■

The Bulls' first-round opponent in the playoffs is the Miami Heat. People are talking a 15–0 Bulls charge through the postseason, just a stampede of skill trampling all foes into the dust. Jackson laughs at the notion.

"We don't anticipate going through undefeated," he says. "Our youngest player on the roster is [27-year-old] Toni Kukoc." He adds that just today in practice, Longley went down with a minor injury. "But it's nothing," he quickly continues. "Jack Haley wasn't even around."

They will slaughter the Heat. That is a foregone conclusion. So what do you ask players on a team like this? I ask Wennington about his boyhood again, because he is a fine storyteller.

When he was 16, he says, he moved with his family to Long Island from Canada. I interrupt him.

"You have a green card?"

"Yeah," he says.

"Got it here?"

"Yeah. Wanna see it?"

"Sure."

He ducks into the locker room here at the Berto Center and returns a minute later. He hands me the card. It says "Resident Alien Card." There is a picture of him on it: a younger Wennington with sideburns.

"Amazing," I say. "Does Luc have one?"

"Yeah."

"Toni?"

"I guess so." He looks at me quizzically. "I mean, what do you think, we're like criminals and we can't do anything?"

No, I tell him. But why play basketball in America, live in America, and spend American dollars all these years and not just become a damn American?

Wennington smiles his devilish smile.

"So I can play on the Canadian Olympic team," he says.

"That's a good idea," I say. "That makes sense. So you're on this year's team and ready for Atlanta?"

"Uh, no. We didn't qualify."

The TV people are in full bloom now, and they are everywhere. My old friend Tim Weigel, the sports anchor for Channel 2, is wearing a powder-blue sportcoat and florid tie. Weigel used to be a newspaperman, and it's for sure he didn't pick up his sartorial style in the world of the ink-stained.

John Salley comes out of the locker room in his usual grinning manner. He lays a couple of karate kicks just shy of my face. Then he demonstrates some cheating, hide-from-the-ref defensive moves on slender radio reporter Cheryl Raye. He spots Weigel and stops abruptly.

"Hey, man," he says. "I *love* your jacket." He walks closer, shaking his head. "What, Sammy Davis, Jr., died and gave you his stuff?"

Jordan pokes his head out, surveys the scene. He has a cigar tin in his hand. He smiles, disappears back into the locker room.

On the overhead TV monitor a midday-news reporter is describing a raid by federal agents on a militia's "bomb-making factory" in Georgia, bombs that supposedly may have been intended for the Olympic Games in Atlanta. Interesting as that news is, it is interrupted by an on-the-scene report from none other than Tim Weigel, live at the Berto Center.

Startled, I look around, and there is Weigel standing just outside the window, only a few feet from us, giving viewers all the news they can handle on this slow news day.

■ ■ ■

Before the game I see Lindsey Buechler, looking very pregnant, in the hallway of the United Center.

"I saw you on TV last night," she says sweetly. "You and some other men were talking about baseball. I turned the channel."

"Understandable," I say.

On the floor I hear someone yell, "Hey, Rick!"

I turn around. It's Dwight Manley.

He's staying in town, he says, for the duration. Whatever is needed. The book—the *book*—is coming out in five days.

"Dennis is pretty much on a gag order until Wednesday," he states firmly. He then tells me of all the wonderful riches that are raining down on his formerly destitute client. Rodman is healthy as a horse, from a fiduciary standpoint.

"Fabulous," I say. "How about his mental health?"

"Great! Great!" Manley gushes. "He's with a team he feels is behind him, one that will work as hard as he will." Dwight says that he himself is just beginning to appreciate the star power of the Worm.

"He was on *Oprah* twice! Oprah loves him! And the book is coming out. Perfect timing. We're sending T-shirts to all the reporters."

"Why such a secret?" I ask. "What's the big deal about the book cover? Who hasn't seen this guy naked?"

"Yeah, but you don't really appreciate the cover until you see it," Manley says knowingly.

Please. Worm is half-nuts. Too sensitive for this world. And yet this naive, cunning, exploitative, ambitious, baby-faced, mysterious, first-time agent is selling him like a farm commodity, lock, stock, and hairdo.

But then, Manley is doing what nobody else would do. And he hasn't gotten in the way of the team. And he seems to be Worm's friend as well as his adviser. And he hasn't put him into any terminally sleazy ads or condo deals or swampland grabs. But just for the record, how smart is it to bring out a star athlete's X-rated autobiography at the very moment the author's full attention is needed on the field of play? How much pressure can the author take? How much money can he rake in? How much is enough?

The league itself is so healthy, it makes one wonder about finances up and down the line. The salary cap for each team is $24 million, divvied up among a dozen or so players. That's huge. But the other day, April 17, the 7-millionth fan visited Arco Arena in Sacramento, where the dog-squat Kings have now sold out 451 home games in a row. Seven NBA teams sold every ticket for every home game this season, including such sorry franchises as the Hornets and the Warriors; the Bulls, needless to say, did not play in front of an empty seat anywhere, home or road. Nearly 21 million fans attended NBA games this season, a new record. And the money from NBA licensing and product sales is flowing like a mountain river. Gross sales of licensed NBA products have grown to a staggering $3 billion annually, with a large amount of that revenue coming from Bulls and Jordan items. Jordan's 1990 video *Michael Jordan: Come Fly With Me,* for example, is the best-selling sports video of all time, making *Billboard* magazine's best-seller chart for an astonishing 304 weeks. NBA telecasts are hugely popular in Europe, Canada, Asia, where there are vast markets ready to be sold sneakers, T-shirts, balls, videos. China, for God's sake, has 250 million TV sets with 600 million viewers, most of whom watch the *NBA Action* highlight show and an NBA game every Saturday morning on the government-owned channel. The Chinese are flat-out in love with Michael Jordan, whom they call "Air Qiao Dan."

So what's the bottom line? I can't even imagine.

The Bulls wipe out the Heat, 102–85, in a game that is as ugly as a car crash: 56 fouls, 3 double fouls, and 8 technical fouls are called. Jackson doesn't even start Rodman, because he is so fearful of Heat coach Pat Riley's status as a man who will turn his players into human jackhammers if needed, devices that could be applied to Worm until he cracks. As it is, the rough stuff only works against the Heat, frustrating the team even more because of its ineffectiveness.

The first player to get tossed is the Heat's center, Alonzo Mourning. He storms off in the fourth quarter with his two T's, applauding referee Steve Javie, saying, "Fantastic, Steve! Really great!" He is quickly followed by Riley himself, who gets the heave-ho for protesting Mourning's heave-ho. As Riley walks off the court in his elegantly tailored suit, detective Bob Scarpetti goes to escort him. Riley tells him to take a hike.

"I'm only here for your security," says Scarpetti.

"I don't give a fuck!" Riley snaps. "I don't need you."

The Heat's Chris Gatling makes his early exit next, maxed out on regular fouls and T's.

Phil Jackson, in his shirt, tie, and fly-fishing suspenders, looks relieved to have this game behind him. Riley brings up too many bad images for him ever to relax against the former Knicks coach. The two men do not like each other. Riley, like Doug Collins, does not feel Jackson is the benign, mellow philosopher he is often portrayed as being. He resents Jackson's ceaseless complaints about the rough tactics of Riley's old Knicks teams. Before this series he even accused Jackson of being the real master of dirty tactics, calling the Bulls' style of play "push, push, push, shove, shove, shove."

The Bulls romp again in Game 2. It is Clacker Night, and the clattering of the thousands of little noisemakers handed out to the United Center crowd is unnerving and at times deafening. The Bulls take the lead, 63–38, at the half, and then just wait for the game, and the racket, to end.

Unfortunately, Jackson puts Rodman back into the game late in the third period. Until now he has played just 13 minutes and has collected 2 points, 2 fouls, and a technical for elbowing the Heat's Kurt Thomas. Most importantly, perhaps, he has only 5 rebounds. Upon returning, he promptly begins to tangle with the much bigger Mourning, rapidly earning 2 more personal fouls and then a technical for his efforts. The second T gets him ejected from the game. As he walks slowly toward the sidelines, Rodman tells Mourning what he can do with himself.

He then slowly removes his jersey as he saunters toward the Heat bench. He moves in front of Riley and gives him and his boys the one-armed up-yours salute. He then hands his jersey to a kid in the stands and departs. The entire procedure takes just 33 seconds of game time, but it's scary in its implications. Since the headbutt, he's been on his best court behavior ever but now Worm may have crossed the line once more.

Was the meltdown okay, because the Bulls were up 33 points at the time?

"No," says Jackson. "It's embarrassing is what it is. In that situation, I told him, 'We need you out there to play.'"

Why even put Rodman back in the game against this volatile club?

The reason, Jackson says, is that you can't suddenly stop playing your best men midway through a big game. Moreover, he thought Rodman could deal with the Heat's heat. "The first half, I was a little concerned. But the second half, I didn't think anything was going to happen. I thought Dennis was going to work his way through it."

But he didn't. And now he's the target his enemies always want him to be.

"You know how it is," says Jerry Reinsdorf glumly outside the locker room, when I ask him about Rodman's behavior. "You just hope and pray he doesn't go off."

But off he went.

I find Manley.

"Okay, Dwight," I say. "How about *that* performance?"

He shrugs. "Talk to Kelly," he says. "Kelly, what did we say?"

Kelly Davis, the cop-bodyguard, is standing next to Manley.

"When Phil put Dennis in, we both said, 'He's going to get in foul trouble and get a technical,'" Davis states.

That night on his TV show, Rodman acts drunk and stupid. The visiting Jay Leno is on with him, and the two end up in a food fight, with Rodman burying his own face in a large birthday cake. He comes out grinning insanely, looking like a clown in whiteface.

Two days later the *Sun-Times* runs his cake-plastered mug in full color on the back page, under the heading "Fine Mess." That was in reference not only to Worm's appearance, but to the fact that the league has just fined him $5,000 for his obscene gesture to Riley. Coupled with the automatic $1,000 fine he received for being ejected, Rodman's total fines this season have now reached $34,000. Plus the $183,000 in salary he has lost for the headbutting suspension.

"We're not comfortable with Dennis's mental state right now," Jackson says. And why should they be? Rodman missed Monday's practice because he had to have cake removed from his ear by a doctor.

But fans and voyeurs everywhere are loving the whole thing. I open today's paper and find a large ad that reads, TONIGHT ON 2-NEWS AT

10. RODMAN'S ROOTS. HIS CHILDHOOD. THE EARLY YEARS. THE TURNING POINT.

PR man Tim Hallam walks through the bowels of the United Center, walkie-talkie in one hand, a can of Diet Coke in the other. He seems totally unfazed by the shenanigans of this team. None of it bothers him. He's seen a lot worse. Just now he's thinking about going out for a smoke. Caffeine and nicotine have replaced pot and booze for him.

"The day we're out of the playoffs is the day I'm quitting," he says, tapping his Marlboros. "Or at least trying to."

In Miami for Game 3 on May 1, Jordan speaks sternly about Rodman's antics. "From a team standpoint, we don't want to tolerate it. He gives the referees and the league ammunition to attack him."

What about stepping in personally, then?

"I'm *trying* to calm him," Jordan says. "But he has such a temper. I can't baby him. I'm not gonna grab him by the hand and lead him to the bench. I'm not gonna do that."

It is the rarest of occurrences, but suddenly all the reporters who have mobbed Jordan out here on the floor at the Miami Arena drift away and swarm another person who has just come out: Rodman. In a minute only Cheryl Raye and I are standing with Jordan. Then it's just me. I use the moment to tell him I was shocked to see him play Chris Wallace one-on-one on a recent *PrimeTime Live,* that I thought we had something special.

"Chris is a wimp." He grins. "Off the record."

Then I tell him of the proposal I've been constructing in my head, a contest in which we can actually compete fairly. We'll play one-on-one, but he can only shoot 3-pointers, and he can't come inside the arc, even on defense.

"Okay. And?" he says.

"And I can shoot from anywhere, but you can't come inside to do anything to me."

He looks bored.

"You think you'd win?" I ask, figuring he hasn't grasped the restrictions.

He looks at me in disgust.

"Hell, yes."

"Why? How could you?"

"Because it's my game, and you couldn't handle the pressure."

■ ■ ■

I leave the Arena, recalling abruptly what today is: Book Day.

There is no complimentary copy in my room at the Mayfair House, so I walk to the corner bookstore and buy a copy of *Bad As I Wanna Be* for the already discounted price of $20.

I go back to my room clutching the thin slice of literature with Rodman's resplendent nude form on a Harley Davidson, a basketball in a strategic place, on the cover. The phone rings. It's Dwight Manley.

"You didn't *buy* a book, did you?" he asks.

"Yes."

"You were supposed to get a review copy. I'm really sorry."

I tell him it's no problem, and he begins to crank up the hype machine once more.

"Two hundred thousand advance copies, biggest in sports history. Another hundred thousand ready to go. Oprah guaranteed a million sales to me. She held it up to the camera. *This* is Howard Stern level."

"What else you selling, Dwight?" I ask.

"Everything," he says. "It hasn't begun. The book signing [in Chicago] at Borders, they're talking the biggest in history. Bigger than Schwartzkopf."

I tell him I find it all a little mercenary, trading on a guy's insecurities and psychological problems.

"Dennis is a showman, too," he insists. "He's not just an athlete."

"He made a fool of himself on Sunday. Cake all over his face. Drunk."

"Didn't Leno egg him on?" Manley asks. "Didn't he make a fool of *himself*?"

"Yes." I think for a few moments. "Don't you think that at this point in the season it's moronic to get thrown out of a game and get a five-thousand-dollar fine for telling Pat Riley to go to hell while making an obscene gesture?"

"Dennis was defending his own teammates," Manley says. "And he wasn't swearing at Riley. It was directed at an assistant coach who said 'Fuck you' to him."

"In the papers Dennis said he told *Riley* to go to hell," I point out.

"He's emotional; he takes things personally. Those assistant coaches shouldn't be talking to players."

Forget it; today is Book Day.

"The *New York Post* just picked up the second rights to twenty-five hundred words of the Madonna part on Sunday," says Manley, continuing his report. "The *Post* is Madonna Central. The book signing is going to be covered exclusively by SportsChannel; we've sold them the rights. Plus we've been discussing his entrance. It will be amazing. You can't guess."

"On a Harley, in a dress," I say immediately.

"That's one of his possible modes of transportation," Manley replies crisply.

I can't help laughing.

"It's like Barnum and Bailey," I say. "P. T. Barnum said, 'There's a sucker born every minute.' Good old Barnum."

"Is that Dennis?" the agent asks.

"No, it's you," I say.

"Oh, stop!" he says, giggling.

■ ■ ■

David Stern and I talk before Game 3.

"I hate to say it, but the joke's on the media," says the NBA commissioner of Rodman and his book. "The guy is a master salesman. He says how troubled he is, how he is working through his problems, and all the rest of it, and the people eat it up."

"You're in the book," I say, opening my copy. "Let me see if I can find it."

Stern looks at the cover and laughs weakly. "I'm never writing a book," he says. "No notes. Nothing. I want to live in the present."

"Do you want Rodman out of the league, as he suggests?" I ask.

"No," says Stern. "We're the NBA family. Some families have an Uncle Moe, some have a Cousin Dennis. We have Cousin Dennis. You know, a lot of players and coaches like that us-against-them mentality. It's a tried-and-true sports motivation technique. Rodman may have taken it to a new art form, but the Celtics did it, Pat Riley does it, the Michigan team that went to the NCAA Final Four did it."

"Here's the part," I say, showing Stern pages 98 and 99, the section that includes a photo of a mean-looking Stern and starts, "The guys making the rules are guys like David Stern—fifty-year-old white men who didn't come from where I came from, and didn't come from where most of the NBA players came from. They don't understand anything. . . . They're too fucking white collar to bother with some lowlife bum like me."

"Let me see that," says the 49½-year-old Commish. " 'Fifty-year-old white men . . .' " He scoffs in irritation.

A couple of hours after the Game 3 victory, another blowout for the Bulls, I spot Longley and Buechler walking through the mall in front of the hotel. "I got Li'l Haley in my back pocket," says Buechler, chuckling.

But the real Jack Haley, who now has his own clothing contract with Bigsby & Kruthers and is having his likeness painted on the company's building with all the other B & K sports and entertainment stars, is standing next to a dark-windowed limousine that's parked in the hotel turnaround. He is not on the playoff roster, but he is certainly on the roster of the pretty young woman he is speaking to. He has a cigar in one hand. Rodman is there, too. And there is another young woman nearby. Kukoc stands on the sidewalk away from the action, observing, looking amused. George, the cop, stands at the ready, keeping people away, smoking a cigar of his own.

The limo is ready to motor. A night out appears to be in the offing. Playoff pressure—it's fan-tastic.

24

BY 2:30 THE CROWD IS NEARING HYSTERIA.
Some of the people have been waiting more than 15 hours to see their hero. The other folks surrounding the Borders Books & Music store on swank North Michigan Avenue and funneling west on Pearson, then north on Rush in a thick line of book-clutching humanity, past Chestnut

and into the distance, have been waiting long enough to prove that this particular author is something special indeed.

I have been here for some time myself, wandering through the tight security, whipping out my Chicago Police Department News Media Identification Card like a pistol when necessary, wondering like everyone else when and how the new literary sensation is going to arrive. It is a cold, clear day in early May, and I spend time out on the sidewalk, absorbing sun rays, talking with veteran publicist Joe Goldstein, who has been flown in from New York by Delacorte Press to help promote the book and work the media into a feeding frenzy. He's a nervous little guy, on edge because he has no idea where the man of the moment will be coming from. If at all.

"Could he come up that street?" Goldstein asks me, pointing down Pearson. "Somebody said he might be arriving in a garbage truck."

Also with us is Alan Trask, the young manager for Delacorte's Chicago operations. He is tall and slender and is wearing a blue suit, white shirt, tie, wingtips, and an earring.

"This, allegedly, is the highest-volume bookstore of any kind in the country," Trask says, as we all continue scanning the horizon for a glimpse of Rodman, who is now 45 minutes late. "They're trying to beat Colin Powell's record for a single signing, something like twenty-three, twenty-seven hundred books. That was in Virginia. Schwartzkopf was also huge. He was here."

On the other side of Pearson a staggering man in filthy clothes taunts the line of people that stretches for more than five blocks. "You waiting to see that sissy?" he says. "That right? That big ol' sissy?"

To take his mind off his anxiety, Goldstein talks about other sports books he has "worked." There was Dick Schaap's monster book with Bo Jackson. "I said, 'Dick, it's not moving. What can I tell you?' Two weeks later the Nike ads came out. Foosh. Through the roof."

"Then there was Pat Riley's book. Two hundred eighty thousand copies. Huge," says the publicist. "I did *Ball Four,* too. Bowie Kuhn banned it. I mean, what's he going to do next, burn it? Hah! Straight through the roof."

What's moving *this* book? I ask.

Goldstein shrugs in amazement. "Normal people," he says. "I look at these people and they're not weirdos. They're people who spend their vacations camping in the Adirondacks. Look at them. The only person I've seen with an earring is him." He points at Trask, who is staring keenly into the distance.

All around us the mob is throbbing with expectation, about one notch below insurrection. Trask notes, "As they say, nothing draws a crowd like a crowd." And that is a big part of the rush: being where the action is. Goldstein sees an armored car making a stop across Michigan.

"A Brinks truck?" he asks.

It is now after 3 P.M.

At 3:20 we hear sirens in the distance. Police cars are driving from the north down Michigan, their lights flashing. All at once the roar of a motorcycle cuts through the air. Dennis Rodman slices out from behind the lead squad car and turns his big chopper onto Pearson, into the crowd being held at bay by dozens of policemen, many of whom are on horseback.

With the blast of his Harley drowning out the fevered neighing of the animals and the screaming of the fans, the 6'8", silver-haired, heavily made-up drag queen parks his hog near the front door of the store and then minces for the adoring crowd and TV cameras. He has on a low-cut silver leotard, a crucifix necklace, leather pants, and silver motorcycle boots. His fingernails are silver, his eyes are done up like a luna moth's, and something that resembles a segment of bicycle chain dangles from his right ear. He could be the king of the gay machinists' ball. Right behind him is Dwight Manley, catching it all on a camcorder, documenting history. With a flourish, Rodman flips his fuchsia boa, tipped with black faux feathers, over his shoulders and enters the store to sign his name to his new book, the one that states, "If I want to wear a dress, I'll wear a dress."

And why not? I ask myself. Really. Why not?

Howard Stern, Rodman's predecessor in commercial self-display, wore a dress. Dustin Hoffman wore a dress. So have, let's see, off the top of my head, Patrick Swayze, Wesley Snipes, Robin Williams, Pee-wee Herman, Jack Lemmon. They're all actors, entertainers, sure. But so is Rodman. Dwight Manley is right: Dennis is a showman. And his stage, here in the thick of the NBA playoffs, is approaching global di-

mensions. These people lined up for a glimpse would be tickled to see
the rebounding champ appear in a cocktail gown. Or buck naked, as he
has said he would someday like to play hoops.

While I was waiting I spoke to the first person in line, a 45-year-old
woman named Tanya Loveless, who was wearing a Bulls jersey over
her sweatshirt. Having arrived at 11:30 last night with two relatives,
Loveless shivered through the night on the sidewalk, wrapping herself
in a black garbage bag and huddling behind an umbrella to block the
wind before she and the other hundred or so early arrivals were allowed
into the building late this morning.

"A guy came up last night and gave us cigarettes," she said. "People
thought we were homeless."

But why, I wanted to know, would she subject herself to such indig-
nities just to get close to Worm for a few seconds?

"I like him because he's sexy," she replied. "I admire his straightfor-
wardness. I wish I could lead my life that way."

I noted her tattoos. She displayed her newest one, on her right forearm, the one that said in script "Mi Vida Loco."

"My Crazy Life," she said. "Dennis has one, too."

I took her word for that. I thought I had read him well, but apparently
I didn't know everything.

As Rodman settles in at the varnished maple library table, where he
is flanked as always by cops Triantafillo and Davis, I think about what
it all means, if anything.

Maybe the fact that a famous American is showing that he can wear
just about whatever he wants and say just about whatever he wants is in-
spiring to some. His style could be seen as another of those occasional
symbolic affirmations we need, the ones that remind us we are not ro-
bots and that this country, despite its rules and taboos and referees, is a
place that is fairly tolerant of rebels and wackos. That the Bulls can accept this goofiness on the eve of their playoff series with the hated
Knicks says a lot about the tolerance of their organization, at least.

But where is the planking beneath Rodman? There is no there there
that I can see. In *Bad As I Wanna Be,* amid all its profanity and trash-
talking (please, does anyone think those things are new?), he says:
"When I realized I could turn my back on everything teammates say and

coaches say and society says, I felt free." Fine. So what does he do with that liberation? Well, besides engaging in random sexual exploits, turning his back on his child, continuing his legendary fiscal irresponsibility (God bless Dwight for showing up in his life when he did), and wearing Halloween outfits and punker hairdos and acting the occasional fool, he does nothing. Except play the part of the outcast. And rebound his ass off.

Take away basketball and Rodman is just a tall, lonely, tattooed guy with funny hats. As he writes of himself and his occasional sex partner, Madonna, "We are two people who do whatever we want in life and get away with it." Hell of a policy. But it resonates with anarchic joy for many.

I asked Tanya Loveless's son-in-law, Romelle Scott, 23, what he likes about Worm. "Everybody has a little Rodman in them," he said. "But they can't bring it out. He can do it."

Behind the Loveless contingent sat a man of Asian descent and his two daughters. Why were they here to see Rodman?

"We love him," the dad said.

Perhaps all Rodman says to people is that a manly athlete can be androgynous. Or a tough guy can be soft. But more than anything, what he says now is, *I want to sell more books than Stephen King.*

Rodman is signing books, and books only, as fast as he can. No posters. No talking, no eye contact. Outside, policemen keep the crowd from breaking down the doors.

"Get off the ladders!" a frazzled clerk screams to kids who have climbed halfway to the uppermost shelves. Security men squeeze through the store, barking at people like prison guards. Books are trashed, lying in the aisles like debris. A crying little girl whose foot has been trampled in the crush is comforted by her mother. I find myself jammed into the "Mystery" section, my face just millimeters from *Murder in Grub Street* by Bruce Alexander and *Contagion* by Robin Cook.

In the center of it all, the fellow with the head like a punked-out Tin Man's scrawls and scrawls, saying nary a word. After 95 minutes and 831 books signed, Rodman takes a break and goes to the back room, to stretch and to collect his thoughts, and perhaps to reapply that darned silver lipstick that keeps smudging. Dwight Manley looks content.

"Get everything you need?" he asks during the lull.

I laugh. He looks so serious. Or rather, he looks as though he is witnessing a serious undertaking.

"Who did his hair?"

"A makeup artist," he says.

"You're too much," I say. "Barnum, from Barnum and Bailey."

"I've been using that, telling friends."

"I guessed he'd be coming on a Harley," I say. "Wearing a dress. Remember?"

Dwight looks at me superciliously.

"It's not a dress."

25

JUST MINUTES INTO THE FIRST QUARTER OF GAME 1 AGAINST the Knicks, Rodman is called for a foul when he literally does nothing except fall to the floor after the Knicks' Charles Oakley elbows him.

I turn to Bernie Lincicome, the *Tribune* columnist who is seated next to me here at the United Center. Lincicome stares straight ahead. "There is," he says, "a certain penalty that comes with being Dennis Rodman."

How true.

But Rodman is playing hard, very hard. And he seems sane. It's as though he is making every effort to be just as straight-ahead tonight as he was bent yesterday.

Before the game I talked to my favorite insider, Jerry Krause. I had already walked throughout the press area and around the floor, showing the glossy 8 x 10 full-color photo that one of our *Sun-Times* photographers had snapped of Rodman at the book signing 24 hours ago. To a man, or woman, each press member had said, precisely, "Oh, my God." Rodman bodyguards Davis and Triantafillo had shrieked with delight. Tim Hallam had said, "I have to have one of those."

The Sleuth, however, simply shrugged. Like he was looking at a shot of a sailboat on Lake Michigan.

"All that matters is what he does on the floor," he said. Odd, coming from a "character" man like Krause, but also true.

Krause, in his fanatical approach to talent collection, is the most tolerant of men. If you can play, *wear* a freaking tutu.

I tell Krause I still can't believe he signed Worm.

"He felt the other general managers [of his previous teams] lied to him," he says. "That Bob Bass lied to him. That Billy McKinney lied to him. I haven't lied to him. We talked for a long time, Dennis and I, before we took him. Believe me."

The game tonight is, as expected, a hot one. In the second quarter Jordan and the Knicks' Derek Harper go at each other and earn technical fouls. Phil Jackson stands up and yells at the ref. Harper looks over at him and says, "Fuck you, Phil."

"Right back at you," yells Jackson to Harper specifically, and to the Knicks generally. "He's intentionally holding him! You know you are!"

At the half, Jordan has 23 points and the Bulls are up 54–47. The Knicks are rough, but the Bulls can be rough, too. Jordan himself is the master of hooking defenders with his elbows on his offensive moves, of shoving when nobody notices, of putting his hip to unsuspecting guards and slapping wrists so quickly that only a slow-motion camera can detect it.

I run into June Jackson during intermission, and I show her the Rodman photo. She studies it.

"Beautiful," she says. "They really gave him shit in the locker room this morning." She looks at the boa, the eye shadings. "Did he do this himself?"

"No."

"He's not that good-looking, but he's beautiful here," she says. "Just shows you what makeup can do."

The Bulls win, 91–84, and I decide to venture into the Knicks locker room, just to test the waters. Hubert Davis talks a little. John Starks is helpful, but rather quickly says, "I'm done." So I move on to Charles Oakley, the former Bull, kidding myself that he might have something insightful to say about the contest, about anything. "I'm not talking," he grunts.

So, feeling great about my professional-interviewer skill at drawing out my fellow humans, I take a shot at center Patrick Ewing, the guy who was once the subject of a lengthy *Sports Illustrated* piece by Rick Reilly and contributed nothing at all; Reilly had to write the whole thing based on other people's observations.

"We expect to win," says Ewing, head down, the way you might give your name, rank, and serial number. "I'm sure they expect to win, too."

Any more?

"It's not about one game."

Could he elaborate?

"That's it."

Allrighty, then.

But the ever-helpful Dwight Manley is waiting in the hallway.

"Dwight, I need to write a column about you," I say. "The man behind the Worm."

"I'm not behind him," he says.

"Well, you're Barnum."

"He pedals, and I steer."

"I want to write about you."

He looks dubious, shy almost.

"I'll have to ask Dennis," he says.

■ ■ ■

"It doesn't mean anything," Rodman says to Oprah Winfrey.

It's Monday night, and I have tuned in the *Oprah* show. The Chicago-based talk show diva has just asked Rodman about his tattoos or hair or clothes or something.

The interview is juvenile, smarmy, manipulative, titillating. Perfect TV. Rodman is barefoot. He is wearing a purple crushed-velvet shirt, orange hair, a necklace, and his big Cat in the Hat hat. Oprah asks him a serious question, or a seemingly serious one, then a philosophical one, to which he answers, "It's very difficult to sleep with a woman and get up the next day and say, 'Damn, why did I do that?'"

He gets the audience hyenas behind him when he says all the young NBA players are overpaid, and "they can go wherever and kiss my whatever." No mention, of course, that he himself has demanded the Bulls pay him $10 million next season or he'll retire.

Chuck Daly, the Pistons' former head coach, comes onstage and says of his former player, "I love him. I love him."

With time running down, and the lovefest building to a gooey crescendo, it's obvious Oprah will be going for the emotional kill pretty quickly. And, by gum, she doesn't disappoint. She asks Worm who he respects, and he says, lips quivering, "I respect . . ." and then his face contorts and the tears virtually shoot from his eyes. Behind him a huge photo of his daughter, Alexis, is projected on a screen.

Oprah has a sated, drained look on her face. Like a person who has just split a cord of wood and is firing up a well-earned cigarette.

"He wants to break the cycle," she says, looking at the camera. Rodman is still weeping. Is that a tear in Oprah's eye? Is Oprah breaking down, too?

And out!

The next day I run into Fred Mitchell, a sports columnist for the *Trib,* and a man I have known for years. He has seen Rodman's divorce papers, where ex-wife Annie alleges that Rodman beat her. Fred, one of the calmest, quietest, most reasonable writers I've ever met, reminds me that it is all alleged, the beating stuff, not proven fact. But he also knows that Rodman's relationship with his daughter is not all Oprah might have us believe.

"Her First Communion was on Saturday, and Rodman had his publicist call and say Dennis couldn't make it," says Mitchell. "Then that night the little girl saw him on TV [at the book signing] in drag."

I tell Fred that I didn't buy the Oprah cry-in, and that Annie had told me two and a half years ago that Rodman didn't come to any of his daughter's big events.

"Annie and the daughter were here in Chicago, flown in for the Oprah show," Mitchell adds. "But they didn't come on because the girl was afraid."

■ ■ ■

In Game 2, another rough, ugly contest, Ewing gets into some serious jawboning with Bulls assistant coach Jim Cleamons. *Fuck you!*s begin flying, both men point at their groins, and Ewing starts toward the Bulls bench, real evil in his eyes. Jordan gets in Ewing's way, then Longley comes over and acts as a barrier. "Come on, motherfucker!" Ewing screams at Cleamons, who is about half his size, but ever so feisty.

I wonder why, as a strategic measure, the Bulls don't just let Ewing have his way with Cleamons, since that will get the star center tossed for the remainder of the series; Cleamons is off to be the head coach of the Dallas Mavericks, anyway. The old pawn-for-a-king trick.

The Bulls win, 91–80, and in the tunnel postgame everyone is asking Cleamons who started the verbal fight, him or Ewing, and what exactly was said. Cleamons says it was a big to-do about nothing, shrugs it all off. Ewing, of course, is silent. But I walk along with Cleamons as his old pal, Cal Ramsey, the Knicks' color commentator, asks him what happened out there.

"I told him to hum on my nuts," says Cleamons quietly. "And he said, 'Produce 'em.'"

■ ■ ■

The announcement came today that Phil Jackson has won his first NBA Coach of the Year award. He received 82 votes from the 113 sportswriters and broadcasters polled, far ahead of second-place finisher Mike Fratello, who had 22. Doug Collins and Rodman's enemy Bob Hill tied for third with three votes each. The award "does not begin to describe Jackson's duties as front man for this rolling carnival and sporadic freak show that is the Bulls," writes Bernie Lincicome. "Mystic, ringmaster, wet nurse, immigration adviser, Jackson has had to be all these and more."

Jerry Krause has won the NBA Executive of the Year award, and it, too, is much deserved. It seems like a good day to chat him up, so I ask the Sleuth why the Bulls didn't take young power forward Jayson Williams of the Nets when he was a free agent last summer instead of Rodman. It was because of money, right?

Krause sniffs indignantly.

"[Williams] had a lot of things wrong with his game," he says. "We had big questions about him."

"He had a lot of rebounds this year," I venture.

"Shit," says the Sleuth contemptuously. "Anybody can rebound for New Jersey, with all their missed shots."

The Rodman acquisition, he continues, was—is—a classic case of
the risk–reward principle, a theorem he learned from "the smartest man
I know, Jerry Reinsdorf. It's starting to look better, that risk–reward
thing. It's a success if we win the championship. If [Rodman] blows up,
then it was not a success."

So right now Perdue for Rodman, even given the latter's current pre-
carious balance, is probably the best trade Krause has ever consum-
mated, no?

"Nope, the best trade ever was Oakley for Cartwright. People said,
'He won't trade his son.'" ("Son" was Oakley, whom Papa Krause
sneaked away from Cleveland in a 1985 draft day swap of Ennis What-
ley and frail rookie Keith Lee for the lug from tiny Virginia Union.)
"Ha!" continues Krause. "The son had to go. But, mmm, this trade
ranks with that. But even the Cartwright one might not be my greatest
trade in this city. That would be when I traded five White Sox for a guy
in the San Diego farm system. Ozzie Guillen."

■ ■ ■

Michael Jordan has a bad back, but he has ignored it to lead the Bulls to
their first two wins over the Knicks. He has scored 44 and 29 points, respectively, in the games, the 44 points being the most scored by anyone
so far in the 1996 playoffs. His total is 40 percent of the Bulls' team
output. He's not doing it by choice.

Toni Kukoc is now 1 for 24 on 3-point attempts in the playoffs, and,
as Jackson has said, Toni needs some "moral courage" to stop playing
so timidly—not just to make his shots, but to charge ahead whether the
shots go in or not. The Knicks have so badly gummed up the cutting
routes of the Bulls' triangle offense that Kukoc and the others look like
pinballs as they bounce off Oakley, Ewing, Anthony Mason, and company. And the offense, except for Jordan's own attack, has come to a
skidding halt.

Longley missed Game 2 with an injury, and Pippen is aching all over.
Kerr can do nothing without getting open; Rodman simply rebounds.
And so Jordan, as ever, is the rock. He is the pinwheel from which the
sparks fly.

The Bulls are leaving today for New York and there is much that each player must do before boarding the plane, but I've found Jordan ready to put off for a couple of hours the things he should be doing and talk.

I ask him why he takes that fallaway jumper, the shot no coach teaches.

"A lot of people think that's new, but I was shooting that before I retired," he says. "I've worked on it, to where it actually eliminates the defense. I forgot where I got it from. I've seen highlights of Elvin Hayes, but that wasn't it. They say your fundamentals are at risk, but I've come to the point where I feel in balance shooting it."

I mention to him that Steve Kerr has pretty much said the same thing about Jordan's shot. And speaking of Kerr, does Jordan find it telling in any way that the two of them, one-sixth of the team, have lost their fathers through murder?

Jordan looks stunned.

"I never knew," he says. "I knew of his closeness to his mother, but I didn't know what happened to his father. He never said anything, and I never asked." Jordan ponders this for a while.

"I'd be pretty sure he does feel the same things I do. Not having a father figure around to help you with family decisions—now you just have to live off what you attained before it happened. The difference is I had my father until I was thirty-two. I was a grown man and had determined my path. He, I guess, was what, still in high school? and had to do a lot of growing up. I think about my dad. Sometimes before a game, I'll think, 'Should I be aggressive at the start or passive?' He always said, 'Show leadership. Be aggressive.'"

I tell him about the time his dad and Tim Hallam and I were in the basement of the old Chicago Stadium, back when Tim was still boozing, and how we stood around and yakked and James was drinking rum and Cokes with limes. And the Luvabulls would march through, and the waitresses pranced about.

"Yeah," says Jordan, laughing. "And he'd be messing around with them. You know, after he pretty much retired when I came to the NBA in 1984, he just lived for the moment. Which is fine. He woke up, whatever he chose to do, he did. He had that option. I loved for that to happen to my parents. I really didn't see, after 1984, a day that he didn't have a happy face."

Jordan has often said how his worst oncourt trait—the habit he has of sticking his tongue way out of his wide-open mouth when he makes an aggressive move to the basket—is something he picked up from his pop. I ask him about the tic again, just to hear him talk about it.

"I would watch my dad working on the car or something, and he would always concentrate with his tongue out, and I tried to emulate that," he says. "A kid wanting to be like his dad."

"So what do you think," I say, "was it learned or genetic?"

"Six, seven years ago I'd say it was a habit. But now I see *my* kids doing it." He and Juanita have three kids. "In fact, my son Marcus reminds me so much of me it's scary. How bad I was as a kid. I did shit just to do it. My parents would ask me, '*Why* did you do that?' 'I don't know.' He's me to a T."

Okay, but back to that tongue. Why doesn't the famed United Center statue have a big old tongue hanging out?

"I didn't want them to," says Jordan. "They wanted to put a tongue on it. But it's promoting a bad habit. It's dangerous. I didn't know any better. Now I can't stop. I tried to stop it. I almost bit it off a couple of times. In college Coach [Dean] Smith my first year said, 'We're gonna have to do something about that tongue.' I said, 'What can we do?' 'Try a mouthpiece,' he said. So I did, for about a week and a half, but I couldn't breathe. Even with my tongue out I breathe through my mouth. That's why I chew gum, so my mouth doesn't get dry."

A few weeks ago I spoke to Lamar Hunt, the owner of the Kansas City Chiefs, and the only original investor in the Bulls who is still active. He told me that he had long felt that Jordan would have made a splendid NFL wide receiver if he had the speed, which Hunt thought he did. Has Michael ever been timed in the 40?

"Yeah, I ran it a few times in college," he says. "For basketball. I ran a 4.3 once. But I never liked running."

I tell him that's Herman Moore, Deion Sanders speed. He shrugs. No big deal. What is transcendent athletic ability to him? Everything he does on the court is transcendent. I still am unsure whether I have ever seen another athlete in a global sport be so much better than those around him as Jordan is better than those around *him.* Of course, there has been a cost.

"It's amazing how the perception of an individual can be abandoned," he says, thinking. "To people who really know you, you're just an everyday person. But people who only see you on TV . . ."

He lets that thought drift for a moment, watching it lead, as it must, to the compromises that have accompanied his superstardom. I ask him whether he's able to go to the grocery store.

"Sure, I can go," he says. "But I know what I'm going to deal with. So I don't."

What are some other things he'd like to do, but can't?

"Well, I haven't flown commercially in about seven years. I can't go to an airport. Can't go to a mall."

How about walking down a street in the Loop?

"I do that sometimes," he says. "I shock people. A lot of times I wear a hat and shades and whatever. And I keep moving, oh yeah. But you know, I'd really like to go walking on a Saturday, a sunny Saturday, just walking. I've never really walked on Michigan Avenue on a sunny afternoon. And I'd love to walk down Lake Shore Drive, right against the lake. I've never done that."

But don't feel sorry for him, he says. It's all a big tradeoff. I tell him that one quality of his that seems to reduce his chances of anonymity is his ability to work a room, like a professional host or master of ceremonies, somebody everybody just wants to talk to.

"My personality is such that I can fit in," he agrees. "I'm a people person. I know how to limit myself, ease my way out of a situation I don't feel comfortable with, so I don't come off in a negative way."

"But you were angry when you told all of us media guys you were retiring," I remind him. That was done in the haze of speculation about his supposed gambling problems.

"Yeah, but I was pissed off because of the accusations," he replies. "I couldn't tell my accusers they were wrong. They wouldn't listen or understand. But it was plain and simple, right in front of them. It's not what *may be* behind the curtain. They wanted to look at what I *must* be doing. *There must be something wrong here.* But it was all right there in front of them. There was nothing, no penalty for any of the things I've done. I feel I've never done anything illegal or against league policy. But it was so frustrating, because people had their own interpretations.

They were picky, so picky." Now he gets a nasty look on his face and whispers in a contorted voice, "'*Yeah! There it is, there's the illegal thing!*'"

He returns to his normal speaking voice instantly. "You want to change what people think, but you can't. If it's something that's completely off the wall, you can clear it up. But if it's somewhere close, you can't do a thing."

Is that why he still won't talk to *Sports Illustrated*? He hasn't allowed himself to be interviewed by the magazine since it put out a sarcastic cover March 14, 1994, that showed Jordan, its No. 1 cover boy of all time, swinging at, and missing by a foot, a minor league pitch. The headline read, "Bag It Michael!" Beneath that was the statement "Jordan and the White Sox Are Embarrassing Baseball."

"Yes," says Jordan. "*Sports Illustrated* blamed me because they didn't know the desire I had for something. I've always tried to be understanding of *SI* and the deadlines for photo shoots and things like that which they have given me. Because of the prestige of being part of it. And then they took what I was doing completely out of context. They didn't know how long I'd had that desire to play baseball. They were criticizing me for what I thought was the opportunity of a lifetime."

"Is there one particular impression of you out there that's wrong?" I ask. "One thing that maybe people think about you that is just incorrect?"

Jordan ponders this.

"Yeah," he says. "I don't think I'm a tyrant. I think it's a misinterpretation of the position I have as leader of the ball club. It goes all the way back to Sam Smith's book [*The Jordan Rules*]." A passage Jordan felt was grossly unfair had him and Pippen bragging about the relative sizes of their infant sons' penises. In the book it sounded mean and quite nearly perverse. In real life, says Jordan, it was guys who are together for months on end, day and night, simply joking in the locker room, the way athletes do. The way eavesdropping journalists can never understand.

"That's the whole point," he says earnestly. "To some extent Sam had correct facts, but the way the facts were stated painted the picture wrong. There is always a lot of joking and kidding. It may be an understanding between you and me that a third person doesn't begin to understand."

Jordan talks almost abstractly of the twin realities that pervade the Bulls' journey: the reality of the team and its honeycomb of interrelationships, and the reality of the team as it is perceived by outsiders.

"I do my best to try to understand the picture that people may see of this. But people who know the game, they can understand my frustrations. It's like, I'll give Luc a push here or there to be a better player. I do it in a joking way—but, I mean, he's missing so many practices, and I wonder how he can come out and still play like that. He's a good kid. And he's so knowledgeable about the game. I say to him, 'If you know everything, *do* it. The game should come simple, if you know it.' But there is that aggressiveness, that killer instinct he doesn't have. And you can't give it to him.

"And Toni. Toni likes to be admired, yes. It's the fame he loves, but he doesn't like to work. Which you have to do for all the consistencies that come with it. He goes through the motions, you know. Like most Europeans, they try to fool you. You watch them, they think they're doing what's right, but yet they're not.

"I mean, we know you can shoot. Help us in other areas. He's such a damn wild card for us. And it's not that he doesn't work on his shot. He shoots every single day. I say, 'Toni, basketball is teaching you a game. It's not always *you*. Sometimes it's us, it's we. Forget about what you're doing here, and think about making the team better.' I tell him every day, 'It's a simple game.'"

What Jordan is saying may look rancorous in print, but it sounds almost wistful as he speaks it. But there's no denying it's got an edge to it, too.

"I wish everybody had that fire," he continues. "But they don't. You have players who have the heart but not the talent, and players who have the talent but not the heart. I'm seeing it a lot more as I get older, and I get frustrated. And that frustration makes me just want to choke the shit out of Toni and say, 'Man, you have a hell of an opportunity; just *take* it.'

"Kerr has heart. He gets the maximum out of what he has. Shooting is his specialty, but he relies on other players to get him open, he needs

Scottie and me to penetrate and dish it to him. That's what I didn't understand at first, didn't have that rapport with him."

And that preseason fight of theirs?

"It was part of my frustration, and part of his, trying to understand each other. I think it helped us tremendously. But right now, here in practice, some guys can't focus. And it's the playoffs. Phil's going through these changes in our offense and things to think about during the course of the game, and everybody is bullshitting around. He's changing routes, and it's confusing. But if you stay tuned, you can pick up all those little components and translate them easily.

"My thought pattern for the rest of today and tomorrow is going to be, 'How do I mentally cover for what some of the other players will be lacking tomorrow night?' My own game plan will be based on my perception of what these individuals are going to do.

"I'm pretty observant. I notice mannerisms. I look at people, not at situations as much as people. I can look at Toni and see he's more worried about his shot than anything else. If he can get his shot off and we lose, he's perfectly happy. But if he shoots the worst and we win, he feels bad."

And how does Pippen fit in here?

Jordan leans forward in his chair. I'd expected him to leave 30 minutes ago, but he seems unaware of time.

"Scottie has heart and talent," says Jordan. "But he wants someone beside him. He's like a little brother. He was lost during that year and a half [of Jordan's hiatus], and I felt so sorry for him. I mean, he was one of the reasons that I really got myself back into the game. I couldn't even watch him. He can understand me better by me being away. Now we're like brothers—we understand each other's responsibilities; we never crowd each other. We pull, we tug, we support.

"When I said he was the best player in the league, I believed it. If you saw his game, his abilities, when I came back? Man, I knew my work was cut out for me to be the top player on this team. He helped motivate me because of his skill progression while I was away. So when I said that, it was motivation for me to get better than him. Scottie does have skill and desire and heart. But does he have that mental consistency to take the challenge and make it happen every single day? I think that pressure got to him this year. When he broke down physically, he broke down mentally.

"I want to play a couple more years. And I know after two years, Scottie's gone. I would want him to leave. To get the money he deserves. It would be a good time for him to leave, not to be the leader of this team, to be a part of another team. He wants to be a good guy now. He's very friendly. I just don't think he's ever had proper guidance to educate him about life. He's learning about women, about how he's perceived. He's really trying to change his whole image."

Jordan leans back in the chair. He looks like a panther in clothes.

"It's exhausting, this game," he says. "I mean, I am tired, man. There always comes a point in the season where I have to find motivation. I start looking at myself, asking, 'Where do I want to go?' This hill I'm having a tough time climbing, somehow I have to do it. I have to battle myself. And then I gotta deal with you guys."

I look at him as he says this. It's almost as though he has defined the enemy, and it is the person sitting quietly across from him, me, and a line has been drawn in the sand between us. It's a line I never can cross. No observer can. None of us one-on-one wannabes and interviewers and buddy-buddies can ever be what we are not. We're watchers. Jordan and his mates in the NBA are doers. But Jordan doesn't even say these words angrily. He means no offense, but he means no false cheer, either. I have always been enthralled by his appraisal of himself and the game of basketball. False modesty? False motivations? Forget it. He exudes an arrogance only a man at the top could have, or justify.

"You guys saying, 'He's lost a step.' 'He can't stand two games in a row,'" Jordan continues. "All that's pushing me. I can't give anybody anything. That's how I get through the season. I'm so competitive, even if I'm not feeling good, I don't want the next man to catch up to me, or beat me, or embarrass me, or make a name for himself off me."

But aren't there times when the game is in the bag and he could just take it easy for a while? "When you have sixty points, why do you want sixty-nine?" I ask.

He thinks I'm referring specifically to the 1990 game in Cleveland when he scored 69 points against the Cavaliers. I wasn't, but he starts off explaining it, and I let him go.

"Because I *hated* Cleveland," he almost snarls. "I went to the hole in the first quarter and Hot Rod Williams knocked my feet out and I landed on my tailbone. I could have been really hurt, and I hear the crowd cheering, yelling, 'Yeah! Yeah!'" And here again he shifts to that fierce whisper, *"Boy, that fucking burned me."*

End of story. You don't mess with Jordan's pride. Which *Sports Illustrated* now knows as well as the Cavs.

But Jordan quickly adds that it's not about pointing the finger at someone after the deed is done; it's about doing it right there in the arena, at the moment, so that nothing more need be said.

"You don't verbally attack a player's manhood. I don't do that. I can't go out and chest-bump, do what Scottie does. Young players do all that, but I think it's bad for the game. What I do is attack your ability. I don't have to stand over you and taunt you. You'll know when it's done that I'm better."

I think about that. In truth, a crowing, obnoxious victor is easier for the vanquished to stomach. The loser can then hate him, plot revenge, consider him lucky rather than skillful. Jordan's form of conquest is more surgical, more scientific. It leaves you nowhere to look except inward. It is a crueler way to kill a man.

And what about Rodman?

"He plays strictly on emotion," says Jordan. "He views himself as being special, unique, an entertainer. I don't buy everything, and he knows it. You can tell by the way he plays he's an asshole. Like getting kicked out of games. You see him at the half or in the third quarter with five, four, three rebounds, you can believe he's gonna go off. Because he doesn't feel he has the spotlight. When he's got nineteen rebounds and everybody's focused on him, this guy's ready to bust his ass. When he's got five rebounds and maybe Scottie and I have the other eleven or twelve, he's losing that focus, so he has to do something to regain it, and he starts acting crazy. The games he gets kicked out of, none are when he has seventeen, eighteen rebounds.

"I mean, there are times when we're fighting against *him* to get rebounds. Sometimes we'll lose it out of bounds because we're fighting him. The way he helps us is offensively. He can get us more than one possession. Offensively, he's the best rebounder, without a doubt. But a lot of that comes from him just aborting the offense."

I tell him that after hearing all this, I'm surprised the Bulls win two games a season. Forget going after title number four. The Bulls have more flaws than Chernobyl.

"Yes, we have flaws," he says. "But we cover them up well. We do have talent, and the leaders are able to compensate for Dennis not being an offensive threat. Harper's streaky, but he doesn't do anything to hurt the team. It's all about understanding. We just know so much about each other.

"Look, I know that I could score as many points as I want to score. If I decided I wanted to average thirty-seven points a game, forty points a game, and I didn't give a damn about wins or what this team does? I could do it. But I want to win. I want everybody to have that same feeling."

At last he seems to realize that most of the afternoon has drifted by, that he now has almost no time to prepare for the New York trip. He stretches.

"I'm tired," he says. "But I can't get tired. This is probably the most pressure I've ever had, because I put it on myself and we put it on ourselves."

He rises to go. "If we win," he says, "I'm going to let it all down."

26

ON THE PLANE FROM CHICAGO TO THE BIG APPLE, I SIT NEXT to *Tribune* sportswriter Melissa Isaacson in first class. I bumped myself up by using frequent flyer miles; she bumped herself up by whining. It's a tactic she perfected last year when she covered the Bulls virtually the entire season while pregnant. Stressed out and swollen, she went into labor during last spring's Orlando series—false labor as it turned out, but she was miserable for most of the season anyway.

She remembers the way Jordan responded to her condition when he rejoined the Bulls in March. She marvels at the way he could read her.

"He would always come up and pat my stomach," she says. "He would ask how I was feeling. Then one day he said, 'You must be feeling better—you're wearing heels.' Who else would have noticed?"

Game 3 sees more of the brutal mashing and grinding that predominated in the first two contests. Kukoc is out with a sore back—injured during the last home practice—and for a time in the first half nobody on either side seems able to stop clutching and grasping long enough to make a basket. Nobody, that is, except Jordan. At one point during a break, he comes to the bench and says to Longley, who is just back in action, "I know it looks like I can do it by myself, but I can't."

As I watch the game, I wonder how anyone could referee it. Everything everybody does is a foul. And then there is the dark, glowering presence of the Knicks' Charles Oakley, who is wearing a protective mask that makes him look like a B-movie human-skin collector. Bernie Lincicome has described Oakley's style of play as resembling "a desert mammal charging the water hole." Late in the second quarter Oakley draws a technical foul for roughing up the increasingly sympathetic Rodman on the free throw scramble. As Jordan lines up to shoot the T, Oakley meanders over toward the Bulls bench, stands next to Pippen, and begins quietly taunting the team, looking for anyone who might take the bait.

Buddha tells him to get lost.

"Fuck you, bitch," says Oakley, looking like an executioner.

The Bulls take their first lead at 51–49 in the third quarter, but it doesn't last long. The Knicks seem to have rallied around Jeff Van Gundy, their short, somber, balding interim head coach. Van Gundy looks nothing like a coach. He looks like the man who might come quietly to the big oaken door, hands folded over his black suit coat, when you ring the bell at the Transylvanian funeral parlor. But forget looks; he's got the Knicks continuing on with the effective rough stuff that peaked under Pat Riley and somehow sifted down through the stewardship of Don Nelson to today.

Seated around the court are many of the big-time swells who always come out for big games: Gene Siskel, of course, and Gary Sinise, Kevin

Bacon, one of the droopy-eyed Baldwin brothers, and a number of fat and/or ugly old men with young babes, proving again that money can overcome even the severest odds.

They are seeing a team put true fear into the Bulls. Jordan scores the Bulls' final 10 points just to draw the game into an 88–88 tie as time expires. Overtime.

But the Bulls don't have it, and they lose, 102–99. Postgame, Phil Jackson is abrupt and refuses to take questions from the press. "That was an exceptional game the Knicks played," he says, then vanishes. Jordan had 46 points, and, more important, played an exhausting 51 minutes. Longley, by far the biggest man on the floor, had 6 points, 1 rebound, 1 assist in 26 minutes.

The next day, Mother's Day, at the Plaza Hotel where the Bulls and their followers are staying, I run into Dwight Manley and Rodman's bodyguards. Manley's business suit and small glasses, his precise, clipped speech give him a professorial air—if professors were young men promoting cross-dressers. Around us, elegantly dressed Mother's Day diners stroll to the Palm Court for the buffet. We are standing near the large portrait of Eloise, the child patron saint of the Plaza, and she gazes down on us in her blue skirt, white blouse, red hairbow, with that impish, oh-so-manipulative grin. It occurs to me that she and her pet turtle would make a fine addition to the Rodman entourage.

"Dennis was on *Saturday Night Live* last night," says Manley. "It was a spur-of-the-moment thing." I calculate for a moment and figure that Rodman must have gotten to the theater fairly quickly after the Bulls' loss.

"He was supposed to be naked in one skit," says Manley, as if this is just another business detail. "He was wearing a towel. But he didn't take it off."

"He was supposed to?" I say.

"Yes."

Let me get this straight. This is on live TV. After a tough loss. In the playoffs. "He was *naked*?" I say.

Manley shrugs.

Bodyguard Kelly Davis steps forward.

"He had small black briefs on," Davis says.

Game 4 takes place later that day, again at a loud and packed Madison Square Garden. Behind me a leather-lunged Knicks fan yells at Rodman in the first quarter, "Keep shootin', sweetheart!"

Pippen's back is hurting him so much that he lies on his stomach on the floor near the bench during his brief periods of rest. Longley is a huge lump taking up space on the floor, immobile compared to the agile Ewing, who shoots deadly jumpers that Luc can't touch. The Bulls are ahead at the half, 51–50, but that means little.

What means a lot is the way Rodman is going after missed shots. He will finish with 19 rebounds, an amazing 10 of them being offensive boards that give the Bulls second chances to score. Also amazing is Jordan, who has a steely look on his face. The critics have said back-to-back games are too much for the old man. Hence the steel.

Jordan will finish with 27 points, 8 rebounds, 8 assists, 2 steals, a blocked shot, and no turnovers in what will be a tight 94–91 Bulls win. But what is memorable about his performance occurs in the third quarter. Jordan accidentally elbows Knicks defender Willie Anderson in the face on a fake, and Anderson goes down like a puppet with cut strings. Does Jordan come to his assistance? Not exactly. He dribbles once to his left, positions his feet behind the arc, rises and buries a 3-pointer over his opponent's prone form. It's something a killer might do.

Early in the fourth quarter, with the game still up for grabs, Phil Jackson earns himself a T from ref Bill Oakes for bellowing, among other things, "Are we watching the same game?"

During a timeout I walk over to where Dwight Manley is sitting and ask him if we can talk soon.

"I'm going home in the afternoon, so I don't know," he says. "It all depends on Dennis's birthday party."

"Are you having it?" I ask. The party has long been scheduled for tomorrow night, Monday, at Crobar, but at this point, with Tuesday being the date for Game 5 of this series, a rational person would have to question the timing.

"If the Bulls win, I've told him to have it and leave early," says Manley "If they lose, cancel it."

"PR is your world," I say.

With 26 seconds to go in Game 4, Rodman drives down the lane and passes to Wennington, who nails a 9-foot baseline jumper for the game-winner. A minute before that, Rodman had driven and dished off sweetly to Wennington for a jam that ended a 6-minute Bulls scoring drought.

Postgame, Phil Jackson says, "Michael did not have the energy to play the way he did yesterday."

Jordan says, "Phil is asking Dennis to expand his offense. We didn't win seventy-two games with me always stepping forward in the final minute."

Rodman, in jeans and a T-shirt that says "Change The Law. Legalize Same Sex Marriage," is typically candid. "Maybe the Knicks think I'm too much of a chickenshit to take a shot, too much of a lazyass to play offense, so every once in a while I surprise 'em."

I take a cab back to the Plaza and decide to try Manley tonight for our interview. It's 11:30, but I call from my room, and Manley says come on down. He's in a huge suite with a corner view, one block up Fifth Avenue from the large sign promoting Jordan and *Space Jam* that rises above the Warner Bros. Studio store on 57th Street. A faux fireplace burns electric orange. Gilt trim flows around the 12-foot ceilings.

The agent himself is decked out in a flannel shirt and Bulls practice shorts. He's lying on a couch, partially wrapped in a blanket, talking on the phone, working a deal. Across from him on another couch Kelly Davis sits with the remote control, clicking the TV from channel to channel. A woman is sitting on a chair near the couch, and I vaguely recognize her. I think she was one of the television producers from my first Crobar foray.

When Manley hangs up, I say to him, "Let's start from the beginning. Who are you?"

In rapid fire I find out that he is from La Brea, just south of Los Angeles, that he is a former rare coin dealer who made his first million dollars by age 23, and that he never went to college. He and Rodman met in Las Vegas three years ago this month—"after the Detroit suicide thing," Manley says—where they played craps at the same table for a half-hour and then said goodbye. Manley was there for a coin auction; Rodman said he was leaving soon, and, Manley recalls, "I never expected to see him again."

Manley returned home to Los Angeles, then flew back to Vegas the following week for a friend's bachelor party, dropped by the Mirage hotel casino, and lo and behold, there was Worm, almost exactly where Manley had left him. "He was having a hard time getting out of town," Manley says with a slim smile. "So I said. 'You want to go see George Carlin tonight?'"

Rodman did. Then they went to the bachelor party together. After that, Rodman began calling Manley, visiting him whenever he happened to be in the Los Angeles area. In this younger man who was so different from him—young Dwight had been the captain of his high school golf team, for God's sake—Worm had found a leader and promoter who seemed to want nothing from him. "I always picked up the tab," Manley says. "I think that was different for him, a new experience. Not to be used. I just liked him for him."

When they became business partners last summer, Rodman stayed at Manley's house for three months. It was something of a coincidence that Rodman showed up on Manley's doorstep just a week after the coin dealer and his wife had split up. I make a joke about Worm maybe suddenly becoming the new woman of the house. Manley snorts. All that kinky stuff is for show, he says. "Dennis is straight as a board," he says. But whatever people want to think is okay with both of them. Manley will soon be handling not just Worm's offcourt dealings, but his basketball business as well, as soon as Rodman dumps veteran agents Phil Pollak and Neil Draddy, which will be pronto. Like everyone else in this world, those two didn't understand the essence of Rodman's vulnerability and pain. And its marketability.

Manley has more hands working than a blackjack dealer. Besides the basic promotions and a possible movie deal and a cartoon show and so on, Manley has this *Bad As I Wanna Be* book that is rapidly becoming a publishing phenomenon. Though it has all the literary merit of vintage Jacqueline Susann, *Bad* has already gone to six printings, with 650,000 copies out there in bookstores, bathrooms, and psychiatrists' offices. Dennis and Dwight get about $3 a copy, and if the book sells a million copies—which Manley insists it will—well, even John Grisham will have to tip his hat to the thing.

"How do we know you're not stealing from Worm?" I ask.

Manley laughs. "I get ten percent. When we formalized our agreement last summer, I overeducated him about the deal. Because he's always been taken advantage of. When I took over, he had a negative net worth. We were with Howard Stern, and he said to Dennis, 'How do you know Dwight might not steal all your money?' And I said, 'Listen, I could steal everything, and he'd be no worse off.'"

Manley was bitten by the coin bug at age six, and after reading a book on the business, he knew it was the career for him. By his sophomore year in high school he was doing his homework, getting good grades, and skipping a day or two a week, he says, traveling by himself to coin shows all over the country.

"Wait a second," I say. "You read a grown-up's book at age six?"

"Yes."

"That's kindergarten age."

"Yes."

"Do you have a high IQ?"

"Yes."

I find myself thinking about him in a different way, re-examining all those hustles he has worked.

"Genius level?" I ask.

"What's genius?"

"Oh, a hundred fifty," I hazard.

"It's more."

He doesn't want to brag, and I have to slowly dredge it out of him. But he's been tested at 166. He says. And why not? Do all big thinkers have to be in the space program?

"I was always very good with numbers," he says. "I could always do anything I wanted. I was in a lot of gifted classes."

But he was a lonely kid, too. He was an only child of divorced parents; his mother worked. He made friends infrequently, and by any means available. "I would give kids ice cream to come over and play," he says. "Or I'd give them a coin."

It strikes me that this is where his and Rodman's growth charts briefly cross, where the threads of unhappy childhoods weave themselves into the very different fabrics of their adult lives. Despite having two sisters, Rodman was alone a lot as a boy, too, and had no clear sense of himself as an individual with value to others. "I can identify with a lot of the things he feels," says Manley, who is still stretched out under that blanket, which he has now pulled up to his chin, making me feel like I'm visiting a consumptive in a Swiss sanitarium. "He *was* an only child."

I know from earlier conversations that Manley actually digs the outrageous things Rodman is doing, and which Manley is orchestrating. The way he talks about Rodman's escapades, it's clear he's getting back at something, somebody, too. It's not just performance, it's fulfillment.

They have so many things up their collective sleeve, including a CD-ROM, clothes, and a date with Howard Stern's sidekick, Robin Quivers.

"For its love prospects?"

Manley hoots. "To talk about it the next day on Howard Stern's show."

Manley takes a moment to remind me that the NBA is show biz. And don't forget it. And, it dawns on me, promoting show-biz people takes a trained eye, just as buying the right coins does. At least for now, this is something Rodman should be thankful for. I think.

"Dennis has never actually *said* thank you to me," says Manley. "It is very hard for him, because he has never been sure who to trust. I understand that, because he has been used by a lot of people."

I think about that as I take my leave, and when I get back to my room, I flip open my copy of *Bad As I Wanna Be*. There on the acknowledgments page, below the tips of the hat to God, Alexis, Bryne Rich, Howard Stern ("for just being the cool dude who lives life his way"), writers Tim Keown and Mike Silver, the Chicago Bulls, Chuck Daly ("for being the one who showed me the way to becoming a man in the NBA"), Mom and Debra and Kim, and Pearl Jam and others, is this statement to Dwight: "Thanks for being a true friend. I know I don't say thanks much, but all that you've done for me has really made a difference in turning my life around. Thank you, thank you, thank you."

27

GAME 5 TAKES PLACE BACK IN CHICAGO, AND THE BULLS BASI-cally just don't lose here. Phil Jackson always hates going to New York, saying, "It's very hard hearing all those boos after being cheered there as a player." This home court feels like a security blanket to him.

"The Knicks can drag you down," he has said. "They can take you out. The way they play? I mean, they can take players out of a series." But nothing evil is going to happen tonight.

Jordan is rested and pours in 35 points, and Rodman is only a bad boy at the end, getting tossed early in the fourth quarter for a very ticky-tack foul that earns him his second technical. As he departs, he is toasted by the crowd, which chants, "New York sucks! New York sucks!"

Now as Bill Wennington fouls the Knicks' John Starks with under a minute to go, Jordan rushes to him and hollers, "Let him go! No way they can stop it now!" The Bulls are running out the clock, clinging to a double-digit lead. It's all over, except for the partying. Krause talked to Manley after Game 4 and urged him to postpone the birthday bash un-til sometime after this game, and Manley did: It's set for tonight. The Bulls win, 94–81.

In the locker room Steve Kerr breathes a deep, smiling sigh of relief, a sigh shared in some fashion by all his mates. "We feel like we're get-ting out of jail," he says. "The Knicks have had us locked up. It hasn't been much fun. It'll be more fun to play Orlando."

Out in the hallway I spot Margot Kerr talking with Jud Buechler.

"Where's the fat lady?" I ask Buechler, meaning his wife, Lindsey.

"She's not fat anymore," he says.

"You had the baby?"

Margot takes over. "It's a girl. Her name is Reily. Eight pounds, one ounce. Born six days ago."

I shake Jud's hand.

"Jeez," I say, "if she just could have waited, she could have been born on Rodman's birthday. Could have named her Worm."

Buechler blanches.

"She *will* wear a dress," says Margot. "They have that in common."
The players stream into the night. Two rounds down, two to go.
Ain't nothin' to do but head for Crobar.

■ ■ ■

Before Game 1 of the NBA Eastern Conference championships against
the Orlando Magic, Phil Jackson sits in his office in the United Center
with no lights on. His feet are up on his desk, his suspenders are loose,
he's literally laid-back. I look in and see that Sam Smith is sitting in the
shadows with the coach.

"Can I come in?" I ask. "Or is this private?"

"Nothing's private," says Jackson.

We talk about all kinds of stuff, but not the upcoming game. We talk
about Phil's old days with New Jersey, when he was an assistant coach
and Bernard King was the star. We talk about King's troubles with making last-minute free throws. "Bernard could do it for three quarters,"
says Phil. "Then at the end he'd get so tight he couldn't make a free
throw."

We talk about David Robinson. "Dennis has told me that David gets
nervous at critical times," says Jackson. "He said they'd call plays for
David at San Antonio at the end of games and his hands would be trembling."

Sam shakes his head at that. "I don't know," he says. "I don't buy that."

Nor do I. I don't think the Admiral has that killer's heart, but I don't
think he's a choker, either. At any rate, how would Rodman know? He
was never in a huddle, anyway.

Jackson does get around to mentioning the game that is now just 80
minutes away, saying that he feels the Magic are "vulnerable." He
thinks Penny Hardaway is vulnerable. "He likes to bring the ball to his
right," says Jackson, musing. "I don't know what his weakness is yet,
but we'll try to find it. I think we'll find it."

There is also the Shaquille O'Neal weakness: free throws. And then
there is Horace Grant. He killed the Bulls, his old team, in last year's
playoffs, hitting the open shots whenever they doubled down on Shaq or
Penny. But the Bulls spent the entire offseason doing things to counter
the Magic's charm, and Horace's presence: They picked up Rodman.
They put an increased emphasis on killer defense. And, of course, they

benefited from the way the Magic had put a thorn up Jordan's backside. It was an irritation that has led him to say, "Now it's just a matter of seeing how I can pay them back."

And pay Horace Grant back. By the end of his time with the Bulls, pre-retirement, Jordan was starting to despise the power forward with whom he had won three NBA rings.

Phil Jackson says Grant was a fragile, juvenile, but sweet person, who was at times "actually afraid of people" on the floor. Jackson was fond of him, although he admits, "I did whip Horace, but I whipped him because I knew the team, Bill Cartwright and others, would take him under their wing and say, 'Forget him, forget him,' nurture him. He was afraid of Karl Malone. I'd say, 'I know you're chickenshit against Malone, but you gotta be the door that stops this guy.' Or Armon Gilliam in one series. He couldn't stop him. I said. 'All he's doing is intimidating you, coming in with his arms. You gotta take that.' He got in an argument with me on the court, and I said, 'Now you're gonna stop playing,' and he started to cry, this anger kind of thing. He's so sensitive.

"I love the guy, but I remember once we were in a race with New York, and his knee was hurt and he said, 'I've got my future to think about.' I said, 'Horace, you're getting paid for *this* year.'" Jackson still describes Grant as "a terrific player." But like many delicate superstars, he brings his weaknesses with him always, just as he brings his gifts.

Jordan, less accepting than Jackson, perhaps, simply got sick of the teammate he felt was way too selfish, saying in private that even if he, Jordan, did come back after the Bulls' third championship, there was no way the team was going to win a fourth crown as long as Grant was on the team.

"Michael said that to me before," Jackson concurs. "Yeah, he said Horace was just too much."

What Jordan said recently about Grant is that the power forward was not satisfied with simply being a spoke in a rolling wheel. "The rift was so strong. We covered it up during the third championship," Jordan says. "But in 1992, when Scottie and I went to the Olympics, and Phil gave us one-a-days when we came back because of all we'd been through, Horace bitched about that. 'Why do *they* get special treatment?'

"He felt he didn't get enough credit. Orlando is finding out about him now. I talked with some guys down there. Horace, if the team's staying in a hotel and he doesn't like it, he'll move out and go to another hotel, miss practice the next day. And that's stuff I never did, never even thought about doing. Never. I always used to call and get an upgrade, use my own money to get a suite. One time, the year after I was gone, the Bulls stayed in Dallas, and the hotel didn't have but one or two upgrades, and Phil got one and Scottie I guess got one. Horace was so mad, he checked out and went all the way downtown to another hotel by himself. Then missed the shootaround."

Now, though, here in his twilit office, Jackson doesn't seem to have a care in the world. He, too, feels let out of prison by getting past the Knicks. The Sleuth sticks his head in the door while we're sitting there. He sees us, registers us all, then says to Phil, "I'll talk to you later."

Jackson doesn't seem to give a damn one way or the other.

■ ■ ■

The Bulls come out hard and take a 10–0 lead before Orlando knows what's hit them. The Bulls do not double-team Shaquille O'Neal unless absolutely necessary, and without the open man the Magic are in deep trouble.

The Bulls are up 32–19 after one quarter, and 81–59 after three. Perhaps responding to the fact that his autobiography has rocketed to No. 2 on the *USA Today* best-seller list (behind only *The Green Mile, Part 2*, by Stephen King), Rodman performs like a superstar. He scores 13 points, yanks down 21 rebounds, and outplays Horace Grant so decisively one has to wonder whether Worm isn't one of those guys who scares the skittish forward.

More important, at the end of the third quarter Grant crashes into Shaq, banging his left elbow on the center's huge arm and hyperextending the joint. He goes to the bench, holding the arm as though it has been crushed by a cement block. The diagnosis: a hyperextension to soft tissue of the elbow, with no evidence of a fracture. Grant also lets it be known for the first time that he injured his other elbow in Orlando's playoff victory over the Atlanta Hawks four days ago.

That injury at least partially explains Grant's pathetic contribution tonight before the collision: In 28 minutes of play he had no points, no assists, no steals, no blocked shots, and 1 rebound. But nothing can explain the odd, embarrassing lack of passion the Magic seem to exhibit as a team. This was the team that was supposed to put fear into the Bulls? The team that was the bright, young, shining force in the NBA? The dynasty in the making?

The Bulls surge so far ahead that Jackson clears the bench, and Buechler, Salley, Brown, and Wennington get some serious minutes. The Bulls win, 121–83, and one rock-solid fact has hit everyone—players, coaches, fans, TV viewers—smack in the face: This series is already over.

And it is. Postgame, Jackson offers his lame excuse on his opponents' behalf: "I don't think Orlando, perhaps, had adequate time to prepare."

Right. The Bulls would be about as mysterious to the Magic as Mickey Mouse. What do they need to know? A day from now Jordan will be announced as the league's Most Valuable Player, his fourth such honor, moving him ahead of former rivals Larry Bird and Magic Johnson, who each won three MVPs. Jordan will receive 97 percent of the first-place votes, the highest percentage anyone has received since the media began choosing the winner 15 years ago. How could Orlando prepare for a hurricane?

Grant misses the rest of the series with his elbow injury, and other of his teammates go down with an assortment of ailments, ranging from Nick Anderson's sprained wrist to Brian Shaw's stiff neck. Shaq tries some gruff talk at the start, saying of Rodman, "He's a gimmick. He'll never be on my level—on or off the court." But it's useless.

The Bulls sweep in four, and the Magic go home, erased as a power in the league, perhaps for years to come. In the final game, in front of the Magic faithful at the O-rena, just to suck a little more blood from the corpse, Jordan fires in 45 points on 16 of 23 shooting.

During the offseason, Shaq, who seems more interested in making rap CDs and starring in movies than in becoming the next lion-hearted warrior of the NBA, will move on to the Los Angeles Lakers for fabulous amounts of money. Penny Hardaway will be left with a team that has no soul, no identity, no Rodmanesque lunatic, no Jordanesque dictator, no Jacksonesque philosopher. "They have the talent to be champions," summed up Worm himself, even before he and his teammates had blown the Magic away. "But they don't know what it takes to be champion."

The only thing I witnessed of note off the court during the series occurred before Game 2 in Chicago. I was standing by my seat on the baseline before the game, when I noticed Jerry Krause carefully checking out the nameplates on every chair in the three rows of media seats. I then saw him get PR man Tom Smithburg and whisper something to him and point to a couple of name cards. The names, I could see, belonged to Dwayne Casey and Brendan Malone, scouts for the Seattle SuperSonics.

I went into the press room for a while, and when I came back the two scouts had been moved away from the middle and two rows back. Tit for tat. When Bulls scout John Paxson had worked a Sonics–Utah Jazz playoff game recently in Seattle, he'd found his seat way up and off the court. My only question was why the Sleuth didn't move the two spies to the 300-level, or have them taken into the parking lot and shot.

■ ■ ■

It's raining as I drive to the Berto Center, where two gardeners are hosing down the sidewalk and watering the plants in the downpour. Orders are orders.

It's early afternoon, and all the players are gone. Media, too. I take a seat in the quiet press room and zone out a while. My mind becomes blank, then I am dreaming. I dream I am in a blue sky, looking down on a green field. Footsteps jar me back to earth.

Phil Jackson walks in. He's wearing jeans, Air Jordans, a zipped-up hiking vest over a flannel shirt, and a Nike baseball cap.

"This is nice," he says, looking around. "Good place to write about basketball." He points to the empty court beyond the glass, the plaques and old newspaper stories framed on the walls. "Surrounded by basketball," he says. "The only thing bad is this."

He points to the lit-up, humming "Chicago Bulls" pop machine.

"Yeah, you're right," I say. "Everything in it is free. But it's empty."

"No," he says, shaking his head. "I meant because it's gaudy."

I laugh.

"It's just like these windows," I say. "They taunt you. The only time the blinds are up is when the gym is empty."

Jackson smiles. Don't think for an instant he doesn't endorse a lot of the Sleuth's clandestine operations.

I tell him how stunned I am at the way Orlando seemed to strike its big tent and hang up its collective jockstrap.

"We said the same thing here," he agrees.

I tell him I felt Horace Grant could have at least made a symbolic return to action, even if he could do nothing with his left arm.

"Well, maybe he could have come back and proven his value, taken a hero's role or something. We said the same thing about Shaw and Nick Anderson. When was the last time Nick did that? You start piecing things together about this thing. I mean, those guys, really . . ."

He looks at the floor.

"I don't know. I was bewildered," Jackson says. "Desire. Maybe it goes to group desire. Whether it's the character of Shaq and Penny, being young and immature, whether it's a coach that can't find the way to get them together—whatever it is, they don't seem to have a core."

What an easy thing to diagnose; what a difficult thing to acquire.

I ask him what he's been doing, and he tells me how he and his coaches have been watching film of the SuperSonics, because they're pretty sure the Sonics will dispose of the Jazz in their series that's still in progress, and then meet the Bulls in the finals. The coaches are making up scouting booklets for the players and patching together a video to show the team.

"We feel very good about playing Seattle," he says. "Very positive."

What about some of the stars on the Sonics? What about, for instance, guard Gary Payton, who just was voted NBA Defensive Player of the Year?

He's not as good a defender as either Michael or Scottie, the coach says.

So why did he get the award?

"They had to give something to Seattle," says Jackson. "It was good for them. We had everything else. Why not?"

True. In fact, Kukoc just won the NBA's Sixth Man of the Year award. It was a title Kukoc said he would never be happy with, since he thinks he should be a starter.

So how is the struggling Croatian these days?

"Toni has lost his mind. I was talking with his fellow countryman,

Ivica Dukan, our European scout, and he said Toni is messed up. But
I'm real proud of Toni. He hasn't begun to pout."

And Rodman?

"Dennis has been better than anybody else. Poised."

And lumbering Luc?

"I tell you, [assistant coach] Tex Winter's like right in my ear during
the course of these games yelling about Luc, and finally I said, 'Tex,
give the fucking guy a *break,* would you? He can hit a jump shot. He can
make a pass when he's in the triangle. Don't expect him to make a *move.*'"

Jackson talks about the problems the Sonics pose for the Bulls, taking my notebook and drawing sharp and impenetrable lines all over two
pages, showing me how the two teams will go at each other.

"They give us a couple matchup problems that hurt us," he says.
"Detlef Schrempf is tough for Scottie, always has been. And Sam
Perkins is very heady and can do multiple things. And they play a trapping defense with a certain fervor. They throw you into disarray, especially if you try to do too much against them."

He diagrams the Sonics' complicated trapping rotation against the
ball, and in a burst of clarity, I say, "What about this guy here if they
double down on that guy there?"

"Well, that's the thing," says Jackson, looking at me with a teacher's
approval. "Too many times in that defense they end up seeing a guard
like Payton on a center. And what are they going to do about this guy
here? We have a triangle. Do they want to run off and double-team anybody in this sequence, and leave another man open? We bait them into
this."

"Hmm. If you have your spacing," I say, "it seems to play right into
the hands of the triangle."

"Perfect," he says. "Perfect. But don't overstate that in the paper,
please. Just say our offensive system seems to be pretty good against
their angle of defense."

There's one other person whose condition needs to be checked.
How's the MVP of the league?

"Well, let me put it this way. [Assistant coach] Jimmy Rodgers is a
guy who really hasn't been around Michael that much, and he said to

him, 'Jeez, now that we're in the finals, our task is really in front of us.' Michael said, 'Listen, I've never been a bridesmaid.'"

Jackson leaves, and I stick around. It's 4:30 now and the day is shot. I make a couple of calls, then just sit. It seems the lights out on the shadowy court are playing tricks on me. Slowly, the court is getting brighter. Indeed, the big bulbs on the ceiling are gradually starting to heat up.

I hear a bouncing ball and then I see Toni Kukoc, Mr. 2-for-32 from the 3-Point Line, dribbling out onto the floor. The press room is dim, and at first Kukoc can't see me. Ivica Dukan walks out onto the floor with Kukoc. Then Kukoc looks directly at me, points at me, and says something to someone out of sight.

Within seconds the mechanical curtain begins to descend, and soon the court is blocked from sight.

28

TODAY PHIL JACKSON HAS HIS TEAM OBSERVE A MOMENT OF silence for LSD experimenter and former Harvard professor Timothy Leary, who died a few days ago on May 31 at age 75 of prostate cancer. The crazed drug guru's motto during the '60s was "Turn on, tune in, drop out." Among his final words were "Why not?" (which he repeated over and over again in different inflections causing people who were in attendance to laugh with delight) and "Yeah." And his very last utterance, according to his stepson, who was at the bedside, was "Beautiful."

Leary was not a hero to a lot of people. But Jackson, as I've noted, was not a wallflower during the flower power years; being a rebel is not a negative in his viewpoint. After all, the title of his first book, done with good pal and future CBA assistant Charley Rosen back in the early '70s, was *Maverick*.

Jackson called Leary "a spokesman for my generation," which is a debatable statement. I found myself, upon hearing this, wondering how

Red Auerbach and John Wooden were treating Leary's demise, whether they felt he spoke for *any* generation.

"Timothy was really maligned," Jackson explains to me now. "People say, 'He ruined a whole generation of America. He's a Communist. He screwed it up.' But he helped change the lives of a whole generation. 'Turn on, tune in' didn't do us that much harm, and in retrospect it probably did us a great deal of good. It gave us another consciousness, a new perspective. That's one of the reasons society has changed so much over twenty years. His influence over Richard Alpert, who became Baba Ram Dass, was dramatic. And that led to more of a spiritual side of the movement. The radical left tuned in to the revolutionary side. I followed the spiritual side of the revolution.

"I always knew you were drawn behind the doors of perception by drugs, but it wasn't the real thing," he continues. "I was aware of that. I only used LSD twice in my life. One experience was remarkable, and one wasn't."

I ask him if he had a bad trip, one of those scary, emergency-room jags.

"No," he says. "One of them was not memorable or enlightening, and one of them was. In that one I was truly in—amidst—the cellular structure of the world, what makes up the world. If you find that space, you can find the harmony, whatever it is you're looking for."

Clearly this coach has interests outside basketball, way outside. In the summers, when he takes off for Montana, he leaves the world of zone presses and salary caps behind. He'll settle back in the land of the big sky, with his Native American artifacts and talismans, and read book after book.

"So many books," he told me during one of our discussions. "So little time."

We talked about Montana, and tarpon fishing, and Key West, and the writers who extol the manly pursuit of self through conquering or submitting to nature. We talked about his favorite writers. He mentioned Thomas McGuane.

But cutting through it all, he stated, was Jim Harrison. "I think Harrison might be the best writer of that type outside of Hemingway," said the coach. "I like what he writes about Montana. And his collection of short stories about Michigan is close to Hemingway's *Big Two-Hearted River*. But he hates being compared to Hemingway. 'Oh, you fly-fish, too?' I really like Jim."

"You know him?" I asked.

"No, not at all. But I know him. Because I've read his works."

I mention that I have met Harrison and that I admire his courage and honesty; that I think much of his pain, alienation, and introspection come from the fact that he is a big, rugged outdoorsman who is tormented by the fact he is blind in one eye, and has been since he was a child.

"Do you know how that happened?" asked Phil.

"Some girl got mad at him and stabbed him, something like that?" I try to recall.

"A neighborhood girl, he had her pants down, and she grabbed a bottle and hit him in the face with it. Not very noble at all. But he was only, like, five or six, doing stuff that kids that age will do."

Phil had given some thought to this particular kind of injury.

"Your whole perception is different," he said. "I played basketball with a guy who couldn't see somebody coming up on his right-hand side. Imagine that. Or Harthorne Wingo; he had a blind spot, because he got shot in the eye with a BB."

That led him to ponder the pain that people use as their fulcrum for success, and novel-writing as a foray into self-discovery. "You can say an awful lot in a novel, but it's like taking a journey not knowing where you're going to end up. My friend Charley Rosen came to me and said, 'I got this great idea! I'm going to write about the Jews who went across the country playing basketball, the House of David, only I'll make up different characters and a different storyline. It'll be great!' And I said, 'Yeah, it is great.' But then you have to *do* everything, the conflict, the scenes. You travel along at three hundred words a day, trying to put stuff down, and you're not getting far down the road at all. All this crap going through your head? For as long as a novel lasts? It would be just like a basketball season for me, only worse. I'd be up, sleepless, at night. I see why those guys smoked and drank and did all that. They did it so they could go to sleep."

Still, Jackson uses novels to move his own life ahead, and sometimes to try to move his players' lives ahead. He recently gave Jordan a novel by John Edgar Wideman, for instance.

"I said to Michael, 'I think you might like this book, because I respect the author.' Wideman's a good writer, a black guy, who played some basketball at Penn. His brother was murdered. And I think he had interviewed Michael for a magazine story a few years ago."

Did Jordan read the book?

"I don't know," said Jackson. "A lot of these guys, they take my books and throw them in the trash. If they do read the book, they know that I put some thought into who they are, what I'd like them to read or what I think they'd like to read. If nothing else, it's just a gift from me to them."

■ ■ ■

It's for sure now: The Bulls will be playing the SuperSonics for the crown. It's a good matchup, an appropriate one. Seattle won the Western Conference regular season with a 64–18 record, second only to the Bulls' 72–10 in the East. These are the two best teams in the league.

The Bulls seem ready for the test. Certainly, they are rested, having had eight days off between the Orlando series and the championship series, which begins tonight, June 5, at the United Center.

Yesterday at practice, Steve Kerr had chatted with former Bull B. J. Armstrong, now with the Golden State Warriors, but currently doing some playoffs work for a California TV station. "I feel like a young B. J.," Kerr had joked to the player whose spot he has taken on the Bulls' roster. A baby-faced 28-year-old, Armstrong is actually two years younger than Kerr. They discussed the 3-pointer technique that has made each so invaluable in this league.

"It's all about one thing," says Armstrong. "Volume. Get 'em up."

Kerr laughs. Then he says to Armstrong, who shared in three NBA titles during his service with the Bulls, "You know, everybody comes up to me and says, 'Hope you get another ring.' Man I don't have *one*."

■ ■ ■

Right from the start, it looks as if Kerr is going to get that first ring for sure.

The Bulls take an early lead in Game 1, then battle back and forth with the Sonics through three periods. At the end of the third quarter, they have only a slim 79–77 lead. But the fourth sees them pour it on in their trademark fashion, stepping up their defense to dog-pack intensity. In the final quarter Kukoc breaks free of his mental prison and bombs in 10 straight points, 6 of them on 3-point shots. The Bulls score 28 points in the final 12 minutes, to Seattle's 13, and win going away, 107–90.

Bruising power forward Shawn Kemp is a force underneath and at the line, making 14 of 16 free throws to finish with a game-high 32 points. But the most notable event of the game is the emergence of Sonics egg-beater Frank Brickowski as the guy who is either (a) not going to take any guff from the confetti-coiffed Rodman, whose book is now No. 1, hardcover nonfiction, with a bullet; (b) going to purposely rile Worm to the point of self-destruction; or (c) get himself tossed from each game for acting like a dim-witted goon. Tonight he clearly follows the third path.

Rodman picks up 5 personal fouls and a technical in the game, but Brickowski, who was sent in by Sonics coach George Karl in the second quarter with the seeming purpose of egging Worm on to a second T, simply blows *himself* up. With less than 90 seconds to go in the half, Brick shoves Worm out of bounds as they battle for rebounding position and earns himself a flagrant foul in the process. Jack Haley, clad in those elegant Bigsby & Kruthers threads for which he has become noted, comes out onto the floor to protect Rodman from the evil Sonic. Or something. At any rate, Brickowski sees Haley and snarls, "What are you, his fucking babysitter?"

That gets him another quick T from ref Joey Crawford, and the automatic heave-ho. As he is escorted from the floor, the flattopped, Fu Manchued forward glowers like Norman Bates being punished by Mommy. He leaves behind him a comical box score line that reads: 2 minutes played, no shots made or attempted, no free throws, no points, no rebounds, no assists, no steals, no blocks, 2 techs, and sayonara.

"We're in the beginning of a learning process," says Coach Karl afterward. "The league will not allow Frank Brickowski to be a player."

And maybe it shouldn't. Asked about the boos that rained down on him from the Chicago crowd, and the boos that will cascade over him every time he plays at the United Center from now on, Brickowski says: "What else is new? I might cry. I might break down."

■ ■ ■

Near the end of the first quarter of Game 2, Michael Jordan rises into the air for an 18-foot jumper, loses the ball on a tip by the Sonics' Hersey Hawkins, then turns and pursues Gary Payton as the guard drives for a breakaway dunk with the stolen ball. As Jordan retrieves the ball after Payton's basket and prepares to take it out of bounds, Payton stands defiantly in front of him and does a blank-faced, "uh-huh-your-mama" number for the old vet.

Seeing this, I want to say, "Aw, gee, Gary, don't do *that.*"

But it is over in a flash, a tiny, unchangeable event, filed away in Jordan's memory bank for future motivational use. Jordan yanks out just a small portion of that motivation to help the Bulls win this contest, 92–88, but it's obvious there's a whole bunch of the same juice remaining. He finishes with 29 points, 8 rebounds, 6 assists, and 2 steals, but it is his ferocity that stands out.

Midway through the game Jordan pulls the relapsing Kukoc to the side and drills him with his dagger-eyed look. Kukoc has been very passive again, hesitant on his shot, and seemingly unsure of what his role is acourt. "Are you scared?" Jordan barks. "If you are, sit down."

Kukoc hits a couple of important shots in the fourth quarter to help the Bulls to the win, one of them a dunk off a Jordan feed. But with the Sonics so down and out after two games, I find myself thinking about the Bulls' offcourt situation.

A man called me the other day and said that he had it on good authority that Reinsdorf was ready to sell the Bulls, either to Disney or a giant communications company. It seemed so logical. Buy low, sell high. Use the building for all its entertainment possibilities. Use the Bulls as programming. And the Bulls never will be higher than they are now, poised to be named the greatest team of all time. So I called Reinsdorf, telling his secretary what I was thinking, wondering if the boss could give me a statement, yes or no, figuring I'd never hear from him.

I was driving down Wabash when my car phone went off. It was Reinsdorf. I pulled to the side of the street. As is typical of our conversations, which have been few, he wanted me to know I was full of baloney.

"I am so tired of these fucking rumors," he said. "Just to calm me down, *quit asking.*"

All right, I said. But what about contract negotiations with Michael, Phil, and Dennis?

"Let's just enjoy these games," he said. "We're only ahead two games to nothing."

This was true. But the simple fact that Rodman had not gone insane, done what he did last year with the Spurs, or even acted as badly as, say, Frank Brickowski made this series exceptional and the Bulls' 2–0 lead something close to a mortal lock.

I knew early that Game 2 was won—that's my prerogative as a know-it-all sportswriter—so I lingered after halftime in the restricted area under the stands, the area that leads to the locker rooms, the wives' room, the press room, and the loading ramp where people like Tim Hallam and NBA press chief Brian McIntyre adjourn for their precious cigarette fixes.

Standing just under the stands, and far enough back so she can see none of the action, is Shirley Rodman, Dennis's mom, who is visiting from Dallas. She is a nice-looking, middle-aged woman in black slacks and blouse, hair up on top of her head in a tight coil, with touches of gold in it.

I introduce myself.

"I know who you are," she says. "I read your work. You're not like that Mallornati guy in your paper. He's mean."

I consider telling her that I have my moments, too, just like Mariotti, but don't. I ask her about her son instead, what he was like back in the early days in Dallas.

"He was always the baby," she says. "He was so short, and he had all these allergies. When his father left, it seemed to be real hard on him. Dennis wanted to know when he was coming back. I took him to a psychologist, and he said Dennis kept too much inside, and doing that was causing the allergies. Kids picked on him all the time, but I never would have known, because he never said anything."

He was so sensitive and so passive, she adds, that she finally transferred him to another school when he was about nine years old. "He was a kid for a very long time. I suppose you could say it was my fault. But I didn't know I would be separated and divorced so quickly. Dennis's father was in the Air Force, and we were together about five years. As for raising Dennis and his two sisters, I didn't know another way. I did the best I could, but I didn't have a clue as to how to raise them. I sacrificed for the kids, and I'm proud that they didn't have unwanted pregnancies, didn't use drugs, that they turned out to be pretty good kids."

Did her son do any of the goofy things back then that have become his trademarks now, I ask, things like slipping into silk halter tops?

"No," she says, shaking her head. "He never dressed in women's clothing. He had his own room, with normal clothes. And it wasn't the projects. He says it was the projects, but that's in his mind. It was an apartment. I was *never* on welfare. Because he didn't have a father figure, I enrolled him in the Big Brothers program, and for four or five years he had that. But he was a mama's boy. So small, and always acted younger than he was. He always stayed at home; he would never leave. He'd just watch TV and play video games."

The roaring of the crowd makes her jump. She is under the stands because watching the Bulls and her son is too nerve-wracking for her in large doses. A kind woman, it seems to me. I try to send my mind back 25 or 30 years ago to another place, to another reality, to try to envision whatever pain her little boy felt, the homely, lonely kid with the skinny legs and the round ears that protruded from his head like doorknobs. I get close, but I can't connect.

I ask Mrs. Rodman whether there was a time when she thought her only son was headed nowhere. Or, conversely, whether there ever was a time when she thought he was headed *somewhere.*

She looks very sad. She is not aware right now that her son is on his way to collecting 20 rebounds, including an incredible 11 offensive boards, which will tie an NBA finals record.

"I thought back then, when he was a little older, that if I did not do something drastic, he was headed toward something bad," she says. "So I put him out."

Dennis has talked about that time when he was a teenager, out of high school, doing nothing, and his mom tossed him from the apartment. "I went from house to house, staying with friends, maybe sleeping on their floor or couch," he says in *Bad As I Wanna Be.* "Many nights I just walked all night, going nowhere . . ."

"He was a follower," Shirley Rodman tries to explain. "It was for about ninety days. But I knew *exactly* where he was all the time. It was very hard for me. I don't think I could do it again."

She lifts her glasses. Her voice was cracking, I noticed. She is taking deep, sighing breaths. She is wiping tears from her eyes.

She is quivering, gentle figure, overwhelmed with emotion.

"Now you see where he gets it," she says.

■ ■ ■

I'm sitting in the press room, typing my night's column, when I see my pal Dwight Manley come scurrying through, carrying his briefcase. Like a modern-day brush salesman, he opens the leather bag, fishes around, then drops a Worm Pop from Custom Confections, Boise, Idaho, in front of me. The purple and white sucker resembles Medusa with earrings and a fat nose. It has Rodman's signature across the plastic wrapper and a box printed on the back that says, "Nutrition Facts." According to the box the sucker contains 140 calories, 25 grams of sugar, and nothing else.

"The company expects to sell fifteen million," says Manley. "Dollar apiece."

Then he hands me six Rodman tattoos. Just peel 'em and slap 'em on.

"They're out in two weeks," he says.

"You're unbelievable," I say.

"Why?"

"You just are."

29

BECAUSE OF THE IMPOSSIBILITY OF PREDICTING PLAYOFF schedules with any accuracy—because rounds can last as few as four games or as many as seven—Games 3, 4, and 5 of this series are coming at a bad time for me. Well, not really bad, just worrisome. All three contests (Game 5 only if necessary) are in Seattle. Which is fine. Lovely city. Nice time of year. Beautiful Puget Sound. But coming as they are in the second full week in June, they catch my family in a crazy pattern of travel. My wife is going to Indianapolis for a week of charity work. My 12- and 13-year-old daughters are going to Toronto for a five-day swim meet; my 9-year-old daughter is going to Oregon to visit her aunt and uncle on their farm. And I am going to Seattle.

That means I can stock the fridge with milk and root beer, lay in a few dozen bags of Chee-tos, fill the kitchen table with bowls of Froot Loops, put out some Dominos pizza money, and hope my five-year-old son Zack is still around when I return. Either that, or I take him with me to Seattle.

The latter it must be. But I can't have a little kid following me every moment as I work. I need a babysitter. But who? In a panic I ask our neighbors across the street, the Colemans, if their 14-year-old son, Chris, would be interested in a working trip to Seattle for the NBA finals, all expenses paid, maybe a ticket to one of the games, with the added benefit of getting to hang out daily with a very enthusiastic, courteous, and athletic young man, Zack.

Praise the Lord! The Colemans agree. Chris packs his bags, I pack Zack's and mine, I collect most of my United Airlines frequent flyer miles and parlay them into a pair of roundtrip tickets for the boys, the Colemans drive us to O'Hare, and the three of us are off to the great Northwest.

I settle the boys into our single room at the Madison Hotel on Sixth Avenue—me in the bed, them on the floor in sleeping bags, of course—and tell them they can go to the hotel pool, order some room service burgers, watch TV, ride the elevators like Eloise at the Plaza, play catch, whatever.

"Dad," says Zack, looking out over the hills that lead down to Elliott Bay to the west and the Kingdome to the south and Key Arena to the north. "We're up high."

"We are," I say. "We're on the eighteenth floor." I give him a kiss and then head out to meet some of my fellow journalists at a bar in Pioneer Square, to get the lay of the land.

I meet up with Dan Bickley and Jay Mariotti from my paper and Dan Bernstein from WSCR radio. We order beers and toast the impending games and the near-certain Chicago championship. "In your book," says Bernstein, "if I am going to appear at all, I insist on going by the name 'Buck.'"

Buck it is, I salute.

We talk about the Seattle music scene, about Nirvana and the departed Kurt Cobain, Blind Melon's Shannon Hoon, Seattleite Jimi Hendrix, and all the other drug-dead rockers like Janis Joplin and, heck, Phil Jackson's hero Jerry Garcia, and we talk about the junkie culture that has infiltrated this city of mellow backpackers and gourmet coffee. *Rolling Stone* dedicated its May issue to the Seattle heroin–rock scene. The lead story is titled, "Junkie Town: They Came for the Music and Stayed for the Smack," with the subhead, "Two years after the death of Kurt Cobain heroin still has a grip on Seattle."

A girl sits down at the table next to ours in this jammed tavern. She looks to be about 18. I get her attention.

"Do you shoot heroin?" I ask.

"No," she says. "And I never will."

She drinks from her vodka and tonic and chats with her group. They look fairly normal. The girl turns back to me. "But two of my best friends from high school are on heroin," she says.

■ ■ ■

The next morning Zack, Chris, and I stop at a Seattle's Best Coffee shop and fuel up, then walk the two blocks to the Four Seasons Hotel, where the Bulls are staying. The boys are wearing their NBA caps and are carrying autograph books. Chris has a camera with him.

They spot Jack Haley in the lobby and go after him. Gracious, do they even want his autograph? The other day Haley was telling a reporter how important it is for him to have that Armani label inside his lapel. And then, too, he said he needs designer underwear for all the locker room scrutiny, and those special moments.

I feel like a fan, being here with the boys. But they seem to be enjoying themselves. They rush around in a frenzy of celebrity sightings. Luc Longley and his father get into the elevator, both men ducking under the door. When Luc comes down again and uses the house phone, the boys nail him. I even get Luc to pose with the pair for a photo. This is not very professional of me, using my sportswriter's status to get access, but so what—following the Bulls is like following a rock tour, anyway. The Bulls seem to be taking the competitive side of the tour quite seriously—after all, the only time they played in Seattle this season they blew a 13-point halftime lead and lost, 97–92—but as they get on the two buses to go to practice, they are engulfed by hundreds of screaming, giddy fans who look like renegade fanatics from a Michael Jackson concert.

As the buses pull away, Chris watches in amazement. "There was a guy," he says, "who had old McDonald's french fry containers he wanted Michael Jordan to sign."

■ ■ ■

Game 3 figures to be a tough game, a revenge match for the SuperSonics. The Bulls are a "beatable" team, George Karl has said again and again. But to prove that, at some point Karl and his boys must beat them. Home courts of good NBA teams are designed for the home teams' success. The quirks of the wood, the basket vision, the seating of the opponents, the introductions, the roaring of the fans, the histrionics of the announcer, the irritating, anti-opponent sound effects, the psychological impact it all has on the refs—all combine to create a huge home-court advantage. In the case of the Sonics, it led to a 38–3 regular-season record at home (second only to the Bulls' in the NBA).

It seems the Sonics are primed to whack the Bulls. Trouble is, Michael Jordan and his mates are obviously primed for something different.

Things start badly for the home crowd even before the game begins. Noted middle-of-the-road saxophonist Kenny G plays the national anthem as though it is some form of new-age jazz/elevator music, trilling all about and then holding the final note for well over a minute. As the sound blares on and on, dazzling folks with G's lung capacity but irritating more than a few people with its sheer arrogance, not to mention the damn noise, Eddie Vedder, the Pearl Jam singer and Rodman's rockin' bro', who is seated near us media types, finally yells, "Bullshit!"

He could have been talking about the home team.

The Bulls come screeching out of the blocks like a pack of dragsters. They race to a 7–0 lead on Jordan's 3-pointer with less than 2 minutes gone, then a 19–4 lead with less than 6 minutes gone, after 5 straight points by Toni Kukoc. The only reason Kukoc is starting is that Ron Harper is out with a bum knee.

But it makes no difference. The Sonics seem lost in another dimension, a world of tiny rims and lead shoes. Amazingly, the Bulls take a 22-point lead, 34–12, on a Rodman jam off a Pippen assist with 1:20 to go in the first period. This is beyond serious for Seattle, this is pathetic.

In the second quarter it seems the Sonics might be in the process of getting their brains in gear and at least attempting to make this game respectable. Gary Payton sinks a couple of baskets and sub Vincent Askew hits a shot to cut the Bulls' lead to 11. But then Jordan enters one of those zones where few other athletes have ever ventured.

In 3½ minutes he scores 15 straight points for the Bulls, and when the dust has settled, they have a 62–38 halftime lead.

Yikes. Seattle fans have already started booing their team. Home-court advantage? Don't think so.

During the break I go into the same crowded washroom as plenty of other ticketholders. While I'm waiting for a urinal to open up, Jerry Reinsdorf walks in.

"You selling yet?" I ask him.

He chuckles. "Thanks for using *freaking* and not *fucking* in your column when you quoted me," he says.

"You're welcome, Jerry," I say. "And it wasn't because we couldn't print *fucking* in the Sunday newspaper. You know, for Jordan this is all part of a salary drive."

"It may work," says the CEO.

Jordan had 26 points in the first half, 6 points more than any Sonics player will score in the entire game. In the third quarter Seattle cuts the lead to 14, but it amounts to nothing. In the crowd is Cindy Crawford, supermodel, eyeing the ever-so-modish Dennis Rodman, sizing him up for a television shoot they will be doing for MTV's *House of Style,* a parchment-deep show that keeps teens informed about developments in the world of hip fashion. "Dennis is going to try on some swimwear," she tells reporters. Maybe even a thong. "It *would* be interesting to see what *that* would be like," gushes Crawford, who has long been promoted as a "smart" model.

In the fourth quarter the Bulls crank it up some more, while Sonics bad boy Brickowski seems once again to be self-destructing in his attempt to be the Western Conference's oncourt answer to the Worm. All of Rodman's sly pushing and arm-hooking and lane-hanging and flopping serves only to frustrate Brick, who cannot do those things the way Rodman can. Or probably more to the point, does not have the mindset to do them the way Worm does.

With about 6 minutes to play, the Sonics forward grows so frustrated he grabs Rodman in a stranglehold, gets nailed with a flagrant-foul call, and is summarily launched from the game. Shortly after that, Shawn Kemp goes after Rodman, who has become the master of passivity. So unnerving is Rodman to the Sonics that, through their anger, they have turned him into something no one would have thought possible: a Sympathetic Guy.

But more than anyone, it was Michael Jordan who made the ultimate, depressing difference against the grasping Sonics. The entire city seemed to acknowledge that maybe their team was just in way over its head, facing a player who had done the same thing to every foe he had met. The lead story in the *Seattle Post-Intelligencer* by reporter Jim Moore the next day said it all: "Last night in Game 3 of the NBA Finals, [the Sonics] were buried by Michael Jordan and the Bulls, 108–86. The series and the season is about to end for the Sonics, who are one game from being swept under the Bulls red carpet.

"Hoping the energy from their home crowd would ignite them, the Sonics couldn't even get a cough or a sputter. The battery was dead, and soon, it would appear, they will be too."

After the game, George Karl said. "The odds are against us. Everybody is against us." He added that the Bulls looked almost scary to him: "I think that's the first time I ever saw Chicago with killer eyes."

Jordan scoffed at that notion. "We have killer eyes every time we step on the floor," he said. Oh, and one other thing. There had been a lot of "conversation" recently, off the court and on, Jordan said. "I must admit trash-talking is part of the game. I talk trash, too," he said, changing his old holier-than-thou tune. "But you can't go out there and just give it 'lip service.'"

That would be for Gary Payton, personally.

∎ ∎ ∎

I tell the concierge manning the stand at the Four Seasons that I want to get a message to Phil Jackson.

"There is no one registered by that name here," he says snootily.

"He's the coach of the Chicago Bulls, the basketball team that's staying here," I say, getting a little Brickowski in my voice. "Maybe you've heard of them?"

"Sir, we don't have a guest under that name."

"He's probably using another name. Some Indian name. He's the coach. And he's here. He's been walking through the lobby."

"There is no Phil Jackson here."

He made a charade of looking at the guest list.

"Don't you see those tall men always walking through, black men coming and going?" I say. "This guy's tall and white, got a beard."

"I'm sorry."

Well, this was leading nowhere, except toward manslaughter, so I write a note—as Jackson had asked me to, so we could schedule a chat session—and give it to the fine young company man.

"Now then," I say, "I would deeply appreciate it if you would get this to Mr. Jackson, the coach of the Bulls." He was starting to give me his spiel again. "Whatever name he's registered under. He's expecting it. Thank you."

That was yesterday. Today I wait and wait and hear nothing from Phil. And I need to talk to him today, because tonight's game for the 3–0 Bulls could likely spell the end of the season for everyone. So I go to the Four Seasons, eat a late breakfast there, see that there's a different concierge at work, and just wander around in the lobby. Suddenly, at noon a kind of whirring sound starts up, coupled with a flurry of activity. The Bulls have arrived! Just back from their shootaround to loosen up for tonight's game, the players make a beeline to the elevators, autograph hounds nipping at their heels. Zack and Chris are right in the mix. They followed me over, after they ate at our hotel. Zack is happy that he got visiting Matt Geiger's autograph in the Madison Hotel coffee shop, bummed that he can't go to the top of the Space Needle.

I see Phil, ask him if he got my message.

"No," he says.

"Why am I not surprised?" I mumble to myself. I ask if we can have that chat.

He looks at his watch, as the last players scurry past him to the elevators. "In a half hour," he says.

"And Phil," I say before he can leave. "What name are you registered under?"

"Swift Eagle."

■ ■ ■

"It's almost biblical," Jackson says as we sit in plush armchairs on the mezzanine level of the hotel. Across from us, just out of earshot but always alert, sits an off-duty, plainclothes Chicago cop who is not going anywhere. The NBA stirs some real passion these days. You just never know.

Jackson is talking about the way the Bulls' foes have been lining up and then dropping with so little fight. "Like Joshua and the walls of Jericho falling down. Earlier in the year people had been saying we were doing it with smoke and mirrors. We *are* doing it with smoke and mirrors. It's true. We present the image that we're poised and strong, that we have no weaknesses."

I can think of a few examples of what could be interpreted as weaknesses. In Game 2, Scottie Pippen, the man with the long arms, was awarded 2 critical free throws in the final seconds. He clanged the first shot. His second shot was so bad, it came within a hair of hitting no metal at all. Fortunately, Rodman was there to retrieve the ball, and the Bulls hung on to win. And Longley—he looks asleep at times. And Harper played 1 minute in Game 3, actually just a few seconds, because of his bad knee.

But Jackson's point is well taken. The Bulls not only are mighty, they *seem* mighty.

"The thought occurred to me today," says Jackson, "that this may be the last practice I have with these guys, all together. It's one of those things I'm trying to remind myself of, to stay in the present, because that's all there is. When it's gone, it's gone. You know?"

Reinsdorf has not been in a hurry to re-sign Jackson, Jordan, or Rodman. "If you don't sign a new contract, Michael has said he won't sign," I say. "Rodman said yesterday, 'If Phil Jackson's not back, if Michael's not back. I'm definitely not coming back.' How is all this going to be re-solved?"

"Well, I know that for Dennis a lot is tied to what I do," he says. "And to give up on a guy like Dennis, who is as popular and effective as he has been, would be a travesty. And Scottie, just the other day, came to me and said, 'Don't leave. Don't leave me here.' But Jerry Reinsdorf believes in a chain of command, in that kind of management where a certain amount of tension exists between positions in the organization. It pushes you toward your best production. Maybe it works. Look at our success. But maybe it's because of other things.

"I take that up with the team, tell them that any one of us can say he's the one that made the team successful. Krause could say, 'I brought the team together.' The coaching staff could claim credit for the way the team plays. The players could take credit for the actual doing of the deed. Michael Jordan could take credit for being the leader. But history has a way of bringing people together in the right place at the right time for whatever reason. So you can't take one issue and pull it out. You have to enjoy being part of the package. I enjoy being part of it. And yet I also enjoy believing that success is coming from my ability to be a lone wolf, a lobo, a maverick inside this organization that prides itself on being a family. I have autonomy without having to have created the situation for myself. They did. Because I'm not signed.

"Michael could say the same thing about being in the last year of his contract. And clearly we've exacted the best possible Dennis Rodman because he's in the last year of *his* contract. Some of this has been created by the genius of Jerry Krause, by seeing Rodman as this risk–opportunity and knowing that Michael would perform at the level he has, because he's been pushed to this point of let's-just-shut-up-and-play. But for me now, with my contract, I have to have a walk-away attitude. If it's not right. All the other coaching jobs are gone, as far as I know, except for Milwaukee. There's nothing wrong with stepping back. The only thing is, I have a relationship with Michael, Scottie, and Dennis." Jackson has said he'll retreat to Montana to weather any storms, for as long as it might take.

"Do you still believe in the journey?" I ask.

"It is the journey," he says. "The goal is obviously wonderful, but the journey is the essence. The steps of the journey are not all extremely joyful, though they are purposeful. The low point in the journey was when Dennis went down with the calf injury before the fourth game [of the season]. That was a concern. We wondered what his mindset would be if he was distant from the team. But he stayed tight during the injury."

There was also the struggle of the second roadtrip west during the last week in January through the All-Star game in the second week in February. "The guys were pushed beyond their limits. It caught up with us and fatigued us. Scottie was hurting, Dennis had a broken finger."

"He did? I never knew that."

"The one he gets taped. The little finger on his right hand. I don't think we made an issue of it. We didn't know it was broken for about a week. He caught it in someone's jersey."

"Oh, I can't believe *that*," I say. It's a joke, but Swift Eagle misses it, because he's saying that the setbacks were *good* for the team, that "people stepped up and filled in. Then when Dennis was suspended, Michael filled in with a lot of scoring."

What about Michael? I ask. What does Jackson think of that rare bird of prey?

"I've never seen him take better care of himself. He gets up in the morning, does his workout, his routine, and just maintains this high energy level. He's always been a guy who had an undue amount of energy—you know, five or six hours of sleep, go golfing—a guy who could push himself to the limit. But I've never seen him like this. Dennis, too, is a great gym guy, always around a gym. But he stays up all night, he'll go to a bar and party, and though he may not do a whole lot of stuff, he's not a teetotaler, either. But Michael is just so consistent with his effort that he has set an unbelievable tone for his team."

And then, Jackson says, there is Jordan's confidence. "I remember Bill Cartwright saying he'd never forget flying out to Phoenix in 1993 to play the Suns, a team that had won, what, sixty-two games that year? Going into the finals against the hottest team in the league, with this impeccable home-court record, and Michael getting off the plane, lighting up a cigar, and saying, 'Don't worry, boys, we'll take care of business.'

And we won two games in a row there, put them in a hole from which they never recovered.

"And he did the same thing when they played Cleveland, and Michael had missed some big free throws in a loss. He was the last one to get on the bus, and he said, 'We'll find a way.' Then he made the miracle shot over Craig Ehlo. There's a buoyancy he brings. That poise."

Hasn't Phil also said he wouldn't mind running his old pal Bill Bradley's presidential campaign, when the former Knick decides to go for the big one?

"I was misquoted on that one," he says. "I said I would *offer* to work *in* his campaign."

I tell him that I heard on the radio that Bradley 'fessed up to smoking pot with Phil way back when.

"He may have smoked it once or twice, but he never, ever really participated. He was a straight shooter. Had great balance."

I mention that Bradley has always seemed kind of aloof. Caring and bright, but somehow aloof. And I know Bradley was an only child, a condition Jackson has talked about from time to time as it pertains to his own sphere. B. J. Armstrong was an only child, as was Will Perdue, among others. And Jerry Krause.

"Yeah, Bill was an only child," says the coach. "They're often spoiled as children. And they tend to be very comfortable alone, and aloof. They're fastidious in some of their manners, or they can be complete garbage pigs if they want to get on the other side. I've found it's harder, sometimes, to pull them into groups. You take Scottie, on the other hand, the youngest of 12, he *likes* to be in a group. When I was Bill's roommate on the road for two years, I was amazed at his microscopic focus," Jackson continues. "During that time he wrote *Life on the Run*, and started his work on the penal community in America. He worked on his book constantly, and of course, in the reviews they all said it was typical Bill: 'He has not revealed anything of himself.' He was also still in the Air Force Reserve. And he was giving speeches all over, flying out at 5 A.M. to give them. I was amazed at his desire, his interest in educating himself."

But these past twelve months have seen three of Jackson's other heroes make more extreme passages than Bradley. Jerry Garcia, Mickey Mantle, and now Timothy Leary have all crossed to the pale beyond since the end of last season. And the most recent of these, Leary, was the one Phil spoke to his team about and held a brief remembrance for. Basketball lessons, Jackson wants his boys to know, can come from anywhere.

30

I THOUGHT IT WOULD BE FOUR AND OUT. BULLS IN A SWEEP. So did everybody.

But it isn't.

The Sonics rise up to play like an authentic NBA-finals basketball club, whacking the Bulls in Game 4, 107–86.

The Sonics seemed inspired by the return of injured veteran guard Nate McMillan to their lineup, which freed up Gary Payton to wheel and deal more than before; he finished with 21 points and 11 assists. Manchild Shawn Kemp also responded with a great game: 25 points, 11 rebounds, and a couple of rafter-rocking jams.

"I told them to go back to playing crazy and out of control," said George Karl of his strategy, making one wonder about the necessity of coaches in general.

But a large part of the Sonics' inspiration came from seeing all the preparations being made for the Bulls' championship ceremony on the Sonics' court. TV crews were working before the game on camera angles to get Commissioner Stern in just the right light for the trophy presentation, and champagne was being stockpiled for the celebration.

"I personally thought we'd lose that game," said disgusted Bulls assistant coach Tex Winter afterward. "I didn't sound off about it. But there were all the distractions, all the stuff affecting the players subconsciously. The anticipation of the sweep. Celebration plans back in Chicago. *The greatest team of all time.* It's a bunch of crap. Media talk."

Scottie Pippen shot 1 of 8 on 3-pointers, Steve Kerr 1 of 6. Ron Harper played 15 minutes, but was ineffective because of his knee.

Even Jordan fell to earth; he was 6 of 19 from the floor, for just 23 points.

"There was terrible karma before the game," said Steve Kerr. "People were bringing boxes of T-shirts into the locker room, we're doing public service announcements to avoid violence in Chicago, people are rehearsing the trophy ceremony before the game. All the questions I was getting asked were whether I was regretful for losing that one game to the Knicks, so we didn't go through the playoffs undefeated. Nobody wanted to talk about just winning *the series*."

Fortunately, Kerr has not lost his wits, or his wit.

"I'm a good shooter," he said thoughtfully. "I've been struggling, but the law of averages will take over. And as Stuart Smalley might say, Doggone it, people *like* me."

I feel compelled to inform Kerr that the 1995–96 NBA All-Interview Team, a serious production of the league, has been announced, and doggone it, he didn't make either the first or second team. Sadly, he missed making the second unit by just one vote, earning 17 votes from sportswriters and broadcasters who were polled by the league, compared to the 18 received by both the Clippers' Brian Williams and the Pistons' Grant Hill.

Kerr hung his head for a moment, then brightened. "I'm devastated," he said. "But I'll work hard on it during the offseason."

I then asked him if he was stunned that the blabber-mouthed and always available Bill Wennington had not made the squad, either.

"No," he replied. "You see, Bill actually is *part* of the media, and therefore is ineligible."

■ ■ ■

So the boys and I are here in Seattle for an unexpected two more days, now that there has to be Game 5.

The kids go off to the Space Needle on Thursday, taking the monorail for part of the ride. I am proud of them, for their independence and the fact they know how to act safely in cities. But when they get back to the room from their jaunt, they have more junk with them than carnival barkers. Among other souvenirs, Zack has a squashed penny with the image of the Space Needle on it. I don't want to know how much it cost. He also now has three baseball caps, a couple of T-shirts, several pins, two towels, a program, a poster, a pennant, and assorted minibasketballs. Plus his precious autographs.

When I leave them at 10 P.M. to have a beer with the gang, the boys are watching a sports show on ESPN, lying on their sleeping bags and playing catch with a green miniature Sonics ball.

At the bar in the lobby of the Madison I see Bob Ryan of the *Boston Globe,* relaxing with a cold one. I ask him how he finds the state of the NBA these days.

"There's nothing wrong with the game that having the coaches sit in the nosebleed seats wouldn't fix," he says.

At Kell's Irish Pub, my fellow worker Mike Mulligan and I and a couple other scribes listen to some fairly authentic ditties from the ould sod, then we go to a place called Crocodile's and hear a wasted-looking female singer with a band called Lucky Me screech about being "the killer of children" and other pleasantries. Supposedly Nirvana started at this joint. It couldn't have helped Cobain's state of mind.

■ ■ ■

One other note: On a Seattle TV newscast tonight the sports announcer referred to Jack Haley as "Bulls assistant coach Jack Haley." An honest mistake, but a big one.

■ ■ ■

On Friday the boys and I head over early to Key Arena for Game 5.

I try to get Chris and Zack into the media area, but am thwarted by the high security. So the two youngsters roam the lower level of the gym rather than take the seats I have acquired for them up near the roof supports. Zack finds me and says he is hungry. So I go into the media lounge and begin slipping him rolls and chicken legs, which he gobbles down as though he has never been fed.

While I'm handing Zack a drumstick, Dwight Manley comes racing in. He is sweating. He just blew in from somewhere distant.

"Trains, planes, and automobiles," he says.

Rodman is so happy these days, Manley says. Worm looks at all the checks flowing in and feels wonderful about them. "Not the material side of them," says the agent.

"The self-worth side of them?" I ask.

He nods.

Out on the floor, Game 5 turns into a repeat of Game 4. The Bulls can't make a 3-pointer, going a collective 3 for 26 from behind the stripe, and their triangle offense looks more like a mushroom cloud than a three-sided figure. The Sonics win 89–78, and back in Chicago the police force is once again taken off riot-prevention duty. Already, preparing for celebrations that haven't come has cost Chicago taxpayers $2 million.

Jordan is one unhappy camper. He has yelled at Luc and he has yelled at Toni, and he has yelled at the refs. He went so far tonight as to stick his jersey in his mouth and do a self-gagging routine rather than risk getting whistled for a technical for protesting what he thought was a bad call.

Rodman has been his usual master-of-diplomacy self, saying of the Seattle community, "Too many people kill themselves around here. They got so many damn coffee shops here because of one reason: People are bored and their lives are miserable."

But Seattleites' lives are getting better with their team's unexpected turnabout. As *Post-Intelligencer* columnist Art Thiel writes, "How about those Bulls? Has there ever been a 72-win team, has there ever been an NBA Finalist up 3–0, that looks so . . . vincible?"

He's got a point. Although no team has ever come back from 0–3 or 1–3 to win the NBA finals, and that is the statistic most people are using to explain that the Bulls have this series salted away, six teams *have* come back from 2–3 deficits to win. If you forget how the Sonics got to 2–3 themselves, it puts a whole different spin on matters.

The Key Arena was so loud for Game 5 that I sat for a good part of the contest with my fingers in my ears, all concerns about looking cool forgotten as I try to stave off any more hearing loss. That exuberance may be something the Sonics will feed off of as they fly to Chicago for the conclusion of this matchup. It could buoy them beyond reason. To say Bulls fans are worried just now would be an understatement. As we pack our bags at the hotel, Zack says to me, "Dad, did you see that circle?"

"Where?"

"In Seattle," he says. "Yeah, it was Dennis Rodman with a line through his face."

There will be lines through all the Bulls' faces if they somehow blow this championship. Not only will the players be labeled losers, they will be labeled epic, choking, worse-than-the-Cubs losers. Their phenomenal regular-season record of 72 wins will be a burden they will drag behind them like prison chains.

■ ■ ■

It's Sunday, June 16. Father's Day.

I wake up to the sounds of food being carried to me on a tray by my youngest daughter, Robin, and Zack. I thank them profusely, and then they giggle and hand me a bill for $1,000,000.

I call my dad and wish him a happy Father's Day, and as I do, I think about Michael Jordan's father, and Steve Kerr's, and even Worm's, the aptly named Philander Rodman, who left his young boy and never came back. I have seen brief interviews with Philander; as I recall, he is living in the Philippines running a seedy bar in the jungle, has something like 27 children and two current wives, and seems badder than Dennis. What would Dennis have become had things been different? Much different. Impossible to know.

"My father isn't part of my life," he writes in *Bad*. "I haven't seen him in more than thirty years, so what's there to miss? I just look at it like this: Some man brought me into this world. That doesn't mean I have a father; I don't."

Labels don't change reality.

But today is Father's Day. That has to mean something to these Bulls. I remember watching Luc Longley and his dad, a man just a few inches shorter than his son, walking through the hotel lobby. "Awesome," Chris Coleman had said. And it was.

I wrote a column for today, in which I acted on the need I felt to assuage a fretting public. I see it now on the front page of the *Sun-Times*. "Relax, all you panicking Bulls fans," it begins.

> This is the way it was supposed to be, the way it should be. Once the world (that being Chicago and satellite provinces such as Texas, New York and China) figured out that the Seattle SuperSonics actually are a very good team and not a stack of coffee-bean-

filled hand puppets, well, they should have just chilled a bit and enjoyed the show.

So the Sonics won Game 5 of the NBA Finals on Friday, 89–78.

Hello, anybody remember Seattle was 38–3 at home in the regular season?

I went on to say that as good as the Bulls are on the road, they are not *that* good. And I pointed out that the only inexplicable thing, the real monkey wrench in the gears of reality, was Seattle's performance in Game 3, their first game on their home court, a game in which they were so putrid, losing by 22 points, that they made everyone believe the Bulls were godlike.

Where did that Game 3 car crash come from? You'd have to ask the Sonics, look into their souls, to find out. I wrote:

> So disconcerted were various national journalists over Seattle's sudden turnaround that the ever-popular NBA-as-conspiracy-kings theories were floated all over Key Arena. *Remember when that envelope containing Patrick Ewing's name was immersed in dry ice before the needy New York Knicks somehow picked it from the barrel? And Penny going to Orlando?*
>
> Evil co-conspirator NBC stood to make $10 million if there were no sweep, and so, says the theory, the Bulls had to lose.
>
> "We just got through with our meeting where we told Scottie and Michael to shoot 20 percent from the field," whispered NBA public relations man Brian McIntyre on Thursday. "We'll be flying in Jake O'Donnell for Game 6, along with Earl Strom."
>
> O'Donnell, of course, is retired. And Strom is dead.
>
> I asked McIntyre if the league had anything else in the works.
>
> "Yes," he said. "We have radio units embedded in our people's molars."
>
> No, the Bulls would win because they were 48–2 at home this season, including the playoffs. And because the Sonics were content with their mini-revolt, with the little dance they got to do at home by preventing the Bulls from celebrating on Seattle's hard-

wood. "Not in our house!" the Sonics fans had chanted at the end. They seemed happy with that. The Bulls would win because they couldn't possibly shoot just 3 for 26 from 3-point range, as they did in Game 5. And because it was Father's Day.

I was sure I believed this. The Father's Day part most of all.

"Dad, let's play ball."

Zack's little voice cuts through my reverie.

I have my laptop and notes and my credentials and stats packed up in my bag, and I'm ready to go to the United Center. I don't want to be late. Heck, I don't want to be on time. I want to be way early. I want to get my mind right for the event. The game starts at 6:30; it's now 3. I have a 50-minute drive in front of me.

But it's Father's Day. I would never have a 5-year-old son on Father's Day again.

So we go to our driveway in front of the garage, and I pitch him an assortment of balls, whatever is lying around, underhand, gently. Whiffle balls and tennis balls and inflatable balls and a plastic ball that is cracked in half but taped up with ankle wrap. He smacks most of the spheres with his oversize orange plastic bat, bouncing them off the porch, the windows, me.

He hits one over the picket fence and into the trees. I direct him to it, and as he runs back, he trips over a root and goes flying. He skins his knee and comes up not exactly crying, but grim-faced, lip quivering, dejected.

He walks back through the gate.

"Dad," he says. "Why does the world have roots?"

It sounds like the kind of metaphorical question a writer would put into the mouth of a child. But it is what he says. He means it figuratively, I think. And I feel my heart breaking, the way a parent's will when mundane things intrude on the perfect world you plan for your kids.

"There are just things like that, that reach up to trip you," I say. "So you need to be careful."

He walks back to the plate, looking down.

"Trees need roots," he says. He's not talking to me. But I say, "That's right."

"If they didn't have roots, they'd die," he says.

He had been literal the whole time.

■ ■ ■

I go into the Bulls' locker room an hour and a half before the game, and there's nobody there except Steve Kerr. The rest of the players have scattered to private places.

I ask Kerr about the team's mood.

"Good," he says. "Confident. What else would we want to be?" Then he leaves.

Are they uptight, cranky, tense? I would say so.

Buddha comes in. He puts on his uniform silently. He picks up his shoes and socks and walks through the door under the sign that says "No Press Beyond This Point."

John Salley walks in from the training room. He is already dressed. He downs his vitamins and snorts from an inhaler.

Are the Bulls going to win?

"Yep," he says.

Why?

"It's time."

And soon he is gone.

Scottie Pippen enters and begins to change into his game clothes. Ailene Voisin of the *Atlanta Constitution* walks up to him, while the rest of the media hang back somewhat timidly, and stands at his elbow as he takes off his pants. She asks him a few questions. Yes, it's weird being in a room where star athletes must get naked in front of strangers of both sexes, but that's how the system works. Equality.

Scottie isn't talking, either.

I leave and promptly run into June Jackson.

"I have a bone to pick with you," she says.

"I wouldn't expect anything else," I answer.

"You told Phil's name in the paper—Swift Eagle."

"Yeah, so?"

"Radio stations, all kinds of people, started calling the hotel, asking

for Swift Eagle. They woke him up at seven in the morning. Finally he
had to have the phone turned off."

She has a cup of beer in her hand. She looks moderately intense.

"I'm sorry," I say. "I just thought—Phil and I both thought—that the
series was over. I never thought it would matter."

She seems to accept this.

"The fire alarm kept going off in the morning," she says, shaking her
head. "Michael set it off from smoking so many cigars."

"You're kidding."

"No. Phil smokes them too, now. And Rodman. And Salley."

"Salley's opening a cigar store," I tell her.

"I know," she says. "What do these guys think—that it's not a nasty
tobacco habit?"

I take my seat on press row, not sure how to feel about this game. I
had just written a column assuring readers that the Bulls would do fine,
that the bickering over bad play and the unfortunate losses to Seattle
were just normal aspects of championship play. Talent, will, and the
home-court advantage would all kick in, and the Bulls would kick butt.

But would they? Or were they two games from becoming one of the
biggest failures in modern sports history?

I thought I was correct in my appraisal of the situation, but next to my
column was Jay Mariotti's, in which he savaged the Bulls. He made
them sound so bad, so out of kilter, so wracked with dissension that they
had no chance of winning. The Bulls had "lost control," he said. They
were "spoiled brats, pointing fingers at each other," showing "no life, no
killer instinct, no mental toughness." They were "an old, achy, jump-
shot-challenged . . . internally-feuding mess."

What a book I would have on my hands if they blew it. The cover
would need a warning label on it: "For losers only."

■ ■ ■

The starting lineups are announced.

For the SuperSonics: guards Gary Payton and Hersey Hawkins, forwards Shawn Kemp and Detlef Schrempf, and at center, Frank Brickowski. For the Bulls it's guards Jordan and Harper, forwards Pippen and
Rodman, center Longley. But except for Longley, positions don't mean
much on this team.

The tension in the big arena is audible, and very nearly visible. The fans who have become so dulled by the Bulls' home-court dominance suddenly seem to understand that if their team drops this one, they are just one game from despair. And if the Bulls should lose this game, who could rightfully feel they *would* win that final game? They would be a team that had peaked, faded, lost its will.

The normally sedate arena is trembling with sound. Up in a skybox some children hold a large sign that reads, "Happy Fathers Day, From Jeffrey, Jasmine, and Marcus." Michael's kids. His father's grandchildren.

The ball goes up, Longley controls it, and the game is under way.

Pippen scores on a layup off an assist by Harper.

Schrempf hits a midrange jumper.

Jordan takes a pass from Rodman and drills a 3-pointer to give the Bulls a 5–2 lead. The Bulls pull ahead 9–6 on a Harper 10-foot jump shot and 2 Jordan free throws.

Then Kemp, the manchild who nearly came to the Bulls two years ago in a trade for Pippen, drains 2 free throws after Pippen fouls him on a shot: 9–8, Bulls. Longley loses the ball out of bounds, and the Sonics bring it upcourt. Payton, a man of quick hands and aloof demeanor, buries one of his slowly rotating 15-foot jumpers. And now the Sonics are in the lead, 10–9.

This is how they did it in the other games. The Bulls are fired up. It is plain to see in their determined, almost angry, faces. But does anyone remember who the oldest team in the league is? The Sonics are not exactly a young team, particularly with the 36-year-old Brickowski out there instead of the disgruntled and soon-to-be-traded 28-year-old center Ervin Johnson. But their stars, Kemp and Payton, are just 26 and 27, respectively. Pippen and Jordan are 30 and 33. Maybe the Sonics are just wearing out the Bulls.

But Jordan feeds to Pippen, who is way outside, and Pippen, the battered Olympian-to-be, hits a 24-foot 3-pointer that ignites the crowd and gives the Bulls the lead again, 12–10, with 7 minutes left in the quarter.

The shot is huge. Pippen went 3 for 8 on 3-pointers in the Bulls' opening win in Seattle. Since then he has shot 3 for 24, including making just 2 of 16 long-range attempts in the two losses. But now his long-levered stroke is back on track. He'll finish today's game with 17 points, including 3 of 7 from behind the 3-point line.

But that single blast from way outside is the big spike. The Sonics will not take the lead again.

The Bulls regroup behind Jordan, who will finish the quarter with 7 points and 6 rebounds, to take a 24–18 lead at the end of the period.

In the second quarter Kerr and Kukoc replace Harper and Longley. Kerr looks hesitant when he has the ball, and the anger on Jordan's face is plain to read. Jordan has been furious with his teammates, whom he thinks do not sense the magnitude of what they can accomplish if they would only follow him and then set off on their own courses.

Kerr stutters for a moment and doesn't shoot a wide-open 3. Then he travels. Jordan smacks him on the butt, and gives him his "Get mean!" look. The next time down the floor, Jordan passes right back to Kerr. It's an assist if Kerr can do what he's been put on this team to do. Kerr does not hesitate for an instant. He buries the 15-foot jumper.

"Yes!" says Jordan. "That's it!"

Kerr's shot has put the Bulls ahead 29–21, and from here it's a cat-and-mouse game, with the Bulls allowing the lead to be cut to as little as 4 points, after Kemp hits a short jumper with seconds to go in the half, and expanding it to as much as 17 points, off a Jordan layup midway through the third quarter.

In the third it is clear that Kemp is ever so sick of Rodman's peculiar, annoying, and effective tactics. Kemp forearms him to the floor, and it seems that if he had a large flyswatter, and no one was looking, he'd thrash Worm into a colorful pulp.

With the Bulls ahead by 14 in the fourth quarter, public service announcements begin to flash on the scoreboard screen. The ads feature Jackson, Jordan, and Rodman, and they urge Chicagoans to stay cool in victory. "Celebrate With Dignity" is the slogan.

Pippen hits for 8 points in the fourth quarter and Rodman cranks his act into overdrive, pulling down 7 rebounds, Jordan's shot is off—he'll finish with 22 points, on just 5 of 19 shooting from the field—but his leadership is on. He ends up with 9 rebounds, a team-high 7 assists, and 2 steals.

But the end comes for Seattle with 4:39 to go in the game. The Sonics' most important player, Kemp, hacks Longley on a fast break for his sixth foul. He's gone, taking his 18 points, 14 rebounds, 3 steals, and 2 blocks to the bench. And with him goes Seattle's hope.

The Bulls start to smile when Pippen hits a 3-pointer to make it 82–66 Bulls. And they go into full grin when he hits another with less than a minute to go, making the score 87–70.

The crowd roar overwhelms the sterility of this huge, clean place. And when the horn sounds and the Bulls have won, 87–75, there is wild dancing in the aisles.

Before the final notes of the horn have faded into the din, Michael Jordan has dived on the ball like a linebacker on a fumble and hugs it to his chest with both arms. Randy Brown dives on top of him. Other players join in. Jordan's eyes are closed and his mouth is set in a fierce grimace of rapture and release and something perhaps unknowable.

When he had first come back to the Bulls from a retirement that had moved him away from the one thing he can do better than any man on earth ever has, he was hesitant. He was reopening a door that had brought him more joy and loss than a man needs. That first game back was against the Pacers, in Indianapolis. Jordan flew to the game in his own plane, the only time he ever did that. League rules forbid taking a private plane when a team plane is available, but this was something different. Jordan's people—his guards and a friend or two—got off the plane. But Jordan did not.

He sat inside, alone. "We were all outside," recalls bodyguard Bob Scarpetti. "No big deal. Then all of a sudden, somebody says 'Where's Mike?' We're out there for fifteen, twenty minutes, and he's still in the plane. He's just sitting there, reflecting about his father. This would be the first time his dad couldn't see him play. We all realized he wanted to be alone."

For a time it was unclear to those who were on the tarmac whether Jordan would actually leave the plane. He could stay onboard, have the others reboard, fly back to Chicago, and the door to all that color and noise would never have to be reopened.

But he got off. And here is the result.

In time, Jordan gets up off the United Center floor and runs through the crowd to the locker room, alone. A TV camera picks up his actions.

While his teammates are at midcourt, celebrating, Jordan is lying on the carpeted floor of the training room, face down, sobbing.

What was today? Father's Day.

■ ■ ■

The sound system blasts "Sweet Home Chicago" as the Bulls players climb on top of the long scorer's table at halfcourt and wave to the fans, to the world. Wennington gets his little boy, Robbie, the four-year-old who looks seven, and carries him with him. Robbie promptly begins to cry.

Harper gets his little girl. Kerr gets his son. Kukoc gets his. In a couple of minutes Jordan, eyes slightly swollen, rejoins his teammates, his fellow oarsmen, his pupils.

The trophy is presented and the cheering increases.

In time the players straggle to the locker room.

Mayhem rules in the depths of the United Center. Cigar smoke, water, champagne suds, beer foam everywhere.

"I have never smoked a cigar in my life," babbles Jerry Krause with a stogie in his hand, his white shirt soaked with whatever, his eyes squinting from the bright lights and fumes. "But this is from Jordan's private stock."

A crush of people, lights, and cameras moves through the wide hallway, trapping and pushing everything in its path the way a plumber's snake moves through a pipe. In the center of the mob is Dennis Rodman, who very casually unwraps a pink and yellow Worm Pop, and puts it in his mouth for consumers everywhere to witness. In a nearby corner Dwight Manley stands with his leather bag and a detached look. Could it be his eyes are the faintest shade of red?

Luc Longley hugs his father. "I pleased you, Dad," he says. "Finally."

Wennington throws wastebasketfuls of tap water at the press and wives and families. Reinsdorf, soaked like everyone else, gives some advice for revelers out in the streets of Chicago: "Everybody should be enjoying themselves and not acting like gangsters."

I move into the crush for reasons that escape me now, but possibly—aw hell, yes—just for the fun of it.

Reinsdorf is yakking for all he's worth, dodging Wennington's water bombs, and I decide to just listen, and fire questions if necessary.

"You get greedier as you go along," the boss says. "They're all hard, but this one we *had* to win or they'd be writing about it for a very long time." The "they," of course, is us, the media. We're the ones who come between effort and fulfillment. We're the ones who tear down monuments. And I often wonder why Reinsdorf doesn't simply run his team privately, in front of no one, behind closed doors, playing in front of vacant stands. How pure that would be.

And what about all those loose contracts, I ask.

"I want Phil back," he says. "Jerry wants Phil back. If he wants to come back, he'll be back."

It's nearly a tautology, I think. And Michael?

"Michael Jordan should never play for another team."

Then Reinsdorf gives his synopsis of Jordan's season. "I think Michael was a man on a mission this year. He was embarrassed in the Orlando series last year. This must have been a tremendous relief for him. I saw him take the ball. I think we'll let him keep it."

It's enlightening to see owners of sports teams at the moment of fruition, to see what the man in the suit feels after having produced a championship business, all the while knowing that he could never do the actual physical work that brought the business to the top. Reinsdorf wipes perspiration, or perhaps some of Wennington's handiwork, from his forehead.

"I have to pinch myself sometimes," he says. "Having Michael Jordan, Frank Thomas, and Bo Jackson work for me. I must have done something right."

The crowd in the locker room undulates as people try to move through the room. Random cries of joy hurtle into the air like champagne corks.

Reinsdorf brandishes a cigar, puffing on it when he is able to get his hand to his mouth.

I ask him whether this is the kind of image he wants to present to children, all these grown men with fuming sticks of tobacco in their mouths.

"Cigar smoking is not addictive," he says firmly. "You don't inhale. As far as I'm concerned, they're not injurious. I know that if I didn't smoke them, I'd weigh four hundred pounds. Michael Jordan's father smoked them, but I believe I introduced them to him. As somebody once said, a woman is only a woman, but a good cigar is a smoke."

Steve Kerr is giddy with joy, but he also has deeper thoughts racing through his mind. "When I look back on Father's Day every year, I'll remember how special this one was," he says.

Over in a corner is his wife Margot with June Jackson. Margot has a cigar in her hand. Both women are completely soaked. Both are blabbering.

"Bill Wennington is insane," states June loudly. "Why doesn't somebody interview me? I want to tell them these people need psychiatric help."

John Salley stands regally above the fray, taking it all in with great pleasure.

He has a cigar wedged into each side of his mouth.

Not far from him is Tim Hallam. The PR man is having that last cigarette.

■ ■ ■

Later that night, Michael Jordan arrives at his restaurant on LaSalle Street. He walks in, soaking wet, still in his uniform, wearing one shoe and carrying a magnum of champagne. He has put a "4-Peat" T-shirt on over his uniform, and he looks for all the world like a little kid who has been roughhousing with pals.

The restaurant is closed, but Jordan climbs the stairs to the small private party taking place on the second floor. He is with his wife, Juanita. Friends of his are there—Ahmad Rashad, Quinn Buckner, Joe Silverberg, the Jordan clothing franchiser, and his wife Sherry, old pals Fred Whitfield and Fred Glover. Everyone is stunned that Jordan has made it here tonight. He looks a mess, but he is happy. He is also slightly distant, reflective, mellow. Outside people are still screaming, though it's now well after midnight. Horns are honking, people are whistling, occasionally the staccato clopping of horse hooves cuts through the drone.

A window is open to the street, and Jordan throws two dozen "4-Peat" T-shirts down to the masses below, tossing them one at a time. He has already given his game shoes away.

The small gathering is quieter than it had been, as each member of the party gauges the mood of the newly elected Most Valuable Player of the NBA finals. He seems both to want to celebrate and to lose himself in reverie. He hugs people for long periods of time. He hugs Sherry Silverberg for so long it seems he may not let go. There is something almost sacred about the atmosphere, though no one can say exactly why that is. On the wall of the dining room there is a large photo of James Jordan. Of course, he has much to do with it.

Michael tells the group that he's in the mood to hear some jokes. He settles back and listens as the partiers crank out good ones and bad ones, juvenile ones and obscene ones. People who never tell jokes tell them tonight. Jordan enjoys them all, seems to delight in the bonding that comes with the telling more than the punchlines themselves. At a point the jokes start to fade away; the well has started to run dry. Then there are no more, and revelers become quieter and break into smaller groups.

Jordan walks around, and after a spell comes up to Joe Silverberg. There are tears in Jordan's eyes, new ones leaking out over the traces of old ones.

"I saw you on TV when you were lying on the locker room floor," Silverberg says.

Some people will say in the days to come that Jordan had somehow orchestrated his singular collapse after the victory. But they are wrong.

"The cameras were on me then?" says Jordan, stunned.

He grows mellow again.

"I was just so happy my kids were there, on Father's Day," he says. "I wish my dad were here now."

31

IT LOOKS LIKE WOODSTOCK TO ME.

From my vantage point here on the stage at the Petrillo Music Shell in Grant Park I can see acres of people spread out on the soaked lawn that stretches into the distance. It's 9 A.M. two days after the Bulls' championship game, and this victory celebration for the masses, for the city of Chicago, isn't even scheduled to begin until 10:30.

It is already very hot, and of course it is muggy. The crowd is younger and less affluent than the dandies who comprise much of the United Center clientele, and they are dressed in jeans, shorts, T-shirts, sneakers, bathing suits, bandanas. They are here out of a wish to honor the Bulls, but also because they know this is probably the only way they're ever going to get anywhere close to their heroes. Handmade signs wave above the crowd that is swelling toward the quarter-million mark. One says "The Fat Lady Has Sung." And there is one that says, "Most Valuable Pop, This One's For You." Beneath the words is a large painting of James Jordan with his arms lifted, looking almost messianic.

I walk backstage and run into one of the Bulls Brothers who perform at home games, imitating the Blues Brothers. It is Lance Haack, the Dan Aykroyd lookalike, and he is lamenting the fact his John Belushi lookalike partner, Fred Bevier, dislocated and fractured his right ankle before Game 6 while dunking off a trampoline. Yessir, I tell him, I know how tricky that can be.

"We had twenty shows booked and a commercial for Johnson's Wax," says Haack sadly. "We've been together fifteen years. I can't replace the second Belushi."

Lovabulls scurry about, along with musicians, cops, and actors. The event is now ten minutes late getting started. Bevier, the injured Bulls Brother, maneuvers his wheelchair into position for his performance. Like Haack, he is decked out in his trademark black suit, white shirt, skinny black tie, black porkpie hat, and shades. He is wearing only one black shoe, however.

The crowd is restless. It is beyond restless, actually; it is eager, sweating, dehydrated, scorched. Chants of "Bull-shit! Bull-shit!" rumble from the masses. Altamont replaces Woodstock in my mind.

Jim Sheahan, the city's director of special events, looks desperate. The holdup has been because of Michael Jordan, who just received his MVP trophy at the Fairmont Hotel before being hurried into a squad car, which has been wending its way to the park. En route Jordan changed from a business suit to jeans, T-shirt, and cap. With Jordan now safely aboard, Sheahan starts the festivities, and none too soon.

The Superfans—George Wendt and Rob Smigel, the comedians who say things like "Dese," "dem," "dose" and "Coach Dikka of duh Bears"—come out and say, among other things, "Duh last two years did not count, my friend!" As the pair praise the Bulls, a spontaneous chant of "New York sucks! New York sucks!" rises from the crowd.

Out come the Bulls Brothers—one boogying, one spinning in a wheelchair—accompanied by the Lovabulls. Then the Dancing Rodmans take the stage: a quartet of neon-wigged male dancers who seem not to have any routine to perform, but simply thrash about to blasting rock music. As the Rodmans do their free-form thing, the Bulls' assistant coaches, scouts, wives, and kids take seats on stage. More singers come out, and pretty quickly the crowd is tired of all this nonsense and begins bellowing, "We want the Bulls!"

Big old Johnny "Red" Kerr, the former Bulls coach and veteran sportscaster, takes the microphone. Shortly he gives way to United Center announcer Ray Clay, who does his legendarily melodramatic "And now . . . the lineup for YOUR World Champion . . . Chicago Bulls!"

The Bulls file on one after another. Haley first, or is it last? Then Caffey and Simpkins. Wennington comes out with his video camera running. One after the other they come. Rodman is wearing an oversize cap and a Chicago Police shirt. Pippen is in bib overalls. Most of the players are wearing sunglasses; Rodman, Pippen, Jordan, and Phil Jackson each carry one of the Bulls' four gleaming NBA title trophies.

Reinsdorf is introduced. To boos. Chicagoans don't like the way he has made Jordan, Jackson, and Rodman dangle for their contracts. Some of them don't like Reinsdorf's White Sox deals. Some don't like the fact that he's from Brooklyn and is rich. But then, Jordan was born in Brooklyn and is rich, too. A lot of fans just don't like owners, period.

Krause is introduced, and—how about it!—there are cheers mixed in with light booing. Krause had been booed lustily at all the other Bulls championship rallies.

Then the speakers begin. First Longley. Then Kerr. Then Kukoc. Then Rodman. Naturally, Rodman can't get two sentences out without using the word *fuck*. Oh well, at least the man's consistent. And he should be accorded some leniency after the way he played in the championship series, averaging 14.7 rebounds per game, and—most of all—

keeping his head attached to his shoulders. Pippen speaks, and as he does so, a water cannon goes off on the right side of the crowd, spraying the parched spectators.

Then it's Jordan's turn. He walks to the stand, and the outpouring of joy washes up from the crowd and over the stage. His words ring out strong and clear. "The city loves me," he says. "And I love them."

Then, quickly, it's over. Four jets fly overhead in formation, and the new anthem, "Only the Bulls," plays over the p.a.

I walk north on Columbus Drive, moving with the crowd as it dissipates and becomes individuals heading in different directions to their homes and offices and factories and schools. I'm one of the last in the procession and I move aside as two shiny new city streetcleaners rumble down Columbus toward the park. They are painted bright red and have "Bulls" written on their sides. On their rear ends, each has a jersey number printed in white paint. The first vehicle is number 91. Worm. The one behind, making sure everything is clean and right, is number 23.

Of course.

As I was leaving the park, I saw Jerry Krause's wife and told her it was noteworthy that her spouse didn't elicit the usual nastiness he gets at rallies like these.

"Maybe people are starting to understand all the good he's done," she said. "But if they don't understand, there's nothing you can do."

She's right. Understanding anything is so difficult. It may be we never can get a look at the whole picture. How, for instance, do you know who really did what, where this man's grip leaves off and that one's takes hold?

A player makes a basket, and that is clear. But he did not do it in a vacuum. A teammate set a pick that freed a cutter, who took a pass that drew the defense to him before he dished to the open man—who made the shot. Layers of assistance.

Then, too, who taught the shooter to shoot? It is the role of a teacher, and a coach, to nurture and inform and then step back into the shadows. But how is the credit ever divvied up just right? There were 12 players on this year's Bulls playoff roster—14 with Simpkins and Caffey; 15 with Haley. There were administrators, coaches, support staff. And there were the rest of us, too, viewers and fans and detractors and mere students of the game. Each of us must be a dot on the vast pointillist canvas that is the Bulls.

Maybe, I think, that's why I feel so light-footed and buoyant as I walk along. We're all part of the sacred hoop, too. Phil says so. I think of all that the Bulls have won this season: Coach of the Year, Executive of the Year, Sixth Man of the Year, leading rebounder in the league, leading scorer in the league, MVP of the league, MVP of the finals, three first-team members of the NBA All-Defensive Team, two members of the All-NBA team, best regular season ever, and—who knows?—best team of all time.

Even Jack Haley played a part in this triumph. Even though the players will vote him only a pittance of a share of the earnings from the playoff pool, even though Kerr gives Jordan, as a present for winning the MVP, a sleeve of golf balls with Haley's face on them—even still, Haley's karma contributed. If Rodman had not attended Haley's child's birthday party and given the boy a live ferret, who can say how the spheres would have shifted?

I cross the Chicago River and take a left, heading west. To my right along lovely Michigan Avenue, the Magnificent Mile, is the Tribune Tower, a stunning and graceful 35-story gothic masterpiece with a statue of patriot Nathan Hale in the plaza in front of it. Hale, his hands tied behind his back, is saying proudly to his captors. "I only regret . . ."

And there ahead of me on less-swank Wabash Avenue, hard beside the river, lies the Sun-Times Building. The squat, seven-story lump of cheesy mid-1950s metal and glass, designed to resemble a tugboat (oh, what lofty dreams the architects had!), is my rest stop, my abode. On the flat roof, just above the yellow "Chicago Sun-Times," sits a huge inflatable red and raging bull. That's my building.

I hope there is room in this world, always, for two papers, two styles, two ways of thinking. No matter what, I know there is always room for the river. It flows almost imperceptibly here, turgid and gray, heading south and west. In time it connects with water that is blue and sparkling. And all of it circles around and around in an endless web, not that much different, it strikes me, from the pattern on a basketball itself.